Hacking
World of Warcraft®

Hacking
World of Warcraft®

Dan Gilbert and James Whitehead II

Wiley Publishing, Inc.

HackingWorld of Warcraft®

Published by
Wiley Publishing, Inc.
10475 Crosspoint Boulevard
Indianapolis, IN 46256
`www.wiley.com`

Copyright © 2007 by Wiley Publishing, Inc., Indianapolis, Indiana

Published simultaneously in Canada

ISBN: 978-0-470-11002-7

Manufactured in the United States of America

10 9 8 7 6 5 4 3 2 1

For general information on our other products and services or to obtain technical support, please contact our Customer Care Department within the U.S. at (800) 762-2974, outside the U.S. at (317) 572-3993 or fax (317) 572-4002.

Library of Congress Cataloging-in-Publication Data is available from the publisher.

Wiley also publishes its books in a variety of electronic formats. Some content that appears in print may not be available in electronic books.

For my parents

—Dan

For my parents

—Jim

Credits

Executive Editor
Chris Webb

Development Editors
Maryann Steinhart
Julie Smith

Technical Editor
Jim Whitehead II

Copy Editor
Mildred Sanchez

Editorial Manager
Mary Beth Wakefield

Production Manager
Tim Tate

**Vice President and Executive
Group Publisher**
Richard Swadley

Vice President and Executive Publisher
Joseph B. Wikert

Compositor
Chris Gillespie, Happenstance Type-O-Rama

Proofreader
Sossity Smith

Indexer
Ted Laux

Anniversary Logo Design
Richard Pacifico

Cover Design
Anthony Bunyan

About the Authors

Dan Gilbert is the creator and developer of the Atlas addon for World of Warcraft. He also maintains atlasmod.com and the forums there, and encourages you to stop by and say hi. When he actually has time to play WoW, you can find him on the Jaedenar server as Razark (his Shaman) or Nine (his Mage). Dan also sometimes works as a web developer, a graphic artist, and a cinematographer. He designs T-shirts at `threadless.com`, where his designs "I Heart Color" and "Release" have been printed.

Dan recently graduated from Hampshire College in Amherst, MA where he studied film production. For his thesis project (or Div III) he created a film called *The Nightingale Princess* with his co-conspirators, Christopher Dreisbach and Owen Granich-Young. The three of them have websites at `thenightingaleprincess.com` and `ocdproductions.net`. So far the movie hasn't gotten into any festivals, but Dan has his fingers crossed. He currently lives in Northampton, MA. In his spare time, he enjoys sleeping.

Jim Whitehead has been an active member of the UI community since December 2004. He initially became an active developer on WatchDog unit frames, and eventually created PerfectRaid and Clique, and spearheaded the creation of the Dongle addon framework. When he's not developing addons for World of Warcraft, he can be found playing the game with one of his many characters on the Stormrage server.

Jim is a graduate of Syracuse (NY) University, holding an MSc in computer science. Although he has been a resident of cubicle-land for the past few years, he will soon retreat to the halls of academia to pursue his PhD in computer science. He lives in Syracuse, where he spends a disproportionate amount of his life's savings on keeping his house warm.

Contents at a Glance

Contents

Chapter 8: Class-Specific Addons 185

Part II: Advanced Hacks: Creating Your Own Addons

Acknowledgments

David Fugate, thank you for bringing this project to me, and for your constant positive support. Jim Whitehead II, thank you for saving my butt more than once, and for being an awesome and knowledgeable coauthor and technical editor. Chris Webb and Maryann Steinhart, thank you for your wonderful flexibility, for putting up with my "optimistic" schedules. Julie Smith, thank you for all your editing work behind the scenes.

Adele Gladstone-Gilbert and Michael Gilbert, thank you for everything, and then some. Deborah Gilbert, thank you for all your love and encouragement. Christopher Dreisbach and Elyse Bellamy, thank you for providing constant inspiration, for making me remember that there's more to life than World of Warcraft, and for renaming my cat. Sebastien Bolea, Matthew Bamberg-Johnson, and Owen Granich-Young, thank you for all the good times both in and out of WoW. You've been the best housemates I could hope for. Alison Wilson, thank you for putting up with WoW in our house, and for cheering me up when I've been awake all night. Chris Bishop, Evan Viera, and James McGuire, thank you for distracting me with existential conversations, which are way more fun than actually working. Ben Fiske, thank you for the late night board games. Jay Sgroi, thank you for being the best AD ever, and for teaching me how to procrastinate with style. Nuala Sawyer, thank you for giving me permission to forget to thank people.

Northampton Coffee, The Haymarket, and Rao's, thank you for the liquid motivation, and the free (and intermittent) Internet access. Matthew Dayton and Michael Goodman, thank you for the summer fun. Nathaniel Adams, Soulhoof, Buddaz, and everyone else from Shimrra, thank you for the good old days. Lincoln Baxter III, Nathaniel McVicar, Eric Browne, and everyone else from Northfield, thank you for the good older days. I miss you guys.

To everyone who has translated and contributed to Atlas, thank you so much. You guys rock. To those of you who have sent me donations, I am eternally grateful. Christopher Davies, thank you for your consistent and amazing work on both Atlas and AtlasLoot. To the Atlas forum regulars, thank you for the assistance, suggestions, and discussion. To all of you wondering why Atlas hasn't been updated fast enough, you can thank this book.

—Dan Gilbert

Tom Harper, thank you for being such a special part of my life. You've stood by me for the past three years, and my life will be changed forever as a result. You've given me confidence, kept me focused, and supported me the entire time. Kelley and Steven Ganoung, thank you for being amazing roommates, and my best friends. Lee and James Whitehead, thank you for being a constant source of inspiration and letting me know when I've gotten ahead of myself. Robert Whitehead, thank you for always watching out for me, and helping to keep me grounded. Gregory Whitehead, thank you for always giving me the opportunity to nerd out, in a way no one else really has. Michelle Hastings, thank you for being the brightest person I've ever met in my life. Your smile shines through even the worst cell phone connection, and I'm a lucky man to have you as my sister. Julia and Kevin Hastings, thank you for being a constant source of smiles and grins—any time you need someone, I will be there. Levi Hastings, thank you for giving me a home away from home, and being a great older brother-in-law.

Karen Hobson, thank you for getting me involved with this project, and for everything you've done for me; I'd be lost without you. Sam Latinga, thank you for all you do for the World of Warcraft community, and for dealing with my endless questions. Matthew and Juliella Orlando, thank you for taking time out of your busy lives (at the auction house) to help a friend in over his head. Matt Richards, thank you for letting me call you at all hours to work through coding ideas. David Shafer, thank you for being . . . you. Peter Provost, thank you for pushing me to start writing, even when the deadline is a half hour away.

AnduinLothar, Beladona, Cairenn, Cide, Cogwheel, Esamynn, Gazmik, Gello, Iriel, Kaelten, Krka, Legorol, MentalPower, NeuroMedivh, Norganna, Qzot, and Tem, thank you for letting me bounce ideas off you at any hour of the night. I've definitely appreciated it. Thanks to everyone from #wowi-lounge for giving me an excuse to step away from my work. Thank you to everyone on the Dongle development team.

Chris Webb, thanks for putting up with me during the planning stages of this book. Dan Gilbert, thank you for being a great coauthor and allowing me to share in your vision. Maryann Steinhart, thank you for leading a clueless idealist through the writing process, and Julie Smith, thanks for all your feedback and encouragement.

Thanks to all of my friends who dragged me out of the house, especially my 829 boys and girls; you help me stay real. Thanks to Jalepeños for the sangria and letting me spend my money week after week. Thanks to all the loyal PerfectRaid, Clique, and WatchDog users for your patience.

—Jim Whitehead

To all the programmers whose addons appear in this book, thank you for your hard work and dedication to projects that make World of Warcraft more enjoyable for everyone. In fact, thank you to *all* addon authors, everywhere.

Finally, thank you Blizzard. You have, for good or bad, changed the world.

—The authors

Introduction

Since its release in November 2004, World of Warcraft (WoW) has become one of the most popular video games on the planet. According to a recent press release from Blizzard (the company that makes WoW), its service has more than 8.5 million active subscribers. For many, WoW is a way of life. The experience is immersive and addictive, thanks to the sheer number of things to do: Fight, quest, socialize, craft, explore—and mod. Modding appeals to players who are more technically minded, and allows the interface—and even the functionality of the game—to be vastly extended. Blizzard has encouraged this practice from the start by including an addon system in its product, and a large modding community has developed over the years. Because WoW doesn't allow user-created content—even the degree to which you can customize your character is limited—creating addons is one of the most creative ways you can leave your mark on the World of Warcraft environment. It also provides an excellent framework in which to learn the basics of programming, object-oriented design, and GUI (graphical user interface) development.

Many WoW players have never used an addon, but those who have never go back. Map enhancements, auction house analyzers, raid communication tools, ore location trackers—addons are capable of changing the WoW experience fundamentally. Addons are modular, small in size, easy to develop, and ideal for distribution over the Internet. In the wake of the game's release, websites have appeared that cater specifically to both addon authors and users alike. However, these websites can be difficult to navigate if you don't already know what you're looking for. It's almost impossible to figure out which addons to pick and how to install them if you don't have a knowledgeable friend sitting next to you.

This book presents a selection of some of the most interesting and useful addons that are currently available. The goal is not to be a complete catalog—something that would be impossible to create because thousands of addons exist and many new ones are released every day—but rather an entry point into the world of addons and a primer on their use and development. Separated into a number of categories, including combat addons, loot addons, chat addons, and map addons, the first half of this book introduces you to a decent cross section of premade addons that you can download, install, and use immediately.

As World of Warcraft rapidly enters the mainstream culture, the demand for high-quality addons is only going to increase. Addon websites are getting more hits now than ever before. The knowledge needed to create addons is freely available, but somewhat fragmented and inconstant. This book is aimed at potential addon developers as well as users. If you have a good idea for a mod, but don't have the programming knowledge to implement it, the tutorials in the second half of the book are the perfect place to start. If you're already a programmer, but don't have any experience with event-driven interfaces and want to learn how they work, WoW is an ideal environment; your programs don't need to be compiled, they can be reloaded as often as you want without restarting the game, and there's a comprehensive framework full of windows, buttons, and widgets to play with, not to mention user-created development libraries like Ace.

This book will teach you the basics of using addons, serve as a guide for helping you choose which ones to use, give you inspiration for your own addon ideas, provide insight into how addons are structured and created, explain how to create your own addons, and expose you to what it's like modifying existing code to suit your own needs. On top of all that, you'll explore the revamped macro system introduced with The Burning Crusade.

Note

I wrote this book because I believe in the power of online worlds. They've always fascinated me. When I look at WoW, I don't see "just another video game," I see an infinitely complex system that's full of contradictions just like the real world. It's a beautifully crafted visual environment and also an escape from the mundane. It's sparked a robust virtual economy as well as created a huge market for illegal currency trading and power-leveling. It's a path to personal success and an endless string of ethereal rewards that become harder and harder to achieve as time goes on. It fosters communities among thousands of people from all over the world yet isolates us from the environments in which we live and work. It's a casual distraction and an addiction, a blessing and a curse. It's making its creators more money than they ever dreamed of, and it's the most fun I've ever had online. More than anything else, it's a glimpse into the future of the Internet and society; not just for gamers, but for us all. —Dan

Whom This Book Is For

First and foremost, this book will appeal to you if you've never used an addon before. You might have heard of them and be curious to learn more. The current WoW addon websites, while comprehensive, are hardly approachable. This book introduces you to the concepts you need to understand to use the existing websites and try out addons that interest you.

This book will also appeal to you if you're a casual addon user who's looking for the best addons out there. Sorting the wheat from the chaff can be a difficult process because addon reviews are pretty much nonexistent. By cataloging and discussing much of what's currently available, this book provides you with information that exists nowhere else. You might also have questions about the legality of addons, a topic that this book addresses right off.

If you're a more advanced user who's interested in addon development, you'll find this book useful, especially if you prefer learning from a guided process instead of from trial and error. Getting a solid foundation of information from one place on this topic isn't the easiest thing in the world. This book augments the reference guides and tutorials that already exist on the web. In the second half of the book you're guided through a couple of addon projects from start to finish. You'll create an addon from scratch, and then hack an existing piece of Blizzard's interface code to suit your own purpose.

This book is *not* for established addon developers who already have a good sense of what's available and how to put it to use. It's not for advanced Lua programmers, nor is it a WoW API (application programming interface) reference manual. In fact, no programming knowledge is required to follow along with the presented projects. However, it is assumed that you own or have access to a copy of WoW and have an active subscription. You also need to have some pretty basic computer knowledge. You should be able to create text files and move them around, and you should have administrator privileges on your machine.

How This Book Is Organized

This book is separated into two parts.

For people who have never used a WoW addon before, the first part of the book covers all the basics: what addons are, and how you can obtain, install, and use them. This part also goes into more detail about the modding community and addon websites, giving you all the skills and knowledge necessary to find and install virtually every addon in existence.

The chapters in this part highlight more than a hundred addons in a number of categories, serving as a nice starting point for new users who are confronted with thousands of existing addons. It's also a handy reference guide for more experienced players. Screenshots abound, short tutorials, and configuration examples are provided for many of the more complex mods, and common slash commands are available at a glance.

The second part of the book guides you through the internals of an addon. WoW addons are written in the Lua scripting language, which should seem familiar to you if you've ever been exposed to a C-like programming language. Addons rely heavily on specific WoW API features, which are covered in depth as each one is put to use. Don't worry; no prior programming experience is assumed, and you'll be guided step by step through the creation of a simple addon from start to finish. In fact, addon development provides a gentle introduction to computer programming because you don't need any special software beyond a text editor and the game itself.

Because of the nature of the book, a few varying approaches are used. Addon installation and programming topics are covered step by step, and should be read from start to finish. However, the addon guides are organized more like a directory, and should be enjoyable to flip through.

Conventions Used in This Book

The following conventions are used throughout this book.

Icons

Throughout this book, a few different icons are used to highlight particular pieces of information. These icons include:

Notes provide additional or critical information on the current topic.

These direct you to web addresses that lead you to more information about the topic, or the official website for a particular project. As is the nature of the Web, as time goes by the addresses might stop working. That's why we have Google.

Tips provide you with extra knowledge that separates the novice from the pro.

 Cautions point out procedures for which you need to be extremely careful, as well as pitfalls that you can avoid. They indicate that something is potentially dangerous, and you should carefully consider whether you want to proceed. You might be looking at lost time, legal troubles, or destroyed in-game items. There aren't many of these.

In addition, the addon guide chapters contain badges (as shown following this paragraph) that indicate which of the three main addon websites are hosting an actively updated version of the particular addon at the time this book was written. Over time, it's possible that other sites will pick up the addon or that it will stop being updated at a particular site. Remember, they're only guides.

Key Combinations

When you are instructed to press two or more keys simultaneously, each key in the combination is separated by a plus sign. For example:

Ctrl+Alt+T (Command+Option+T)

The preceding tells you to press the three listed keys for your system at the same time. You can also hold down one or more keys and then press the final key. Release all the keys at the same time.

Typographical Conventions

New terms may appear in *italic* type.

A special typeface indicates code, as demonstrated in the following example:

```
<html>
<head>
<title>Untitled Document</title>
</head>
<body bgcolor="#FFFFFF">
</body>
</html>
```

This code font is also used within paragraphs to designate tags, attributes, and values, as well as filenames and URLs.

The code continuation character (↵) at the end of a code line indicates that the line is too long to fit within the margins of the printed book. You should continue typing the next line of code before pressing the Enter (Return) key.

In some sections of the book the authors have used bold in code to indicate new material you are to add to existing (non-bold) material. For example:

```
<head>
<title>Untitled Document</title>
</head>
```

What You Need to Use This Book

You need a high-speed connection to the Internet. Unless you're very, very patient, a dial-up connection isn't recommended. Although most addons are small in size, some are multiple megabytes. You must be logged in to WoW to test your own addons.

You also need an active subscription to World of Warcraft. If you're interested in using or developing addons, connecting to an emulated (free) server is not recommended. First of all, it's a violation of Blizzard's Terms of Use. Second, many addons cause errors on nonofficial servers, and their authors cannot provide support for them under this circumstance.

Finally, you need administrator privileges on the computer you're using. To install or create addons, you need full read/write access in your World of Warcraft installation directory. Furthermore, you should be able to create text files and install programs.

Change Is Inevitable in World of Warcraft

Blizzard is constantly refining WoW through the regular release of patches. As well as affecting the game, these patches often include fixes, updates, additions, and changes to the addon API. Because this book doesn't cover too many advanced topics, these API changes shouldn't severely endanger its technical content, but it is possible that something could break. If you are having trouble with the tutorial section of this book, feel free to contact me (Dan Gilbert) at loglow@gmail.com.

However, these API changes *will* inevitably cause some of the addons you download and install to break. When that happens, you should first look for updated versions. Most addon authors are pretty communicative when it comes to fixing incompatibilities. Patches cause the most chaos, so you might want to wait a bit after they're released to let the dust settle.

Most important, be aware that WoW addons have a high turnover rate. Authors come and go all the time, projects switch hands, and many addons don't survive the test of time. While this book was being written, WoW saw the largest patch in history: the transition from 1.12 to 2.0, which included massive API changes. This patch also—for the first time ever—didn't allow out-of-date addons to be loaded at all, and as a result many addons died off entirely because they'd never been updated. Some of the addons covered in this book *will* die, even though they're all considerably well established. They all managed to survive the 2.0 patch, so that's saying something about them. Many addons had to be cut from the book because they simply aren't being updated anymore and no longer work.

If and when you encounter an out-of-date addon, do some web searching. Sometimes addons are updated only in one or two places. You can try to get in touch with the addon's author as well, but remember: these people create this software in their free time for no money, so always be friendly and supportive.

Finally, all of the addons in this book will be updated, eventually. They'll gain features, lose features, break, get fixed again, rearrange their options, get rewritten from the ground up, or change authors. Don't take the words in this book as gospel. Instead, use them as a guide to improve your understanding of what an addon does and how it works. As your collection of addons grows, you'll learn to adapt to change gracefully.

Hacking
World of Warcraft®

Simple Hacks: Addons, Macros, and More

part

Introduction to WoW Modding

What is an addon?

An addon is nothing more than a bunch of markup files, scripts, and textures in a folder.

These files are identical — in form — to the ones that define the default interface designed by Blizzard. That means they have the power to do anything Blizzard has done, barring a few intentional limitations. Because addons exist as discrete files on your hard disk, they can easily be archived and distributed online. Since the game's release, thousands of addons have been created, and a large community of developers continues to grow.

In fact, members of the community have had an impact on Blizzard's own interface development. Many features that originated as user-created addons have made their way into the default interface, including (but not limited to):

- Extra action bars on the bottom and right side of the screen
- Quest-goal tracking from outside the Quest window
- Numerical values for reputation status
- Built-in scrolling combat numbers

At the same time, many addons haven't been assimilated into the default user-interface and have matured on their own over the years. Here are a few examples of the most popular addons:

- **Gatherer:** Remembers the location of every mine, herb, and chest you discover, marking each one with an icon on the world map and minimap.

- **Auctioneer:** Scans the auction house to determine the market value of your items. It also highlights items that are for sale below their market value.

- **KLHThreatMeter:** Enables you to see who in your group or raid has accumulated the most threat over the course of a fight.
- **Atlas:** Provides you with maps for every instanced dungeon, each marked with the locations of bosses and other points of interest.

Blizzard has made it a priority to support addon developers by responding to their concerns in the forums. Each patch contains numerous updates and additions to the underlying framework on which addons are built.

You might think addons are too much of a hassle to be worth your time. In truth, they're incredibly simple to install and use. However, before jumping into the specifics of addons, let's clear up some confusion about the legality of WoW modding in general.

Examining the Legality of WoW Hacks

Many players are worried about getting banned. Blizzard announces thousands of account cancellations each month in connection with the use of third-party programs. These illegal third-party programs are often confused with addons, but they're not the same thing.

Third-Party Programs

Third-party programs are executables that modify the game's data files or interfere with communication between the WoW client and Blizzard's servers. This is how speed-hacks were created and how most bots work. You can expect to be banned for using any of these programs. It's important to understand that these programs are *not* addons; they're executables that run at the same time as the client and interfere with its data in memory.

Note Blizzard has a support page to help you understand what constitutes a third-party program. If you're interested, visit `http://blizzard.com/support/wow/?id=aww01657p`. For the record, it uses the word "hack" very differently from this book. They use it to imply a malicious act, whereas this book uses it to describe an interesting (and legal) technical project.

Certain statements in the World of Warcraft Terms of Use document — that you agree to before playing the game — make it sound like no modding of any kind is tolerated. However, it's important to distinguish between the modifications Blizzard wants to prevent and the kinds of modifications this book is about. Blizzard is concerned only about programs that mess with the game's data files and memory directly. You won't ever touch these.

It's important to note that Blizzard reserves the right to prohibit the use of any mod at any point in time. However, in practice Blizzard is supportive of addon use and development, and cracks down only on modifications that result in some kind of unfair advantage. All of these delicate distinctions may make it seem like addons are a liability, but the bottom line is that pure addons are completely legal.

What exactly is a *pure* addon?

A pure addon resides in a folder in the World of Warcraft directory. It's not an executable file. It's fully managed by the WoW client and is restricted by the limitations of the addon system. *No one has ever been banned from the game for simply using a pure World of Warcraft addon!* This is important. You will not be banned for using an addon, we promise. If an addon ever allows players to do something that Blizzard disapproves of, Blizzard has the power to disable its functionality forever. It will not ban anyone for using it (however, abuse and harassment is another matter).

Fortunately, you don't have to take our word for it. Drysc, an official Blizzard representative, made the following clarification: "Due to the UI and macro restrictions and our ability to control the use of functions within each, you will not be banned for any use of a pure UI addon or macro that wholly runs within the confines of the game."

Not All Executables Are Bad

Just to make things more confusing, there are some legal executables that you'll come in contact with in the WoW modding world. These programs are fundamentally different than the unauthorized third-party programs mentioned previously.

Some addons are distributed as Windows installers. These are not considered unauthorized or dangerous because they don't interfere with the WoW client, nor do they modify core game files. Be careful, though; and always make sure your installer is from a trusted source. Executables can do literally anything to your computer. Legit installers do nothing more than place addons' files into the proper place on your computer.

Also, some addons include an executable component that's used to provide automatic updates. Again, they're okay to use because they don't mess with core installation files or data in memory while the game is running. For example, a popular addon compilation called Cosmos ships with an auto-updater. There's no risk in using it.

In most cases, common sense will dictate whether a program is okay to use. The technical distinctions between legal and illegal mods are subtle, but become easier to understand as you gain familiarity with them. You can safely assume that every hack discussed in this book is legal, and will *not* endanger your account.

What's So Special About Addons?

To reiterate: Addons are legal because they run entirely within the WoW client. They're not executables. Instead, they exist as source code that's dynamically compiled by the game. Because all addon code passes through the client's interpreter, nothing remains outside of Blizzard's control. That means if and when an addon becomes too powerful, Blizzard can disable its functionality instead of banning anyone.

For example, about a year after the game's launch, an addon was released that would automatically run your character from place to place. No one who downloaded or used the addon was banned, but Blizzard responded with a patch that disabled the addon.

Remember, even though addons are legal, you're still responsible for your in-game behavior. If you abuse an addon that spits out spam, you'll be banned for spamming. Once again, common sense is the bottom line. If it feels like you're cheating, you probably are. If it feels like you're harassing other players, then you're at risk.

Hammering Home the Legality Issue

Because the legality of addons is one of the most frequent inquiries from players, I'm including the following two posts from a thread on the official Blizzard forums. Trimble is not a Blizzard representative, but he provides a very accurate overview of the situation. Slouken, however, is a Blizzard employee, who confirms the accuracy of Trimble's post, yet clarifies that inappropriate behavior won't be tolerated under any circumstances.

Trimble's Post

UI addons fall into two categories:

- **Macros:** *Macros aren't really addons at all, but they can use Lua code to do neat things in game. These are found ENTIRELY inside the game, and the code is run by Blizzard's interpreter, so [Blizzard makes] the rules on what macros can and cannot do. Therefore, Blizzard won't ban someone from using any macros.*

- **Addons:** *Addons are extra files, put into the WoW Interface directory on your hard drive, which supplement the existing Lua and XML code that Blizzard created that makes up the user interface that everyone uses. Addons are made up of Lua files, and XML files, both of which are also run by Blizzard's interpreter. Therefore, Blizzard won't ban someone from using any Addons.*

Third-party programs are actual programs that get loaded into memory and executed using their own code. They run separate from the game similar to how ICQ or MSN Messenger runs in the background. The difference is that third-party hacks try to read or change data coming into or out of the WoW game client (to the network card), or they try to read or write to memory space used by the WoW Game client.

Speed hacks, for example, often interfere with data flowing from the game client to the network card by intercepting the "I am here" signal that the game client sends to the server and making it seem that the player is moving faster than he should be. The server accepts this as truth because Blizzard left it up to the game client to limit how fast you can go. (Oops, Blizzard?) This strange design is caused by a need to let the game client do some of the work because the server is too busy to be expected to do everything.

Anyway, the distinction in third-party hacks is usually the fact that hacks run as their own programs and interfere with the game client.

Addons aren't anything more than really extravagant macros.

(Note: Cosmos is known to have an external EXE file that gets run as its own code — however, it doesn't interfere with the game client. In fact, all it does is download Lua and XML files, put them in the right places, and then QUIT long before the WoW game client even starts.)

Slouken's Response

This is a very good explanation of things as I understand them. However, I am not involved in policy and I'm not a lawyer.

While we've done our best not to penalize people who use the scripting interface, even in ways that aren't intended, it's conceivable that at some point someone will find a way to use them that is against the terms of use (e.g. is hurting other people's play experience), and is something we can't disable. In that case it's possible that we might warn people that using the addon is against the terms of use, and if they continue to do so, some action would be taken.

If you haven't been explicitly warned by a GM, or seen an official Blizzard response about an addon or UI modification, then don't worry about it.

How Does Blizzard Enforce Its Terms of Use?

You may be wondering how Blizzard prevents the use of illegal third-party programs. If they're not sending data to Blizzard's servers directly, how does Blizzard know about them at all? Well, a part of the WoW client is called the Warden. The Warden monitors the other programs running on your computer and reports this information back to Blizzard. Thousands of accounts are banned each month based on this collected information.

The Warden is looking specifically for programs that are reading or modifying the game's memory. It scans for the signatures of known cheating programs. The code that powers the Warden is updated often, and is downloaded each time you connect to the WoW servers. The Warden cannot be successfully removed or disabled.

Many people have raised concerns about privacy because the Warden can monitor just about anything your computer is doing while you're playing WoW. Blizzard has stated that it uses the information reported by the Warden only for enforcing its Terms of Use and discovering illegal programs. Many people accept the Warden as a necessary aspect of an exploit-free game. Many more people are unaware that the Warden even exists at all.

Who Watches the Watchers?

In late 2005, a programmer named Greg Hoglund released a tool that monitors the activity of the Warden. This program is called the Governor, and is freely available at:

```
www.rootkit.com/newsread_print.php?newsid=371
```

Caution: No one has ever been banned for using the Governor. However, Blizzard will know that you've used it because the Warden will tell them. The author of the Governor has stated that his tool "is not designed to assist cheaters, and offers no mechanism to help cheaters hide their programs." Just remember, Blizzard reserves the right to ban you for using any third-party program at any time, so if you do use the Governor, you do so at your own risk.

You probably shouldn't bother actually using the Governor because the information it provides isn't exactly crystal clear, as the following figure shows.

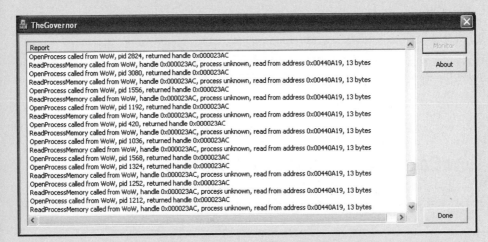

It's much more important to understand the concepts at work here, and accept the fact that if you play World of Warcraft you're consenting to give up your privacy.

Many people in the Internet community believe that the Warden represents a dangerous violation of personal privacy. However, many legitimate WoW players support the Warden for cracking down on illegitimate behavior that would otherwise ruin the game. No matter which side you agree with, you need to be aware that Blizzard is monitoring all activity on your computer while you're playing World of Warcraft.

Exploring the WoW User Interface

Now that you know you're allowed to use addons, what exactly are they? To help answer that question I'm going to explain a little bit about how the WoW User Interface (UI) works. To start with, the default UI isn't hard-coded into the client; it's scripted. Pretty much everything that makes up the interface is one of three things:

- Markup files that describe the layout of interface elements
- Scripts that define the behavior of onscreen objects on their underlying logic
- Texture files that determine what interface components look like

This kind of UI implementation has many benefits, the most important of which is flexibility. Because everything is built with high-level elements such as frames, buttons, and sliders, the interface is easy to tweak. Blizzard knew they were going to be constantly updating the game, so this freedom of modification was absolutely necessary. They also wanted to make it easy for *you* to modify.

Scripts and the WoW API

Embedded within World of Warcraft is a powerful scripting language called Lua. There's also a bridge between Lua and the game's environment called the WoW Application Programming Interface (API). The WoW API includes a collection of functions that can be called from within Lua scripts. This allows scripts to interact with the game environment.

Because Blizzard scripted almost everything in the default interface, it was natural for them to open up the framework and allow their users to create their own scripts. They went one step further and developed a nice system for installing and managing user-created interface modules. These custom modules are known as addons.

Addons and Macros

Macros are basically just tiny addons that are implemented in-game. Although they're streamlined to work with slash commands, they have the same access to the scripting system thanks to the /script command. In addition, macros have the following limitations:

- You can store 18 global macros that are shared between all your characters and another 18 that are character-specific.
- Each macro has a 255-character limit.

Unlike macros, addons have no size limitations. Furthermore, addons are able to utilize eXtensible Markup Language (XML) files to define the layout of their interface elements.

Because addons are just a collection of files in a folder, you don't really need to know anything about the UI, API, or scripting to install and use them.

Modding Limitations

Blizzard has placed some intentional limitations on user-created scripts to prevent certain kinds of addons and macros from being written, including the following:

- **Character movement can't be controlled:** All the functions that control character movement are protected, which means only addons signed by Blizzard can use them. Basically that means they aren't available to you.

- **World coordinates are unavailable:** WoW uses a few different coordinate systems, one of which is world coordinates. These coordinates are the most accurate representation of your location. Unfortunately, they haven't been available since the `GetPlayerPosition()` function was removed from the API in a patch shortly after the game's release.

- **You can't tell which way you're facing:** The `UnitFacing()` function can no longer be used to determine which direction a character is facing. It was removed from the API in the same patch.

- **Data on disk isn't updated during gameplay:** Addons can store and access their own local data, but it's only updated on disk when your character leaves the world. This prevents third-party programs from legally monitoring in-game actions by simply reading files on disc. Remember, sniffing the client's memory would be a violation of the Terms of Use.

- **No mod can choose a target for you:** You are unable to use Lua's conditional statements to select another unit; it must be an explicit decision on the part of the player.

- **No mod can choose a spell for you:** Similarly, you cannot use conditional statements to pick which spell should be cast; this decision must also be explicit.

The last two limitations were introduced with the 2.0 patch and were highly controversial. However, most of the controversy was because of a lack of understanding about what exactly was being changed. Fortunately, some of the new slash commands that Blizzard added to the macro system are powerful enough to offset those restrictions. Furthermore, most addons can be designed a little differently to take them into account. A limited number of addons (like Decursive) were severely crippled by them and are no longer available.

Creating a Simple Macro

Most people use macros to combine two or more simple actions. As mentioned earlier, macros are like mini-addons. You can get a lot of mileage out of them, especially once you learn Lua scripting and can effectively utilize the `/script` command, as well as the numerous new slash commands added with the 2.0 patch.

Let's start with the basics and create a simple macro that casts a spell and announces the action to your group (see Figure 1-1). Of course, you should replace the name of the macro and the spell that it casts with one that your character actually has. The following macro would only be appropriate for a Priest.

1. Type the slash command /macro to bring up the Create Macros window. You can also press Escape to open the Main Menu and then click the Macros button.

2. Click the New button. A small window opens to the right.

3. Name your new macro. For a healing spell, "Heal" might be a good name.

4. Choose an appropriate icon for your macro from the huge list. If you select the question-mark (?) icon, then the icon associated with the first item or spell referenced by your macro will be used instead.

5. When you're done, click the Okay button.

6. Type the following lines into the textbox.

```
/cast Heal
/p Healing %t
```

The %t is a special code that inserts the name of your target into the comment. Below the textbox is a reminder of how many characters you've used.

7. Drag your macro's icon into an open action bar slot.

8. Click the Exit button or press Escape to close the window.

FIGURE 1-1: The Create Macros window and the newly created Heal macro.

In all macros, each line of text is interpreted as a separate command. Each command is executed near-simultaneously, so you can't cast two spells in a row unless the first one doesn't activate the global cooldown timer.

Note that the /cast command works with any spell or ability, so even if you're not a caster, you would still use it to perform many of your actions within a macro. For example:

/cast Fireball

You can even get more specific:

/cast Fireball(Rank 1)

Notice the lack of a space between the name of the spell (or ability) and its rank. If you don't specify a rank explicitly, the highest rank your character knows will be used.

Note   Blizzard overhauled the macro system with the release of WoW 2.0 and The Burning Crusade expansion by adding a huge number of slash commands to the game. See Chapter 16 for more specific information about creating your own advanced macros.

Finding Downloadable Addons

There are literally thousands of addons out there. Fortunately, a few websites have popped up offering addon hosting and organization. Many of the larger addon projects have their own websites, too, but if you're not sure what you're looking for yet, it's best to start with one of the generalized sites. The one you choose to use most often is entirely up to you, although you'll probably end up visiting them all from time to time. Each of the "big three" sites — Curse.com, UI.WorldofWar.net, and WoWInterface.com — host thousands of active addon projects. We asked representatives from each site to summarize what they offer.

Read each site's statement, and then fire up your web browser and check them out. All three offer regularly updated news and files, but each one has a distinctive feel and exclusive features. Once you're comfortable navigating around, download a few addons that look interesting to you. If you're worried about picking an addon that's too complicated for a beginner, grab Atlas. It's simple to use.

Note   I'm the author of Atlas. Excuse the shameless plug!

UI.WorldofWar.net

http://ui.worldofwar.net/

"About six years ago we set up the first Warcraft III maps site (maps.worldofwar.net), which is actually still running, and as soon as WoW was released we thought we could use the same in-house site system to help the WoW modding community and also add a specialist section to WorldofWar.net for modding. The site was fairly rudimentary to start, but with great feedback from the community we updated and added new features to the site continually. With user input, we managed to create an absolutely awesome site that not only helps WoW players but just as importantly the mod authors.

"UI.WorldofWar.net (see Figure 1-2) takes a different approach than most sites. We are very hands-on. We could have just created a file hosting site and left it at that but having worked on the Warcraft III maps site for well over four years we realized the importance of the community and also giving authors and visitors features that are actually useful. Because of that we have created many features that you won't find anywhere else such as multi-zip downloading for users to download all their favorites in one go, visual aids to notify users when mods are suitable for use with the current version of the game, accurate lists of popular mods, special bug reporting features, community awards for outstanding mods, and many more features users will find useful.

FIGURE 1-2: ui.worldofwar.net.

"From day one we have worked with Blizzard to make sure that we comply with its EULAs and TOS agreements. It's important to us that we can support Blizzard and the community by making sure that everything on the site is legal and falls into line with Blizzard's policies.

"Most importantly, we have a real sense of community and great dialogue between site administrators, mod authors, and WoW players."

— Paul Younger (Rushster)

Curse.com

www.curse-gaming.com/

"Our website started up around January of 2005 as a guild website for Curse in WoW. The members in WoW had been complaining about not having a centralized place to update addons from, so we took the initiative to make one and get authors submitting addons to Curse (see Figure 1-3). It took off instantly, and traffic skyrocketed in a matter of weeks.

FIGURE 1-3: Curse.com.

"I believe that the main thing that sets our website apart from the other modding sites is that we are not dedicated exclusively to addons. Our users may find news and submit news, and share images and videos with each other as well as find guides, strategies, and relevant game information on our wiki. The fact that we are always looking to expand our functionality as well as broaden our areas of service is definitely something we consider to be a great asset to modders and WoW'ers alike.

"While almost all of our content isn't unique, we do try our best to make it stand out and be the best out there. We do, however, get exclusive images, videos, and information from various game developers."

— David Cramer and Christopher Carter

WoWInterface.com

www.wowinterface.com/

"Now a part of the Zam.com network, WoWInterface.com was started by Dolby, Kudane, and Cairenn, the same team that brought you EQInterface. The site is a proud member of the Blizzard Official Fan Site Program and has quickly become one of the biggest UI sites for World of Warcraft. We have more than 7,500 people making use of our site at any one time.

"Our sites are extremely proactive in supporting UI authors. We feel strongly that the authors deserve all assistance that we can provide. From having the fastest approval time on submissions of mods to the site to assistance in protecting authors' intellectual property rights, we are here for the authors. We do more than just host mods.

"We are the only site to run an IRC channel dedicated specifically to WoW UI authors. Authors from across the globe are welcome to join us in the channel, sharing coding practices, learning from one another, assisting each other with mod debugging and testing, and just plain hanging out, kicking back, and relaxing with like-minded people. And we have two in-game author guilds, and a Portal system that enables authors to have, in essence, their own site where they may post news and FAQs about their mods, and have version control resources such as Feature Request and Bug Report tracking among other things.

"WoWInterface.com (see Figure 1-4) also hosts four major projects: the Ace and CT mod sites, both of which are so hugely popular that they have to maintain their own sites in addition to being available via the mod sites; WoW UI Designer, a program that makes it much easier for beginning (and advanced) authors to create mods; and the WoWInterface Development Network (WDN).

FIGURE 1-4: WoWInterface.com.

"Lastly, in over four years in operation, with three of the largest UI sites for each of their respective games, we can proudly say that we have never released a User Interface that contained any trojan or virus. Our approval system for files has helped us create an outstanding record for preventing the spread of trojans and viruses.

"We're extremely proud of the reputation and trust we've built with our users, our authors, and the gaming companies themselves and we continue to work hard to maintain them."

— WoWInterface Administrator

Installing and Managing Addons

You've had a chance to look around the addon sites, and maybe you've downloaded an addon or two. If you've never used an addon before, install only one to start out with, just to make sure you get the process down and everything works. Then you can go ahead and install more.

Installing an Addon from a Compressed Archive

Use the following steps to get a typical addon that you've downloaded installed and working properly in the game. The majority of addons are distributed as ZIP compressed archives. A few use other compression formats (like RAR), for which this guide is still applicable, although you may need to download additional compression software to uncompress them. A few others have installers; for those, simply follow the instructions that come with them.

1. Locate the downloaded addon archive.

2. Extract everything in the archive into a new folder on your desktop. Performing this step depends on the OS that you're using:

   ■ Windows XP or Vista: Double-click the file. Then select File ⇨ Extract All and follow the directions.

   ■ Mac OS X: Simply double-click the file and extraction will begin automatically.

   ■ Older Windows: If you don't already have compression software, you'll need to download and install some. I personally recommend 7-Zip (7-zip.org) because it's free and open source. You can also check out WinZip, PowerArchiver, or WinRAR (for RAR files), although they're all commercial programs that you need to buy.

3. Now you need to locate the addon folder or folders. Each addon module consists of one folder, but some addons are comprised of multiple modules. Open the folder that contains the extracted contents of the archive. Once inside:

   ■ If you see a folder with the name of the addon, check to make sure that it contains a .toc file. If it does, select the folder and all other folders at the same level in the directory structure. Then copy everything you have selected to the clipboard.

   ■ If you see a folder called Interface, open it. You should then see another folder called AddOns within it. Open it, too. You should now see at least one folder with the name of the addon. Select all the folders you see and copy them to the clipboard.

4. Locate your WoW installation directory as follows:

- Windows default:

  `C:\Program Files\World of Warcraft\`

- Mac OS X default:

  `/Applications/World of Warcraft/`

5. Open the Interface folder.

6. Once inside, open the AddOns folder.

7. Paste the contents of the clipboard into the AddOns folder. Figure 1-5 shows what this folder should look like with a number of addons installed. Note that all the folders starting with "Blizzard_" are present by default. If you ever delete them, they'll just come back the next time you run the game.

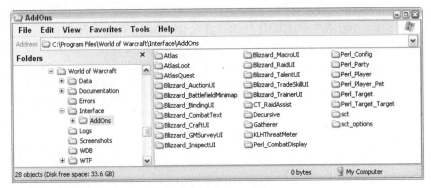

FIGURE 1-5: A typical Interface/AddOns folder in Windows.

8. You can safely delete the folder on your desktop and the original archive.

Now that the addon is installed, you can test it out in the game! Some addons have a drastic effect on the interface and some leave no visual mark whatsoever. In either case, you might want to verify that the game is properly recognizing the addon.

Making Sure an Addon Is Installed Correctly

Once you've installed an addon, you can check to make sure the game is recognizing it properly, and that it's an up-to-date version. Follow these steps:

1. Start World of Warcraft and log in to your account.

2. On the Character Select screen you should see an Addons button in the lower-left corner. If the button isn't there, then there aren't any addons installed correctly.

3. Click the Addons button to open the Addon List.

4. If you see your addon in the list, it's installed correctly.

If your addon doesn't show up in the list, then chances are it's installed in the wrong place. Go back and make sure your directory structure is correct. Extra levels of folders will prevent addons from being recognized. Each module (aka each folder containing a `.toc` file) needs to be *directly* within the `Interface/AddOns` folder.

Uninstalling an Addon

Sometimes you'll test out an addon and decide it's just not for you. Instead of disabling it (which you'll learn how to do in a minute) and leaving it to clutter up your AddOns folder, you might want to uninstall it altogether. This is really easy to do:

1. Return to your `Interface/Addons` folder in the WoW installation directory.

2. Simply delete the addon's folder. If an addon came with more than one module (which the game actually recognizes as multiple addons), simply delete them all.

Using the In-Game Addon List

The Addon List is a control panel built into the World of Warcraft client that allows you to manage all of your installed addons as well as a few important settings. It provides the best way of disabling specific addons without uninstalling them. You can also use it to enable older addons that haven't been updated since the most recent patch.

The Addon List is opened with the Addons button in the lower-left corner of the Character Select screen. This means you need to be logged in to use it. Also, you need to have at least one addon installed or the button won't even show up. Once opened, the AddOn List will present you with a list of your currently installed addons and a few settings. Figure 1-6 shows the Addon List with a bunch of addons installed.

Figure 1-6: The Addon List is used primarily to enable and disable addons.

The list of installed addons is color-coded by status:

- **Yellow addons:** Enabled; will be loaded automatically.
- **Grey addons:** Disabled; won't be automatically loaded.
- **Red addons:** Out of date or missing dependencies.

Take note that authors can change the default color of an addon's name, so some entries in the list may be colored abnormally. If that's the case, you can always see an addon's status to the right of its name; if nothing is written there, it's enabled.

To enable or disable addons, simply check or uncheck the box next to them. By default, you're marking which addons are enabled for the currently selected character only, because WoW keeps track of this information on a per-character basis. If you want your current settings to apply to all of your characters, select All from the Configure Addons For drop-down box.

Enabling Out of Date Addons

An addon is considered out of date if it was written for an earlier version of the game and hasn't been updated since the most recent major patch. There's no guarantee that these addons will work. However, many of them run just fine because usually only a few UI-related changes are made in each update. To enable these addons, simply check the Load Out of Date Addons checkbox near the top of the window.

The client performs the out of date check by comparing an internal interface number to one that's included in an addon's .toc (table of contents) file. Some players advocate simply changing an old addon's interface number so the game recognizes it as up to date. I don't advise this practice. If an addon is marked as out of date, look for an updated version of it. If you can't find one, just enable out of date addons. If you ever ask for support from an addon's author, it's important that you know if the addon is truly out of date.

There are out-of-game programs that run through all your installed addons and automatically update their interface numbers to match the game's current value. These programs completely defeat the purpose of the version-checking system, and should be avoided entirely. However, if you plan to create your own addons, you should be aware that they exist and that many players use them regularly.

About Addon Dependencies

As you know, addons are designed to be self-contained and modular. However, they're also able to communicate with each other, which allows for all kinds of nice developments such as:

- Addon function libraries (like Ace, Sky, and Chronos)
- Modular info bars (like Titan Panel and FuBar)
- Addons for addons (like AtlasLoot and AtlasQuest for Atlas)

It follows that if one addon depends on another, it shouldn't be able to run unless the addon it depends on is installed and enabled. Fortunately, Blizzard supports dependency checking.

When you mouse-over an addon in the Addon List, its dependencies will be listed beneath its description. If an addon is disabled, then any addon requiring it will also be disabled. An addon missing any of its dependencies can't be enabled.

You might have noticed that some addons list optional dependencies. Addons with optional dependencies will run on their own, but have certain features that require other addons. Any addon with optional dependencies should perform its own checks to see if the addons it works with are present.

Dealing with Errors

When a script that's running (via an addon or macro) tries to do something illegal, references something that doesn't exist, or has a typo in it, there's a high chance that an error will be generated. Historically, a dialog box would pop up immediately containing the name of the offending script and the type of error it generated (see Figure 1-7). However, as of the 2.1 patch, errors are no longer enabled by default. This means they occur silently in the background; you never see them.

Enabling or Disabling Script Errors

If you're developing an addon, having script errors enabled is more or less necessary. If you're just using addons, the choice is up to you. If you leave them turned off, an addon (or a specific feature of an addon) may very well silently fail. You won't necessarily know something's wrong, but you also won't be bothered by dialog boxes popping up. If you turn script errors on, you'll always know immediately when something isn't working the way it's supposed to.

To enable script errors, type the following in-game:

```
/console scriptErrors 1
```

If you ever want to turn them off again, type:

```
/console scriptErrors 0
```

Alternatively, you can use an addon that catches errors and displays them to you, overriding the default interface. If you use one of these addons, the status of the scriptErrors setting doesn't matter. A few of these error-catching addons include BugSack (which was created by Rabbit and uses Ace2 libraries), Swatter (which is included in the Auctioneer package; see Chapter 5), or ImprovedErrorFrame (which is covered on its own in Chapter 4).

What to Do When You Get an Error

If you have script errors enabled, sooner or later you'll enter the world and see one of them appear. Errors can also occur while you're playing the game or tweaking with an addon. It comes with the territory and it's nothing to worry about because it can't affect your WoW installation or characters. It's extremely unlikely that the default UI will ever generate a script error, so it's almost always the fault of an addon. If an error is ever driving you crazy, you can always go the Addon List and disable all your addons; the error will most likely go away immediately. You can also disable script errors as described previously; however, this is a Band-Aid solution and doesn't really address the problem. It's a much better idea to get to the root of the problem, rather than ignore it.

You may be wondering what causes errors in the first place. There are a few possibilities:

- **An addon has a bug, plain and simple:** This isn't the most common reason because most addons are thoroughly tested before being released, but it's still a possibility.

- **An addon is old:** This is much more likely because Blizzard changes the API with each patch. If an API function is removed, an addon that calls it will generate an error.

- **Addons are conflicting with each other:** This is also common. If more than one enabled addon uses the same global variable name or hooks the same function, things can go wrong.

Installing one new addon at a time will help you know right away which addon is causing a problem. Also, you can sometimes figure out which addon is responsible by looking at the error message itself, although this isn't a foolproof method. For example, take a look at the error in Figure 1-7; it's pretty clear that the Atlas addon is responsible because the error references the `Atlas.lua` file.

FIGURE 1-7: An out of date version of Atlas generates a script error after a patch.

In any case, when you get an error, you want to figure out what's causing it and how to get rid of it as soon as possible. Most of the time you can click through the error and keep playing, but it's bound to return sooner or later and something's probably not going to work.

Take the following steps to diagnose and solve the problem:

1. Determine which addon is causing the error. If the answer's not immediately obvious, disable all your addons. Then turn them back on one by one until you get the error again. Try running that addon alone (as the only one enabled) and see if the error persists. If it does, you've found your culprit. If not, it's probably an addon conflict. Try to determine which other addon is responsible using trial and error.

2. Check to see if there's an updated version of the addon. Many addons are updated regularly with bug fixes, new features, and improvements. Don't contact the addon's author with an error report before checking for (and testing out) a new version.

Caution

Steps 3 and 4 are destructive, and you'll lose all of your addon settings if you delete the files in step 3, and all of your WoW settings if you continue on to step 4. You can always move the files listed into another place (such as your desktop) instead of deleting them. This way you can restore them if necessary.

3. If there's no new version (or it didn't help), remove the addon's saved variables by deleting the files in which they're stored. If these saved variables become outdated (because of an addon update, for example) they may cause script errors. You'll find the variables stored in two possible locations within your WoW installation directory:

```
WTF/Account/<username>/SavedVariables/
WTF/Account/<username>/<server>/<character>/SavedVariables/
```

4. If that doesn't help, you may want to try removing your WTF folder altogether. Simply drag it to the desktop (if you don't want to delete it) and restart the WoW client. Your customized game settings will be lost, but the error might go away. You can always drag the WTF folder back to its original location to restore your settings.

5. If removing saved variables didn't work, check the web for other reports of the same error. See if there's a fix or an official comment from the addon's author.

6. If all else fails, submit an error report directly to the author of the addon. Include the text of the error itself and a screenshot if you can. Give a detailed account of when the error is occurring. Include any other information that might be helpful. Be friendly; the people who write addons are volunteering their time to help you out.

Using Interface Skins

As mentioned earlier, the appearance of the WoW interface is determined entirely by individual texture files. These texture files are stored in MPQ archives in the WoW installation folder. Interestingly, the WoW client looks for the files it needs in more than one place.

If you place properly named texture files in a few specific folders, WoW will use them instead of the default files. This process lets you replace the default look and feel of the interface. Figure 1-8 shows a comparison between the default UI and two other different skins.

FIGURE 1-8: UI skinning lets you change the look and feel of the WoW interface.

Are Skins Legal?

Because UI skinning is much less popular than addon development, it seems to have slipped under Blizzard's radar to some extent. A careful review of the Terms of Use seems to indicate that there's nothing inherently wrong with skinning.

Because all you're doing is placing new files into a folder, and not modifying existing files, it's hard to categorize a skin as an addon, program, or mod. One could argue that a skin is certainly "designed to modify the World of Warcraft experience" but given the ease with which skins are installed, it almost seems like UI skinning is an intentional feature. No one has ever been banned for using a skin.

Where to Find Skins

There aren't *nearly* as many skins as there are addons. In fact, there's really only one artist who's created them. This is partly because the interface contains such a huge number of intricate textures that need to be redesigned to make a successful skin. Furthermore, there isn't exactly a skinning system built into the game, just a convenient way of replacing which files are loaded. Finally, no one (yet) has written a program that manages the difficult task of creating WoW skins.

Despite these obstacles, the artist T.King (tkingart.com) has created a number of beautiful WoW skins including Gothic, Castle, Winterwood, and Elfwood. These skins are exclusively available at WoWInterface (www.wowinterface.com) in the Downloads section. At the time of this writing they're the only pure skins available.

Note Several other packages are available that essentially re-skin the interface. These packages are built around collections of addons, and are capable of drastic changes to the layout of the UI. They're covered in Chapter 9.

Installing a Skin

After you've downloaded a skin, follow these steps to install it:

1. Locate the downloaded skin archive.

2. Extract the archive directly into your root WoW installation directory. Skin archives contain a precise relative directory structure, which ensures that each file will end up in the right place.

   Alternatively, you can extract the files onto your desktop first (Mac OS X does so automatically when you double-click the downloaded file). Afterward, locate the Data folder, which will either be the outermost folder or one level deeper. Drag the Data folder into your World of Warcraft folder. If prompted, tell the operating system to replace files. Don't worry; you're not actually replacing anything. The OS only asks this as a precaution.

3. To verify the installation, take a look in the Data/Interface folder. You should see a ton of folders in there.

4. Start the game and enter the world. The interface elements should look a bit different!

Uninstalling a Skin

You can have only one skin installed at a time, so if you want to change skins you have to uninstall the previous one first. If you get tired of a custom skin, you can always uninstall it to revert back to the game's default artwork. Follow these steps to uninstall a skin:

1. Return to your Data/Interface folder in the WoW installation directory.

2. Delete everything in there except for the Cinematics folder.

3. Restart WoW and the interface returns to normal.

That's Only the Beginning . . .

This concludes your introduction to the basics of WoW modding!

In this chapter, you learned about what addons are and how they're perfectly legal to use from Blizzard's point of view. You also learned how they differ from illegal third-party programs. You were introduced to the difference between addons and macros, as well as some of their limitations. The three primary addon websites presented themselves, and you had a chance to download some addons, install them, and figure out how to enable and disable them using the built-in Addon List. You learned about dependencies and how to deal with errors. Finally, you learned how to use (the very few) interface skins that are out there.

The next chapter is the first of eight that cover specific addons, what they do, and how to use them. It focuses specifically on combat-oriented addons. You can either read the next eight chapters straight through or flip through them at your convenience.

Combat Addons

The most common thing you do in WoW is fight, so combat is a natural place for us to start. Azeroth is filled with hostile animals, monsters, and NPCs just waiting to kill you, so you'll want as much of an advantage against them as possible. The addons presented in this chapter can give you that extra edge.

They fall into three broad categories (although most are found in the first):

- Addons that display information differently from the default UI or provide information that you don't typically have. Examples: OmniCC displays numerical cooldown timers directly on your action buttons and MobHealth3 provides estimations of how many hitpoints your enemies have.

- Addons that help you perform certain combat-related tasks. Example: WeaponQuickSwap makes it easy to write weapon-swapping macros.

- Addons that analyze your combat history and provide statistics or breakdowns. Examples: CombatStats gives you an overview of your battle performance and SW Stats monitors everyone else in your party or raid.

Addons can't fight your battles for you, but they can help you win. All combat in WoW is numerical, from the amount of damage you deal to the duration of your spells. Many combat-oriented addons take advantage of this fact, providing you with statistical analyses of the long lists of numbers generated during a fight. The results are often quite useful when trying to compare pieces of equipment or figure out which spells or abilities to use in certain situations.

Combat can also be a chaotic experience where one split-second decision means the difference between life and death. Many addons attempt to give you a clearer representation of how your fights are progressing. How many hitpoints does your enemy have? How many seconds are left until the spell you need becomes available? This kind of information can give you a tremendous advantage in a sticky situation.

However, there is such a thing as too much information. I don't recommend using all of the addons in this chapter at the same time. It's easy to have so many progress bars onscreen at once that you'll be too overwhelmed to win even a straightforward fight.

Note While many of these addons can be useful when raiding, many of them are specifically tailored for very large groups of players. Raid-specific addons are covered in Chapter 7.

Displaying Combat Events with Scrolling Combat Text

Addon created and maintained by Grayhoof

CURSE-GAMING	WORLDOFWAR	WOWINTERFACE

Scrolling Combat Text (SCT) is one of the most widely-used addons out there. Basically, it makes small numbers (and messages) constantly pop up above your character's head during combat, making your fights feel a little more like Final Fantasy. It's not only more fun to see this extra information, but it can be extremely useful. I have a much easier time following everything that's going on when using SCT (compared to reading combat messages out of the chat window). Also, SCT allows for a huge degree of customization.

Using SCT

SCT needs no configuration, although you'll definitely want to play with the settings to get the most out of it. Go find an enemy and start a fight. Typically, you'd see floating numbers only for the damage you're doing to the enemy. With SCT, you can see all the damage you're taking as well (see Figure 2-1).

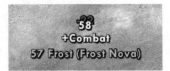

FIGURE 2-1: SCT displays damage you're taking, among many other things.

In addition to damage, SCT can display the following information:

- Incoming and outgoing heals
- Spells (damage, resists, and type)
- Misses (dodge, block, immune, and so on)
- Buffs and debuffs (gain and loss)
- Low health and mana warnings
- Rage, mana, and energy gains
- Combat states (entering or leaving)
- Combo points (with an alert at five)
- Class skill alerts (Execute, Overpower, and so on)
- Honor, reputation, and skill gains

Configuring SCT

Scrolling Combat Text is highly configurable through the use of its tightly packed options window (see Figure 2-2), which you can call up with the command:

`/sctmenu`

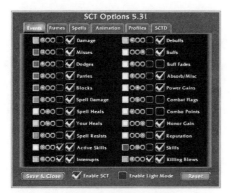

FIGURE 2-2: The options frame lets you customize SCT's appearance.

Here you can configure which messages are displayed, the color they appear in, and the frame they're sent to. The various frames (SCT, SCT2, and SCT Message) are used to distinguish where different messages will be displayed onscreen. You can move frames around individually, as well as change their sizes, fonts, and animation styles.

SCT also has support for profiles so you don't necessarily need to reconfigure your settings for each character (although you might want to). Just click the Profiles tab at the top of the options frame to display a list of the stored profiles for each of your other characters. You can also select one of the pre-built profiles. These presets are a good way to explore some of the things SCT is capable of. Definitely check out Grayhoof's personal profile.

SCT also has a few basic command-line options, which are described in Table 2-1. Use them with the command:

```
/sct <option>
```

You can type /sct alone for an in-game list of these options.

Table 2-1   Scrolling Combat Text Command-Line Options

Option	Description
menu	Displays SCT option menu
reset	Resets SCT options to default
profile	Sets profile for this addon
standby	Suspends/resumes this addon
about	Prints out addon info

Source: documentation by Grayhoof

Looking at the SCTD Extension

Greyhoof, the author of SCT, has created a separate addon called SCT-Damage (SCTD) that allows SCT-like handling of the damage done to your enemies. Typically, the default interface manages this, but SCTD provides additional customization and features that bring these numbers into line with the rest of SCT. Simply install the addon like any other, and you'll see the SCTD tab appear on the top of the options window to the right of the Profiles tab.

Creating Custom SCT Message Events

The nuts and bolts of SCT are just as customizable as its appearance. You can define your own custom SCT message events based on text that appears in the chat frame. Grayhoof provides detailed documentation for this feature (as well as a ton of examples, many of which are enabled by default) in the file you'll use to define these events. The file is named sct_event_config.lua and can be found directly inside the SCT folder. Simply load it up with your favorite text editor to get started, and be sure to read the instructions carefully.

Blizzard's Own Floating Combat Text

Shortly before the Burning Crusade expansion was released, Blizzard integrated its own stripped-down version of SCT — called Floating Combat Text (FCT) — into the default interface. FCT has limited configuration and is a good choice if you need only the most basic features of SCT. I recommend playing around with FCT before deciding whether SCT is right for you.

You can enable FCT on the Advanced tab of the game's Interface Options panel. From the Main Menu (press Esc), go to Interface Options, and then the Advanced Options tab. On the right you'll see the FCT settings (see Figure 2-3). FCT enables you to toggle which events are displayed and to choose the behavior of the text (whether it scrolls up, down, or arcs), but it doesn't let you tweak sizes, colors, or fonts.

FIGURE 2-3: Blizzard's Floating Combat
Text is a simplified take on SCT.

In most cases, SCT's frames, animation styles, fonts, and overall tweakability make it vastly preferable. FCT is a good choice only if you don't want to get your hands dirty with SCT's comprehensive settings.

Calculating the HP of Enemies and Players with MobHealth3

Addon created and maintained by Neronix, based on work by Wyv and Telo

MobHealth3 (MH3) is an addon that attempts to calculate how many hitpoints your enemies have. Because the game doesn't report this information to the client on its own, MH3 employs an algorithm that estimates the actual value. Essentially, it keeps track of how much damage you do and how much that damage affects the reported percentage of the enemy's health.

Knowing exactly how much HP your enemies have isn't the most important thing in the world, but it's often useful, especially because you already know exactly how much damage you're doing. Plus, MobHealth3 is low-profile, it integrates nicely with several other addons, and can even report the estimated health of other players.

The MobHealth3 addon itself doesn't actually display anything; it just does all the necessary calculations. It has its own API so that other addons (such as target frame replacements) can latch on and display the data however they might want to.

Note At the time of this writing, the primary addon sites aren't hosting an up-to-date version of MobHealth3. For the latest version of both MH3 and MH3 Blizzard Frames (see the next section), please visit the list of Ace addons at `http://files.wowace.com/`. Scroll down to find these two.

Using MobHealth3 Blizzard Frames To View the Data

If you don't already use an addon that replaces the default target frame and supports MH3, then you'll need to grab a separate addon by Neronix called MobHealth3 Blizzard Frames (MH3B). This addon simply adds MH3 support to the default Blizzard target frame (see Figure 2-4) and provides a few options for configuring how the value is displayed.

FIGURE 2-4: MH3 estimates how many hitpoints a raptor has; MH3B displays the result.

You can use the following two slash-commands for the MH3B options (see Table 2-2):

```
/mh3blizz <option>
/mh3b <option>
```

Either one, when used alone, displays the help.

Table 2-2   MobHealth3 Blizzard Frames Command-Line Options

Option	Description
abshealth	Toggles showing absolute health on the target frame
abspower	Toggles showing absolute mana/energy/rage on the target frame
healthx	Adjusts the X offset of the health text
healthy	Adjusts the Y offset of the health text
perchealth	Toggles showing percentage health on the target frame

Table 2-2   Continued

Option	Description
percpower	Toggles showing percentage mana/energy/rage on the target frame
powerx	Adjusts the X offset of the power text
powery	Adjusts the Y offset of the power text
about	Prints out addon info

Source: documentation by Neronix

Configuring MobHealth3

MobHealth3 has a few options of its own, which affect how it calculates and stores data. The default values should be fine for you; however if you'd like to see a health estimate earlier, you can lower the precision value. MH3 also has two slash-commands, and you can use either one (see Table 2-3):

```
/mobhealth3 <option>
/mh3 <option>
```

As usual, you can use them alone for in-game help.

Table 2-3   MobHealth3 Command-Line Options

Option	Description
precision	Adjusts the accuracy of MobHealth3 to your liking (a number 1–99). For example, this is the percentage that a mob's health needs to change before you will trust the estimated maximum health and display it. The lower this value is, the quicker you'll see a value and the less accurate it will be. Raiding players may want to turn this down a bit. If you don't care about accuracy and want info ASAP, set this to 1.
reset	Resets the session cache and the DB if you have saving turned on. Basically, because the addon is performing the same calculations over and over again, it can create a cache of the HP values it derives that persists from one session to the next. However, the calculations are easy, so this cache isn't necessary for most players (see the save command).
save	Saves data across sessions. This alternative is not really necessary. A cache is always kept with data for every enemy you fought this session. Remember, recalculating an enemy's health is trivial.
stablemax	When turned on, the max HP updates only once your target changes. If data for the target is unknown, MH3 will update once during the battle when the precision percentage is reached.
about	Prints out addon info.

Source: documentation by Neronix

Viewing Detailed Enemy Information in the Tooltip with MobInfo-2

Addon created by Dizzarian, maintained by Skeeve, incorporating work by Wyv

CURSE-GAMING   WORLDOFWAR

MobInfo-2 keeps track of everything you kill, where it was, how much health it had, what it dropped, as well as a ton of other stats. Whenever you encounter an enemy you've seen before, any data that's been collected earlier is placed in the tooltip. Over time, as you kill more and more of the same kind of mob, this data becomes more accurate. For example, after you've killed 50 of the same mob, you'll see a pretty good breakdown of how often certain items drop from it. Certain calculations are performed as well, such as how many times you would need to kill the mob in question to level up. MobInfo-2 also calculates how many hitpoints enemies have (much like MobHealth), but its other features extend considerably further.

Using MobInfo-2

Like most addons, MobInfo-2 comes with a very usable set of default values. The first thing you'll notice is that the tooltip contains more information when your mouse is hovering over a mob that you've killed before (see Figure 2-5). As you kill more of the same mob, each value will begin to stabilize. For example, the rarity of a certain item dropping won't become accurate until you've killed a few dozen of that mob. Over time, you'll develop a valuable database that you can use to figure out where to obtain items or which mobs are most worth your time to hunt.

FIGURE 2-5: MobInfo-2 places additional enemy information in the tooltip.

Configuring MobInfo-2

You can open the MobInfo-2 options window with either of these two slash-commands:

```
/mobinfo2
/mi2
```

All settings are controlled here; there aren't any additional command-line options. You can mouse-over any setting to view a detailed explanation of what it controls. The options window consists of four different tabs:

- **Tooltip:** Controls which statistics are displayed in the tooltip and how they are displayed
- **Health/Mana:** Adjusts how HP and mana values appear in the target frame
- **Database:** Enables you to adjust or reset the database, and to import data
- **Search:** Provides a simple way to browse through the database

Importing an External Database

It takes a long time to develop a good (and complete) MobInfo-2 database, so you might want to get a head start by finding someone else's to import. When you import a database, any new data is merged with the current database. You can ask a friend to send you a backup copy of his or her database or you can search for one online. Follow these steps (provided by Skeeve) to perform the import:

1. Close the WoW client.

2. Back up your MobInfo-2 database (see the next section) just to be safe.

3. Rename the file you want to import from `MobInfo2.lua` to `MI2_Import.lua`. If you downloaded the database, it will probably already have the correct name.

4. Copy the file into:

   `World of Warcraft\Interface\AddOns\MobInfo2\`

5. Start WoW and enter the world.

6. Open the MobInfo-2 options and go to the Database tab. If there's valid data to import, it will be indicated and the Import button will be clickable.

7. Choose whether you want to import everything or only unknown Mobs. If a Mob already exists in your database and you choose to import everything, the data of the new Mob will get added to the data of the existing Mob.

8. Click the Import button. You'll see a summary of the results in the chat window.

9. Log out to save the new database.

10. Delete the `MI2_Import.lua` file; otherwise it wastes memory.

Backing Up Your Database

In case you ever need to switch computers or reinstall WoW, you might want to back up your MobInfo-2 database so you don't lose all your hard-earned data. You might also want to share your database with other people. Simply locate the `MobInfo2.lua` file in the following location:

```
World of Warcraft\WTF\Account\<account name>\SavedVariables\
```

Copy the file and save it in a safe place.

Seeing All Your Cooldowns Numerically with OmniCC

Addon created and maintained by Tuller

Omni Cooldown Count (OmniCC) is an awesome yet simple addon. Any spell or ability will display its remaining cooldown time on top of its icon (see Figure 2-6). If it's not cooling-down, nothing extra is displayed. It works everywhere: the default action bars, your inventory, the character sheet, and with most other addons. No setup is necessary.

FIGURE 2-6: OmniCC adds cooldown values to spell and ability icons.

Configuring OmniCC

If you're the tweaker type, OmniCC gives you a bunch of appearance settings to fiddle with, all of which are pretty self-explanatory (see Table 2-4). The `model` command toggles the default rotating cooldown timer. The slash-command is:

```
/omnicc <option>
```

Use the command alone for help.

Table 2-4   OmniCC Command-Line Options

Option	Description
size	Sets the font size. The default value is 20.
font	Sets the font to use.

Table 2-4 *Continued*

Option	Description
color	`<duration> <r> <g> <b>` Sets the color to use for cooldowns of `<duration>`. Duration can be `vlong`, `long`, `medium`, or `short`.
scale	`<duration> <value>` Sets the scale to use for cooldowns of `<duration>`. Once again, duration can be `vlong`, `long`, `medium`, or `short`.
min	Sets the minimum duration (seconds) a cooldown should be to show text. The default value is 3.
model	Toggles the cooldown model.
shine	Toggles a brighter flash on finished cooldowns.
shinescale	Sets the size of the bright cooldown flash. The default value is 4.
reset	Goes back to default settings.

Source: documentation by Tuller

Enabling OmniCC Basic Mode

As if it weren't already simple enough, OmniCC comes with a basic version of itself that involves no configuration and doesn't save any variables. Basic mode also eliminates color-coded values (all text is yellow) and text scaling (all durations are the same size).

If you want to switch over to this light version, open up the `!OmniCC.toc` file (no, the exclamation point isn't a typo) and delete the following lines:

```
cooldown.lua
main.lua
```

Then, replace them with the line:

```
basic.lua
```

Save, close, and you're done.

Keeping Track of Your Biggest Hits with CritLine

Addon created by Sordit, maintained by Bloodmoon

`CURSE-GAMING` `WORLDOFWAR`

CritLine is a lot of fun. It adds an exciting element to the game: the ability to keep track of your record-breaking critical strikes! Sure, it's not quite as exciting as leveling or getting a piece of your set, but it's still a blast when it happens. Basically, the addon keeps track of your highest hits (and heals) and alerts you whenever you break a record. This is a great addon for people who like to brag.

Using CritLine

CritLine's primary functionality is automatic. When you break a record you'll know about it. When you first install the addon there are a lot of records to break, because pretty much everything you do is a new record, but soon enough they'll die down as CritLine establishes a good baseline of records, and you'll be alerted only when it's a big deal (see Figure 2-7).

FIGURE 2-7: According to CritLine, it's a new Frostbolt record!

You'll notice that CritLine adds a little CL icon to the edge of the minimap. Click the button to see a nice report of all your high scores. The Show Summary button spawns a smaller, more concise version, although it's still too big to keep onscreen all the time (see Figure 2-8). Click the minimap button again to make the report go away. You can drag either window around the screen wherever you want.

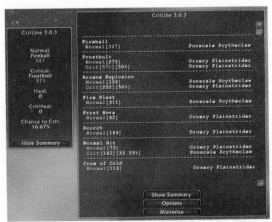

FIGURE 2-8: CritLine tracks your high scores for each spell and ability.

Configuring CritLine

CritLine has its own configuration dialog, which is accessible with the Options button on the main report. The settings in the window are all pretty clear, except for the Use Level Adjustment setting, which requires that high scores come from enemies within four levels of you.

There are also a few command-line options (see Table 2-5) that you can use with the following slash-commands:

```
/critline <option>
/cl <option>
```

In this case no help is available if you use either command alone.

Table 2-5   CritLine Command-Line Options

Option	Description
open	Opens the CritLine window as if you had clicked on the minimap icon
show	Shows the CritLine icon on the minimap
hide	Hides the CritLine icon
reset	Resets the character you are currently playing
resetall	Resets all characters

Source: documentation by Sordit and Bloodmoon

Seeing the Casting Bars of Your Enemies with Natur EnemyCastBar

Addon created by Limited, maintained by Naturfreund

CURSE-GAMING   WORLDOFWAR   WOWINTERFACE

Natur EnemyCastBar (NECB) attempts to replicate your target's spell casting bar. Since the Burning Crusade expansion was released, this functionality has been made available in the default interface (you'll see instructions on enabling it a little later). However, like Floating Combat Text, the built-in enemy cast-bar feature is basic, with almost no configuration. NECB is a mature addon with a huge number of options and features that can give useful information in PvP, PvE, and raid situations.

Using NECB

Under ideal conditions, as soon as a nearby enemy begins casting a spell, a bar will appear on your screen and begin counting down (see Figure 2-9). The bar will be labeled with the name of the spell as well as the name of its caster. If another spell is detected, a new bar will appear right next to the first. When the bars are empty (and the spells cast) they'll disappear.

FIGURE 2-9: NECB imitates your enemies' casting bars and tracks debuffs.

NECB is also capable of tracking debuffs (much like CCWatch, the next addon discussed in this chapter), such as Polymorph, Hamstring, and Chilled effects (some of these are also visible in Figure 2-9). This list includes many debuffs cast by mobs and bosses as well.

Furthermore, if multiple people in a raid are running NECB, events can be transferred throughout the network, effectively extending the range of detection and keeping everyone on the same page. Individuals can also spawn their own countdown bars (with custom messages), and then broadcast them to everyone else in the raid.

Configuring NECB

NECB has a centralized control panel and a whole host of slash-commands. In fact, it has far too many settings to document in this book (see Figure 2-10), so they won't be covered in detail.

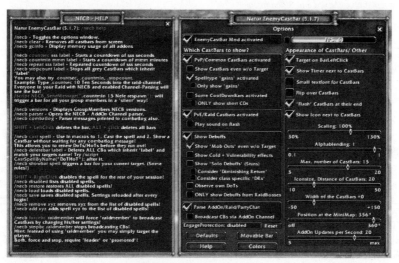

FIGURE 2-10: NECB is feature-rich and has a steeper learning curve than most addons.

The control panel is easily accessed from a minimap button (with red, yellow, and green bars) or with the slash-command /necb. Here's a brief description of a few of the features and settings NECB offers:

- **Easy to disable:** NECB is resource intensive and can sometimes cause poor performance on slower machines or when a lot is going on. The addon can be easily disabled with a checkbox in the upper-left corner of the control panel. Disabling NECB unregisters all events, eliminating the load placed on your computer.

- **Event settings:** The settings on the left side of the control panel primarily determine which events trigger a bar to appear. If you mouse-over each setting, you can read a description of it.

- **Appearance/performance settings:** The settings on the right side of the control panel primarily affect the appearance of the bars and the performance of the addon. Again, mouse-over descriptions are available.

- **Help window:** Typing `/necb help` or clicking the Help button opens a comprehensive help window that details many of NECB's features and slash-commands.

- **Default, position, and color settings:** The rest of the buttons in the lower-left corner let you reset all settings to their defaults, reposition the location of the bars onscreen, and change the bars' colors.

- **AddOn Channel Parser:** Typing `/necb parser` opens the AddOn Channel Parser, which monitors the communication between different people running the addon. This is only of interest if you're using NECB in a raid or group.

- **FPS meter:** In the upper-right corner of the control panel you can enable a nice FPS meter, which can be dragged around the screen.

- **Memory usage monitor:** Typing `/necb gcinfo` opens a window that monitors the game's memory usage.

Fore more information, refer to the documentation that comes with NECB, which can be found split between two files: `Changelog.txt` and `NECB_Interface_readme.txt`.

Enabling the Default Enemy Casting Bars

As mentioned previously, the default interface is now capable of displaying your target's casting bar. There are two modes (see Figure 2-11), one of which places the casting bar below the target frame, and another that places it on the floating panel above a nearby unit's head (if the panels are enabled). The latter is particularly useful because you can see if a nearby unit is casting whether or not you have it targeted.

FIGURE 2-11: An enemy's cast bar below the
target frame (left) and above his head (right).

To enable these features, open the Interface Options panel. On the Advanced Options tab, select the appropriate checkboxes in the Display section (see Figure 2-12).

FIGURE 2-12: The appropriate Interface
Options to enable enemy cast bars.

Monitoring the Durations of Spells You Cast on Your Enemies with CCWatch

Addon created by Elwen, maintained by Phoenixfire2001

CURSE-GAMING   WORLDOFWAR

CCWatch pops up a progress bar whenever you cast a spell that has a lasting effect, like Frostbolt or Polymorph. The progress bar slowly fills, helping you estimate how long a spell will remain active on your target. This kind of information can be crucial for any class with crowd-control abilities, hence the name CCWatch. Be warned, CCWatch isn't perfect, but the info is valuable enough as a guide that any imperfections are easily overlooked. The appearance of the bars is also somewhat configurable.

Using CCWatch

The first thing you'll notice after installing the addon is that it scans through all your spells, abilities, and talents, and then indexes those that are applicable. As a result of this process, you'll see a bunch of messages in your chat window when the addon loads. The durations of spells aren't available via the WoW API, so CCWatch consults its own spell duration database. CCWatch works best with the highest rank of each spell you know.

I recommend heading out to an area with some easy enemies so you can get a feel for CCWatch and how you'd like to configure it. Use one of your lasting abilities on an enemy and a progress bar with the ability's name will appear and begin filling up. Figure 2-13 shows examples of CCWatch's bars.

FIGURE 2-13: CCWatch shows the durations of
your spells' lasting effects.

As mentioned before, CCWatch isn't perfect and sometimes your spells won't trigger a progress bar, especially if you're pretty far away from your target, or if you're fighting many enemies at once. Remember that CCWatch's progress bars only provide an estimate of an effect's length. Sometimes your spell will break before its full duration is up.

Configuring CCWatch

CCWatch provides a configuration interface that you open by typing:

```
/ccw config
```

You can set most of CCWatch's options here, as well as custom-configure the spell duration database. Unlock CCWatch before scaling the bars or setting their opacity so you can see a preview of how they'll look. Personally, I like having the timers count down instead of up.

Most options can also be set from the command-line (see Table 2-6) with either of the following slash-commands:

```
/ccwatch <option>
/ccw <option>
```

Use the commands alone for help.

Table 2-6   CCWatch Command-Line Options

Option	Description
on	Enables CCWatch
off	Disables CCWatch
lock	Locks CCWatch and enables
unlock	Allows you to move CCWatch
config	Shows the configuration menu
print	Prints the current configuration
invert	Inverts progress bar direction
scale	Scales CCWatch, use 0.25 to 3.0
width	Sets bar width, use 50 to 300
alpha	Sets bar alpha, use 0 to 1
grow	Sets bar priority system: down (bars on same spot get pushed down), up (bars on same spot get pushed up) or off (bars on the same spot overwrite each other)
u	Updates improved skill ranks
timers	Sets timers display off, on (counts up) or rev (countdown)
warn	Enables/disables chat warnings
warncc	Sets which communication channel to use (EMOTE, SAY, PARTY, RAID, YELL, or custom)
clear	Clears saved configuration settings (undocumented)

Source: documentation by Elwen and Phoenixfire2001

Creating Easy Weapon-Swapping Macros with WeaponQuickSwap

Addon created and maintained by CapnBry

CURSE-GAMING   WORLDOFWAR

WeaponQuickSwap is unlike many addons in that it's solely designed to aid in the creation of macros. Technically, WeaponQuickSwap adds two functions to the scripting namespace. These functions allow you to write simple macros that will swap the weapons you're holding. The two functions are WeaponSwap() and MageWeaponSwap().

Both functions are used in the following form:

```
/script WeaponSwap("main1", "off1", "main2", "off2", ...);
```

Each parameter should actually be the name of a weapon (names are case-sensitive). The two main parameters represent main-hand weapons; the two off parameters represent off-hand weapons. If main1 and off1 are equipped when the macro is used, then they'll be swapped out for main2 and off2, and vice versa. MageWeaponSwap() is exactly the same except it acts on the main-hand and ranged slots.

You're required to specify at least one set of items (two parameters), which basically just equips those two items, and then does nothing else. You can also specify more than two sets, which will rotate among the sets in order. Most of the time you'll use two sets. Figure 2-14 shows an example macro.

FIGURE 2-14: Swapping from a
two-hander to a dagger and a shield.

If you're referencing a two-handed weapon (or you want one of the slots to be empty) just leave that parameter as an empty string, for example:

```
/script WeaponSwap("Sword", "Shield", "Large Sword", "");
```

You can use an asterisk (*) as a wildcard character to keep a slot unchanged. Whatever was equipped before the swap will remain in place. For example, to swap your main-hand slot only:

```
/script WeaponSwap("Sword", "*", "Dagger", "*");
```

Finally, a comment on WeaponQuickSwap's web page suggested using this macro to remove your weapons before dying so you won't have to pay for repairs:

```
/script WeaponSwap("", "");
```

WeaponQuickSwap comes with good documentation, so check it out for more examples.

Evaluating Your Performance in Battle with CombatStats

Addon created by DmgInc, maintained by Smuggles

CombatStats gives you access to a detailed statistical breakdown of your combat actions. It tracks all your different attacks and heals so you can analyze each element individually or all of them at once. It provides a great way to numerically compare the effectiveness of different spells or to see how you're stacking up against your friends.

Note

The latest version of CombatStats isn't available on any of the primary addon sites (only old, out-of-date versions are hosted at the time of this writing). For the latest version, please visit http://realisticsoftware.com/pages/WoWAddons.html.

Using CombatStats

Initially, the only thing you'll see onscreen is a very small window with a red number on the left and a green number on the right (see the top of Figure 2-15). This is a DPS (damage per second) meter. Because DPS is a measure of damage over time, it's good for comparing different kinds of attacks, like fire versus frost or magic versus melee. You can click and drag to move this little frame around.

The red number represents the amount of damage you're taking and the green number represents the amount of damage you're dealing. The numbers update only while you're engaged in combat.

After installing CombatStats, you need to use it for a while in order to build up a combat history. Your stats, especially percentages, will be way off until the volume of data is large enough. A few minutes of intense fighting will begin to give you useful numbers.

FIGURE 2-15: The CombatStats DPS meter and General Attack Info frame.

The General Attack Info frame (the larger window in Figure 2-15) provides more in-depth information and categories, and can be kept onscreen for as long as you want (you can drag it around, too). Open it by right-clicking the small DPS meter. Just click on the drop-down menu at the bottom of the frame to switch between different categories. There's one for each kind of attack or heal you've used, as well as a Total category. The Defensive category is also accessible here; it shows a rundown of attacks made against you.

Configuring CombatStats

You can't really change the appearance of CombatStats. Most of the options (see Table 2-7) are utility functions. A nice one is target on, which hides the DPS meter when you don't have a target. You can use either of the following slash-commands in conjunction with the options in Table 2-7:

```
/combatstats <option>
/cs <option>
```

Either command alone displays the help.

Table 2-7   CombatStats Command-Line Options

Option	Description
enable on|off	Enables or disables CombatStats
target on|off	Only shows DPS meter when you have a target
mouseover on|off	Shows detailed window on mouseover
endoffight on|off	Shows end of fight information
reset yes	Resets all stats to 0

Source: documentation by DmgInc and Smuggles

Analyzing Your Combat History with SW Stats

Addon created and maintained by Artack

CURSE-GAMING   WORLDOFWAR

Want to see how you stack up against your group members? How about who's doing the most healing in your raid? Or, do you want to know which mobs are hurting you the most while you're soloing? SW Stats tracks combat actions for every fight you witness and displays a real-time bar graph so you can see who's doing the most damage, or taking the most damage, or healing the most, or being healed the most; you can choose from 25 different statistics to track.

Using SW Stats

SW Stats places a small icon on the minimap. Click the icon to bring up the SW Stats main menu from which you can open all of the addon's other windows or reset its data. You can also right-click the icon to open the main window in which the graph is shown (see Figure 2-16). Now, go find a fight. You'll notice that your name appears in the list, as well as the name of whatever you're fighting. By default, the main window is graphing how much damage each participant has dealt. As you attack more enemies, the graph will flesh itself out.

The small checkbox to the lower-left of the window allows you to pause or resume data-collection (data is collected only while it's checked). The R button on the title bar opens a window from which you can send out a text-based report of the data. The S button opens the graph settings control panel. The small row of buttons beneath the window allow you to switch between several groups of settings quickly.

FIGURE 2-16: SW Stats is ideal for real-time combat comparisons.

Configuring SW Stats

The Data tab of the graph settings window lets you choose what kind of information is displayed in the main window as well as how it's labeled and filtered. You can also modify the appearance of the bar graph here with the settings on the Visual tab. Just click another button below the main window to switch between configuring different presets.

You can open the general settings window from the minimap icon's menu or by typing the command /sws gs. From here you can adjust several additional display options. Finally, you can use a chat channel to synchronize data among the people in your party or raid. Open the Sync Settings window from the main menu and enter the name of the channel to use.

SW Stats has a bunch of command-line options that you can use with either of the following two slash-commands in conjunction with Table 2-8:

```
/swstats <option>
/sws <option>
```

Either command, when used alone, displays the help.

Table 2-8   SW Stats Command-Line Options

Option	Description
con	Brings up the SW Stats console.
tlock	Locks or unlocks the windows.
dump	Dumps a var. Usage: `/swstats dump` *nameOfVar*.
vc	Does an SW Stats version check for people in the SyncChannel.
gs	Shows or hides the General Settings.
su	Shows skill usage of people in the SyncChannel in the console. The name of the skill has to be EXACTLY the way it is in game. Usage: `/swstats su` *Name of Skill*.
kick	Kicks a player from the SyncChannel. Usage: `/swstats kick` *NameOfPlayer*.
bars	Shows or hides the main window.
resetwin	Resets the position of all windows.
join	Manually join a SyncChannel. Usage: `/swstats join` *NameOfChannel*.
rv	Starts a vote to reset the SyncChannel.
?	Shows console help.
reset	Empties the Stat tables.

Source: documentation by Artack

Note   The DamageMeters addon provides a slightly simpler alternative to SW Stats. It was originally created by Dandelion and is now maintained by AnduinLothar. It gives you the same sort of bar-graph display, but has fewer options on the whole. It's been around for a long time, and was recently updated to work with The Burning Crusade.

> CURSE-GAMING   WOWINTERFACE

Moving On

In this chapter you learned about several addons that can help you out in a fight, either by displaying information differently or by analyzing your performance. Next, because exploring the world and traveling around are huge aspects of World of Warcraft, this book will take a look at some of the various map-related addons that are currently available.

Map Addons

Maps are vital for getting around Azeroth and navigating its zones. Blizzard's built-in mapping systems (the World Map and the minimap) give most people everything they'll need to explore the world, but they aren't configurable in the slightest. Additionally, their limitations, such as the ones in the following list, can get annoying really fast:

- You can't have the World Map open and control your character at the same time.
- The World Map doesn't show details for undiscovered areas.
- There's no way to mark interesting locations you find.
- The minimap is tiny, and can't be moved onscreen.
- Full maps of instances aren't available at all.

Thankfully, there are addons that address all of these problems. But before we get to them let's discuss a feature — enabled by several addons — that isn't built into the default interface: the coordinates system. Many players don't even know this feature exists.

Looking at the Coordinates System

Your location within a zone is represented by x and y coordinates. Technically, these coordinates are used by the game to determine where to place player icons on the World Map. However, because they're available via the API, they can be used for anything you can think of. The values of the x and y coordinates themselves are decimal numbers between 0.0 and 1.0, but many addons display them to you as integers between 0 and 100.

You can imagine the map of any zone as a graph with the origin in the upper-left corner. As you travel east, your x value goes up and as you travel south, your y value goes up. That means the upper-right corner is [100,0], the lower-left [0,100], and the lower-right [100,100]. See Figure 3-1 for a labeled example of this.

The coordinate system can be a useful tool, particularly for giving other people directions. If you find something interesting at [46,22] for example, then it's easy to pass this information on to other people and it's equally easy for them to find the same exact spot. Furthermore, websites such as Thottbot (www.thottbot.com) take advantage of this data to mark their mob location maps, even though users don't have to know what coordinates are to use them.

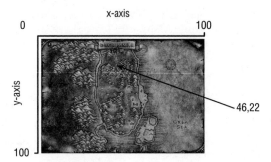

FIGURE 3-1: Each outdoor zone uses the same coordinate system.

There are a few standalone addons that add your coordinates to the WoW interface. In addition to the two addons discussed next, AlphaMap, MetaMap, and simpleMinimap (covered later in this chapter) let you see the coordinates as well as their other features. Often, you'll also be able to get the coordinates of your cursor when the World Map is open, allowing you to determine the coordinates of any landmark in your current zone.

Note

In Chapter 9 you'll begin working on an addon project, in which you'll create a coordinates addon of your own.

Koordinator

Addon created and maintained by Kataris

CURSE-GAMING

Koordinator is capable of placing coordinates on both the minimap and the World Map. It can replace the text displayed above the minimap with your current coordinates, while on the World Map, it displays your coordinates at the bottom of the window. The coordinates of your mouse cursor are also shown. This addon has two slash-command options:

- /koordinator minimap: Toggles the minimap text replacement
- /koordinator worldmap: Toggles the display on the World Map

cMinimapCoordinates

Addon created and maintained by Corgrath

`CURSE-GAMING`

This addon does pretty much exactly the same thing as Koordinator, except the World Map coordinates are displayed in the upper-left corner of the frame instead of the bottom (it also predates Koordinator by about a year). It has two slash-commands as well:

- `/cmc minimap`: Toggles the minimap text
- `/cmc worldmap`: Toggles the World Map display

Navigating Instances with Atlas

Addon created and maintained by Dan Gilbert

`CURSE-GAMING`   `WORLDOFWAR`   `WOWINTERFACE`

For some reason, Blizzard decided to include beautiful maps for every area of Azeroth except instances. You can still see the area surrounding you in the minimap when you're in an instance, but never the overall layout of the entire dungeon. This is where Atlas comes in.

The core of Atlas is basically an image viewer. However, it's the images that come with Atlas that make it worthwhile: a map for every instance in the game. Furthermore, the maps are marked with the locations of bosses and other points of interest. Atlas also includes maps of battlegrounds, dungeon locations, flight points, and outdoor raid bosses.

Note

I'm the author of Atlas. It started off as an experiment (as I'm sure most addons do) and just grew from there. Because I'm a very visual person, I wanted to see what dungeons looked like from the top down. I started off making maps of them by taking screenshots of the minimap every ten feet.

Over the past year, Atlas has evolved a lot, mostly in response to feedback from other players, and the maps have improved as well. I always kind of assumed Blizzard would add instance maps to the default interface, although so far there's been no sign of them.

You can browse through all the maps that come with Atlas at `http://atlasmod.com`.

Using Atlas

After installing Atlas, you'll notice a new icon on the minimap that looks like part of a little globe (you can right-click the icon to drag it around the minimap's frame). Click this icon to open up the main Atlas window, which displays the maps and legend (see Figure 3-2). You can alternatively use the slash-command /atlas. The drop-downs at the top of the window enable you to navigate between the maps. You can also drag the Atlas window around the screen. Lock it in place with the little lock button in the upper-right corner.

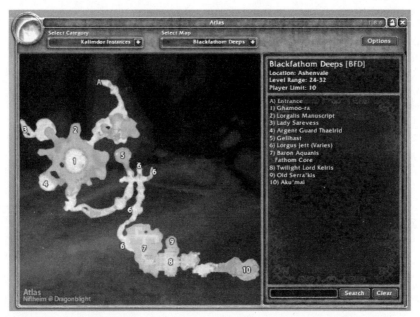

FIGURE 3-2: Atlas includes maps for every instance in the game, plus a few extras.

Configuring Atlas

Atlas has a few simple options, accessible from the Options button in the upper-right corner of the main window, or with the slash-command /atlas options. A few of the settings aren't very self-explanatory so here's some more information about them:

- **Auto-Select Instance Map:** Detects the instance that you're in when you open Atlas, and then automatically switches to the appropriate map. This feature doesn't work in instances that have more than one map, like Blackrock Spire, Dire Maul, or many of the Outland instances. In this case, Atlas remembers the last map you had open.

- **Right-Click for World Map:** Makes the World Map open when you right-click anywhere on the Atlas window. This is useful when you want to quickly switch from Atlas to the World Map.

- **Clamp Window to Screen:** Makes it so that you can't drag the Atlas window off the edge of the screen.

The rest of the options are pretty straightforward. The Reset Position button is useful if the Atlas window ever gets dragged completely off-screen and you can't get it back.

Searching with Atlas

At the bottom of the legend is a small text-entry field as well as Search and Reset buttons. Type part of a word or name in the box and click the Search button, and the legend's entries are reduced to only those that match your text. Note that the search is performed only on the entries for the current map, not all the entries in the database. While not so useful for instances with only a few entries like Ragefire Chasm, the search comes in handy when there are a ton of entries, like for Blackrock Depths or the AtlasMajorCities plug-in. If you want to get the whole list back, just click Reset.

Extending Atlas with Plug-Ins

Not so long ago, I updated Atlas to include a plug-in system that would allow other users to easily create their own map-packs. In fact, some of the maps that come with the main Atlas package have been separated out into their own plug-ins (like AtlasDungeonLocs and AtlasFlightPaths). Unlike the extensions covered later, map-packs don't add new functionality to Atlas; they just provide more maps and data.

For example, check out AtlasMajorCities, which provides maps of all the major cities in Azeroth and Outland, conveniently marked with vendors, trainers, and other NPCs.

After reading through the addon development chapters in the second half of this book, you should be in a pretty good position to create your own Atlas map-packs.

Finding Out What Bosses Drop with AtlasLoot

Addon created by Pernicius, maintained by Daviesh

| CURSE-GAMING | WORLDOFWAR | WOWINTERFACE |

AtlasLoot is an extension for Atlas that makes most bosses listed in the legend clickable. Each clickable boss is marked with a small silver coin; a golden coin indicates which one is currently selected. When clicked, a loot table for that boss is shown (see Figure 3-3). AtlasLoot also includes a nice directory of item sets that you can browse. Each item's tooltip is available as long as that item exists in your local cache; otherwise the word "unsafe" appears next to it in red.

Caution

You can attempt to query the server for an "unsafe" item's info by right-clicking the item a few times (usually twice). This works great for many lower-level items. However, if the item has never dropped on your server before, you'll be disconnected. This doesn't cause any lasting negative effects, but make sure your group isn't counting on you when it happens.

FIGURE 3-3: AtlasLoot shows you the items that bosses drop.

The first time AtlasLoot is loaded it will prompt you for some basic options. It's a good idea to leave it on Safe Chat Links or you might disconnect other players if you link them unsafe items. You can also have AtlasLoot tie in with Lootlink or ItemSync if you have them installed. Daviesh, the current author of AtlasLoot, recommends Lootlink because of the way it handles unsafe items.

AtlasLoot now also comes with a standalone loot-table browser, which you can use without Atlas loaded at all. Just click on AtlasLoot's minimap button (a little treasure chest) to open it, or right-click to access its options panel. Finally, AtlasLoot integrates nicely with AlphaMap, a World Map replacement addon covered later in this chapter.

Viewing the Quests in Each Instance with AtlasQuest

Addon created and maintained by Asurn

AtlasQuest is another extension for Atlas. It adds a pane to the left of the main window that displays a list of quests in the currently selected instance. You can toggle the pane with the new

AQ button next to the Options button and select between Horde quests or Alliance quests at the top of the pane. When you click on an individual quest, its details are displayed in the main Atlas window (see Figure 3-4). A nice addition is the Story button; click it to read about the history of each instance.

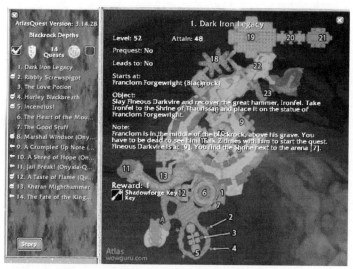

FIGURE 3-4: AtlasQuest shows you the quests in each instance.

Exploring a Satellite View of the World with Yatlas

Addon created and maintained by endx7

Yatlas is the ideal sort of addon: It takes data that's freely available (in this case, minimap textures) and reshapes it into something new and useful. Yatlas is an alternative to the World Map's stylized drawings. It presents a satellite view of the world constructed from the minimap textures. These textures have a good deal more information than the default maps. Furthermore, the map lets you freely zoom and scroll around.

Yatlas has two operating modes:

- **Normal View:** A square, draggable window that can be opened with the slash-command /yatlas or by clicking the minimap icon (it looks a lot like the Atlas minimap icon). You can also map a key binding. Left-click and drag on the map to move it around or use your mouse wheel to zoom in and out (there's also a zoom control in the bottom-left corner). Use the drop-downs to quickly jump to a zone or the Goto Player button to jump back to your location.

- **Full Screen View:** Much more like the typical World Map; it takes up the whole screen and has a familiar layout (see Figure 3-5). It can be opened with the slash-command `/bigyatlas` or with a key binding, and it operates the same as the previous operating modes.

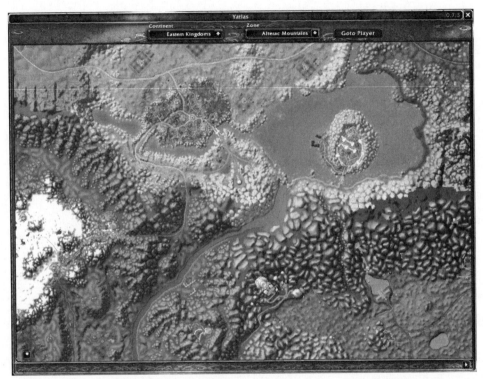

FIGURE 3-5: Yatlas creates its maps out of minimap textures.

Zoom out as far as possible in either mode, and Yatlas slows down considerably as you drag around because it needs to keep track of so many minimap textures at once. It might even seem like your computer crashed, but be patient and you'll regain control. Zoom in a little bit and the responsiveness improves a lot.

In both modes you'll notice several icons on the map:

- **Blue stars:** Large cities
- **Blue circles:** Towns
- **Blue exclamation points:** Interesting locations
- **Gravestones:** Graveyards (same as the minimap icon)
- **Purple caves:** Instanced dungeons

Mouse-over any icon to get a description of the location in the tooltip. These icons can be toggled on or off by clicking the arrow button in the lower-right corner of the window. Yatlas is also able to display information from CT_MapMod, Gatherer, and MapNotes.

The Options button brings up the Yatlas configuration panel where you can control the minimap button's placement and the transparency of the windows, among a few other things.

 Note Although not affiliated with Yatlas, the site `http://mapwow.com` uses the Google Maps API to provide a similar minimap-based view of Azeroth. Furthermore, it can plot the location of herbs, ore, and treasure chests.

Displaying the World Map All the Time with AlphaMap

Addon created by Jeremy Walsh, maintained by Telic

| CURSE-GAMING | WORLDOFWAR | WOWINTERFACE |

AlphaMap is a heavily customizable World Map replacement that can be kept onscreen all the time. It fills the gap between the simplicity of the minimap and scope of the World Map. AlphaMap can access all of the regular zone maps as well as its own maps of instances and battlegrounds. It can be configured to be visible all the time or only when you activate it. Its various transparency settings also allow it to be used as an overlay (see Figure 3-6). AlphaMap's versatility lets it fit into your interface in many different ways.

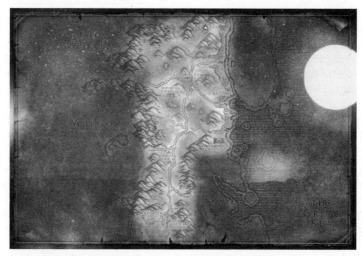

FIGURE 3-6: AlphaMap can be kept onscreen all the time.

Using AlphaMap

The first thing you'll notice after installing AlphaMap is a control box that looks something like the top of the World Map, but with a few extra buttons (see Figure 3-7). This box is called the AlphaMap Selector and it's where you can choose which map you want to view using the two drop-downs (the default map is your current location). To the right are three buttons:

- **Pause/Play:** The pause/play button stops AlphaMap from updating. It also prevents AlphaMap from switching back to the default map when you close and reopen it. While AlphaMap is open, you can click this button twice to switch back to the map of your location.

- **Alpha Symbol:** Clicking the alpha symbol button opens or closes AlphaMap. Right-clicking it brings up the configuration panel. The minimap icon (which is also an alpha symbol) behaves exactly the same way.

- **HotSpot:** The target button is called the HotSpot. You can mouse-over it to display AlphaMap temporarily (clicking on it does nothing). The HotSpot can also be configured to toggle the display of certain markings like notes and icons.

FIGURE 3-7: Use the AlphaMap Selector to switch between maps.

You can drag the Selector around or lock it in place with the lock button on the left. When open, the main AlphaMap window can also be dragged around. Position your mouse at the top or bottom of the window and two yellow bars appear; then click and drag.

Configuring AlphaMap

As stated before, AlphaMap is very configurable. Fortunately, all the options are in a control panel. It can be opened by right-clicking the alpha symbol icon on the Selector or the minimap icon, or by using either of the slash-commands /AlphaMap or /am. There are so many options that instead of trying to learn them all just keep the following tips in mind:

- Make sure you play with the Map Opacity and Map Scale settings in the lower-right corner of the panel, especially if you plan to have AlphaMap open all the time. Make it too small and you won't be able to read anything; too big and it'll clutter the screen.

- Switch to a non-Blizzard map (such as an instance map) to enable two additional tabs. These tabs let you configure each non-Blizzard map separately. The second tab lets you choose whether your settings affect all maps in the same category or just the current map. You can also copy your current settings to other categories with the Apply To buttons. In the bottom-right corner of the options panel you can see which map or category you're configuring in big green letters.

- The AlphaMap Selector can be hidden by docking it to the options panel. This setting is found on the Selector tab. You can also dock it to the map itself.

- By switching the World Map View Mode from Standard to Compact (on the Miscellaneous tab) you can remove the background of zone maps. If you've discovered any areas in a zone, you'll see only those areas; everything else will be transparent. If you're using AlphaMap as an overlay, this is a recommended mode.

- AlphaMap displays your current coordinates in green and your cursor's coordinates in yellow. Coordinates are a good way to communicate the location of something to other players.

AlphaMap includes great documentation; see the Notes.txt file that comes with it.

Adding a Full-Featured Mapping Package with MetaMap

Addon created and maintained by MetaHawk

| CURSE-GAMING | WORLDOFWAR | WOWINTERFACE |

MetaMap is a complete replacement for the World Map that comes with a huge number of extra features. These features are modular (see Table 3-1) and are loaded into memory only as needed (make sure you install all of them though). Some of MetaMap's integrated modules duplicate the functionality of standalone addons such as MozzFullWorldMap or MapNotes (covered later in the chapter), rendering them unnecessary as long as you use MetaMap.

In short, this is a one stop shop for instance maps, map notes, tweaks to the World Map frame, waypoints, boss locations, loot tables, and even a database of mobs that grows as you explore the world. Some players might find MetaMap too bloated, while others will find that it provides all the mapping features they'll ever need in one convenient package.

Table 3-1   MetaMap Addon Modules

Module	Description
MetaMapBKP	Backup and Restore module. Backs up all your data and allows a restore at any time, with ease. Available from Extended Options.
MetaMapBLT	Boss Loot Tables. Displays loot tables when Ctrl+clicking on any map note, or any item in the map SideList.
MetaMapBWP	Waypoint system. Shows direction to selected point, and the distance remaining. Selected from the MetaMap menu. Option to always load on startup.

continued

Table 3-1   Continued

Module	Description
MetaMapCVT	Main Import/Conversion module. Imports many different data files. Any data file must be placed in the MetaMapCVT folder for import.
MetaMapEXP	Export module for exporting User notes, or KB data for others to import. Both Import and Export functions are available from Extended Options.
MetaMapFWM	FullWorldMap module. Shows unexplored areas of the map with custom colors. Option to load always on startup.
MetaMapWKB	WoW Knowledge Base. Stores NPC/MoB data on mouse-over or keypress. Full integration with the Notes system. Option to load always on startup.
MetaMapZSM	ZoneShift module for German and French clients.

Source: documentation by MetaHawk

Using MetaMap

MetaMap's changes to the interface fall into four broad categories:

- The World Map
- The Knowledge Base
- The Note System
- The Waypoint System

These are covered in the following sections, although you should also read the documentation that comes with MetaMap because it goes over every feature and setting in detail. That documentation is found in the main MetaMap folder in the ReadMe.txt file.

The World Map

MetaMap replaces the default World Map, so you can simply press M (by default) to bring it up or you can click the minimap icon (it's the same globe icon as Atlas/Yatlas). MetaMap provides access to all of Blizzard's maps in a window that can be moved around by dragging its title bar. You can navigate the maps the same as you would with the default World Map. There's an extra drop-down menu for instance maps, as well as a button for the options menu and a question mark button. Click the question mark button to open the StoryLine frame, which gives you the background story of certain zones (currently only for instances). Coordinates are displayed at the bottom of the window and on the minimap.

The Knowledge Base

The MetaMap Knowledge Base can keep track of all the mobs and NPCs you encounter, and then display a searchable, sortable list of them (see Figure 3-8). It records their name, type, level, and location. This is one of my favorite features of MetaMap. The recorded locations are stored as ranges in case the mob wanders or spawns in a wide area. Once a mob is listed in the database, you can create a note on the map indicating its position (see more on notes below).

FIGURE 3-8: The MetaMap Knowledge Base lists all the mobs you've encountered.

By default, the database won't acquire new targets as you play. To start collecting information you have to turn on the tracking option, which will add mobs to the database when you mouse-over them. Just follow these steps:

1. Put your mouse over MetaMap's minimap icon to open the main menu.
2. Select Extended Options from the menu.
3. Switch to the MetaKB tab.
4. Turn on the Auto Tracking setting.

By default, you need to be within five yards of a mob for it to be added, although you can increase this distance up to infinity.

The Note System

MetaMap enables you to create custom notes on any of the zone or instance maps, much like the MapNotes addon (see the next section). Notes are displayed as small icons on the map and their associated information is shown when you mouse-over them. Simply Ctrl+click anywhere on the map and a dialog box pops up for you to create a new note. You can also click an existing note to edit it.

Once a note exists, you can use the edit dialog to move it, send it to another player (requires the recipient to be running MetaMap), draw a line between it and another note, toggle it to appear on the minimap, or delete it. If there are any notes on the currently selected map, you can right-click the question mark button to open the SideList, which is basically a map legend. Each note is listed in the SideList and can be clicked to ping its marker on the main map.

Much like how Atlas and AlphaMap include points of interest for instances, MetaMap includes the same information in the form of notes. However, even though the data comes with MetaMap, it must be manually imported before it can be viewed (don't worry; you only need to do this once). Follow these steps to import the data:

1. Select Extended Options from the main menu.

2. Switch to the Imports tab.

3. Press the Load Imports Module button. The two disabled Import buttons on the panel become enabled.

4. Press the Instance Notes Import button. You can also press the BLT Data Import button, which imports loot tables for many of the game's bosses.

5. Press the Reload UI button to complete the import.

Now switch to an instance map and you'll see all kinds of useful markings (see Figure 3-9). If a boss note is marked with the pink letters BLT in its tooltip, then you can Ctrl+click on it to bring up a loot table (similar to AtlasLoot).

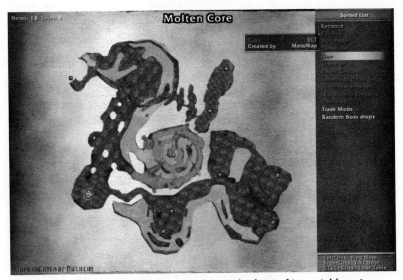

FIGURE 3-9: MetaMap includes instance data in the form of importable notes.

The Waypoint System

Waypoints can help you navigate toward a fixed destination. Setting a waypoint causes a little arrow to show up onscreen, along with a distance meter (see Figure 3-10). Depending on what direction you're heading, the arrow will rotate to point toward your target. When you reach your destination, the waypoint will clear (this can be changed). Using a waypoint is good way to find your way back to an important location.

FIGURE 3-10: The waypoint's arrow rotates to lead you to your destination.

There are a few ways to set waypoints:

- Select Set a Waypoint from the main menu. This opens a new menu that lists all of the current zone's notes. You can access the waypoint options from here too.
- Right-click a note on the main map.
- Right-click on any mob in the Knowledge Base.
- Use the slash-command /bwp <xx,yy> <name>. Both parameters are optional. If you omit the coordinates, the waypoint will be created at your present location. This is useful if you want to find your way back to your current spot. You need to uncheck the option Clear Waypoint on arrival or else it'll disappear as soon as you move around.

Once a waypoint is set, you can click the arrow to open the waypoint options menu or right-click it and drag to move it anywhere onscreen.

Configuring MetaMap

MetaMap has a bunch of configuration options, all of which you shouldn't have a hard time playing around with. Most general settings are found in the Extended Options window, while specific display settings (such as scale and transparency) are found stuck to the bottom of the regular options menu. The options menu is context sensitive, so if you open it from the main window you'll see the appropriate visual settings, whereas if you open it from the minimap you'll be given the option to rotate the button around the frame.

Note An alternative to MetaMap, in terms of features and functionality, is the Cartographer addon created by ckknight (the author of FuBar) that also uses a modular system and includes points of interest, instance maps, and a moveable World Map frame. Cartographer is an Ace2 addon, as well.

CURSE-GAMING   WOWINTERFACE

Adding Custom Notes to the World Map with MapNotes

Addon created by Sir.Bender, updated by ciphersimianand eswat, maintained by Telic

`CURSE-GAMING`   `WORLDOFWAR`   `WOWINTERFACE`

MapNotes allows you to make little marks on the World Map and then label them with whatever information you want. If you're using MetaMap, then you don't need to install this addon because its features are already built in. The standalone version of MapNotes works in almost exactly the same way as the MetaMap equivalent, but there are a few minor differences, especially when it comes to the structure of the menus.

Using MapNotes

To get started, open up the World Map. Ctrl+right-click anywhere on the map to open the MapNotes main menu, and then click the Create Note button. You're presented with a dialog box in which you can choose the icon, colors, and content of your new note (see Figure 3-11).

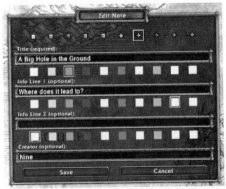

FIGURE 3-11: The MapNotes dialog box for creating or editing a note.

Press Save to continue. The note's icon appears on the map. The red highlighting around it indicates that it's the most recently created note. Mouse-over it to read the information you saved (see Figure 3-12).

FIGURE 3-12: Mouse-over a note to read it.

Note

There is a hard limit of 100 notes per zone.

Now that you have a note on the map, you can left-click it to bring up the main menu again or right-click it to bring up a different menu with the following options:

- **Edit Note:** Reopens the dialog box, enabling you to modify the note.

- **Set As MiniNote:** A MiniNote appears on the minimap as well as the World Map. Right-click the note and select Turn MiniNote Off if you want to switch it back.

- **Send Note:** You can choose a player (as long as he has MapNotes installed) to send it to, or you can generate a slash-command that others can use to replicate the note.

- **Special Actions:** Opens yet another menu with these two options:

    - **Toggle Line:** Enables you to pick another note and then connect them with a line.

    - **Delete Note:** Does exactly what you'd expect.

Configuring MapNotes

You can open the MapNotes option panel from the main menu (Ctrl+right-click on the map or left-click on a note). All the options are self-explanatory, except for the rows of icons (and checkboxes) at the top of the window. Check or uncheck these icons to filter which notes are visible (it takes a click on the map for the display to update). This filtering feature means you can organize different kinds of notes using a consistent icon scheme, and then turn groups of notes on or off at once.

There are several slash-commands you can use with MapNotes, but you'll probably never need to use them, so they won't be covered here. See the README file that comes with MapNotes for a complete documentation of the slash-commands and other notes.

Tracking Herbs, Mines, and Chests with Gatherer

Addon created by Norganna, maintained by Islorgris

CURSE-GAMING   WORLDOFWAR   WOWINTERFACE

Gatherer keeps track of all the herbs, mines, and treasure chests you find and marks their location with icons on both the World Map and minimap. This makes it much easier to find the specific trade skill items that you need, when you need them, and it also lets you raise your gathering skills faster. Gatherer is indispensable for anyone with Mining or Herbalism.

Note Gatherer has its very own website with news, documentation, downloads, forums, and support at http://gathereraddon.com. The front page displays the latest news and updates.

Using Gatherer

Simply collect items as normal and Gatherer will add them to its database right afterward. Nearby nodes will appear on your minimap as red circles with room for the default yellow tracking dot inside them. When nodes are slightly farther away, they'll appear as the appropriate icon for that kind of node (see Figure 3-13). The World Map will display an icon for every node recorded.

Gatherer minimap icon ————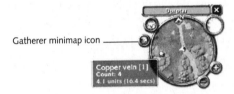

FIGURE 3-13: Gatherer displays the location of a copper mine on the minimap.

Mouse-over the Gatherer minimap icon (it's very colorful) to open the main menu, from which you can bring up the options panel, toggle some major settings, or access the Search and Report features. The default options are great; many players always leave the Herbs, Ores, and Treasures settings on auto. This means Gatherer will look at your skills to determine which types of nodes to display.

The Search and Report windows (actually two tabs of the same frame) give you two different methods of browsing the database of recorded nodes. The Report tab lets you select a zone and see which nodes have been recorded there; whereas the Search tab lets you specify what you're looking for, and then tells you where to find it.

Configuring Gatherer

Select Gatherer Options from the main menu or type /gather options to bring up the options panel. Here are some things to know:

- **Filters tab:** Enables you to pick which nodes will be tracked. Typically you'll want to track everything, so you can leave this panel alone altogether.

- **Globals tab:** Contains most of the display options. The Map Minder feature reopens the World Map to the last map you were looking at if less than the specified amount of time has passed. The rest of the settings control the icons themselves.

- **Quick Menu tab:** Houses settings for the minimap icon and main menu.

- **Zone Match Feature:** For localized (non-English) clients only, so you probably don't need to worry about it.

- **? Button:** Click to access a great in-game help feature. (It's in the upper-right corner of the options panel.)

Gatherer has a slash-command interface that uses either of the commands /gatherer or /gather. Because its options panel is complete, not all of the slash-command options are covered here. You can type either command alone for a list of them.

Tweaking the Minimap with simpleMinimap

Addon created and maintained by arJUna

CURSE-GAMING   WORLDOFWAR

Many players spend a lot of time looking at the tiny map in the upper-right corner of their screens. The minimap is indispensable; it shows the terrain around you, as well as herbs, mines, quest goals, party members, and more. Plus, much like the Windows tray, it's adorned with all kinds of little buttons and notifications,not to mention all the buttons other addons stick on there.

Do you really need to have an icon onscreen at all times that tells you whether it's night or day? Do you need to be constantly reminded what zone you're in? Your screen real estate is precious, and simpleMinimap lets you maximize it by trimming (and even reshaping) the minimap to suit your needs.

The WoW client controls the content of the minimap internally; however, the circle you're seeing isn't quite the whole picture. The complete minimap is actually a square. Its circular appearance is achieved by masking out the corners, which means a clever addon (such as simpleMinimap) can modify the mask to reveal the hidden parts of the image, resulting in the slightly wider view seen in Figure 3-14.

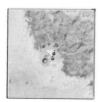

FIGURE 3-14: Use simpleMinimap to
reduce clutter and reveal more terrain.

The simpleMinimap addon is configured through a system of menus. Right-click the minimap to open the main menu. Several basic options control size, transparency, and which parts of the minimap cluster should be visible. Below these options are several modules, each one providing a specific set of features (see Table 3-2). These modules can be turned on and off independently, without affecting the rest of the addon.

Table 3-2 simpleMinimap Addon Modules

Module	Description
autozoom	Automatically zooms out minimap after delay
compass	Places cardinal direction markers on the minimap's edges
coords	Small frame that shows map coordinates
GUI	Drop-down setup menus (default is right-click on minimap)
movers	Allows movement of UI frames attached to the minimap
pings	Pop-up frame that shows the minimap pinger's name
skins	Allows for changing the minimap's skin (square, corner)

Source: documentation by arJUna

If you enable the movers module, a bunch of overlapping semitransparent gray boxes will appear. Each box represents one of the following frames (mouse-over each to see which is which):

- **QuestWatchFrame:** Displays quest-goal information when you Shift+click one of your quests in the Quest Log.

- **QuestTimerFrame:** Displays the timer when one of your quests needs to be completed in a certain amount of time.

- **DurabilityFrame:** Displays the little suit of armor when any of your items is badly damaged or broken.

- **CaptureMover:** Displays bar for capturing territory in world PvP events (like in Eastern Plaguelands and many of the Outland zones).

You can click and drag these around. You can also click and drag many pieces of the minimap, too, as well as the entire minimap cluster. Once everything is where you want it, it's a good idea to lock it all in place; right-click on the minimap to open the main menu, and then select the Lock Minimap option; the gray boxes will disappear.

The main menu is the hub of configuration and is organized logically. Every change you make will be visible right away. The addon enables you to control many things, including the following:

- Changing the shape or border of the minimap with the skins module (main menu ⇨ skins ⇨ skin). Many people like the squares, which show the most terrain.

- Hiding the parts of the minimap cluster you don't need (main menu ➪ show/hide).

- Using your mouse wheel to zoom the minimap in and out (when your cursor is over it). Note that the autozoom feature only works after you've zoomed in with your mouse wheel, but not after clicking the + button.

- Determining the height of the minimap cluster in relation to other windows using the strata setting.

- Using built-in coordinates so you don't need yet another addon to display them.

There are two ways to disable the main menu, in which case you'll need to use alternative means to re-enable it.

- If you disable the GUI module (main menu ➪ GUI ➪ enabled), you can turn it back on with the command:

  ```
  /smm gui enabled
  ```

- If you disable the entire simpleMinimap addon (main menu ➪ enabled), you can turn it back on with the command:

  ```
  /smm standby
  ```

In fact, all of simpleMinimap's options can be configured with slash-commands. Because the main menu (via the GUI module) provides a great visual way of configuring everything, not all of the slash-command options are covered here. You can use either of the slash-commands /simpleminimap or /smm to print out a list of them in-game.

Seeing Unexplored Areas with MozzFullWorldMap

Addon created by Mozz, updated by Shub, maintained by Telic

By default, the World Map displays only detailed maps in areas you've already discovered. This can get a little annoying when you're struggling to "discover" an area that you're standing right in the middle of. Furthermore, the joy of exploring the world with your first character might turn into annoyance when your subsequent characters have to rediscover the same areas over and over just to get them included on the map. MozzFullWorldMap (MFWM) solves these problems by simply revealing the entire map.

Using MFWM

MozzFullWorldMap is a simple addon, from the user's perspective. It adds a small checkbox that's labeled Show Unexplored Areas to the upper-right corner of the World Map. Enabling it does exactly what you'd expect (see Figure 3-15). Because all the textures for the World Map (hidden or not) are stored on your hard drive, MozzFullWorldMap simply makes them visible. By default, when you enable the feature, unexplored areas will be tinted a deep blue so you can still distinguish them from areas you've been to; however, this tinting can be disabled.

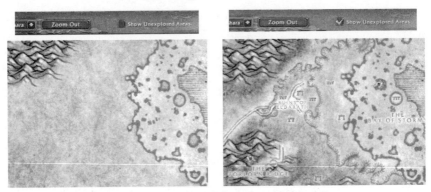

FIGURE 3-15: MozzFullWorldMap disabled (left) and enabled (right).

Note

As you've already seen, many addons provide all kinds of info you wouldn't otherwise have (like your DPS or maps of instances, for example). MFWM is no different, but unlike many addons, it might be capable of destroying some of WoW's magic if you use it your first time through the game. Azeroth is a huge, mysterious world that's worth discovering on your own.

MozzFullWorldMap is fully compatible with AlphaMap, as well.

Configuring MFWM

MozzFullWorldMap is about as simple as they come. Besides turning it on and off, it has a few settings that let you tweak or disable the tinting. Use the options in Table 3-3 with either of the following slash-commands:

```
/mozzfullworldmap <option>
/mfwm <option>
```

Either command used on its own will give you onscreen help. Use /mfwm normal if you want unexplored areas of the map to be indistinguishable from areas you've already visited.

Table 3-3 MozzFullWorldMap Command-Line Options

Option	Description
blue	Shows unexplored areas in blue.
normal	Shows unexplored areas in the normal map color.
trans	(0.0 to 1.0) Controls transparency of unexplored areas. 0.0 is completely clear, 1.0 is completely opaque.

Source: documentation by Telic

Locating Your Guild Members with GuildMap

Addon created and maintained by Bru

CURSE-GAMING

Wouldn't it be nice to know exactly where your guild members are? Well, GuildMap tells you just that by adding dots for them to the minimap and World Map. Because this information isn't available to the WoW client, GuildMap uses a hidden inter-addon communication channel to broadcast each player's location to everyone else in the guild.

Note Unfortunately, for you to see others, they also need to be running GuildMap. Granted, it's somewhat of a challenge to get all your friends to install the same addon, but if you can persuade them, it might be well worth it for all of you. Think about putting together a package of useful addons specifically for everyone in your guild.

GuildMap requires no setup or configuration to work. Just install it and forget about it. When a guild member (who's also running GuildMap) is near, you'll see a little icon for them in the minimap. You'll see the same thing on the World Map. You can even zoom the World Map all the way out and see where everyone in your guild is in the world.

There are just a couple of GuildMap options: You can choose to have arrows displayed on the minimap when people are near to you, and you can configure what happens when you click the minimap icons with your right or left mouse button. You can open up the configuration panel with the slash-command /guildmap.

Getting Detailed Travel Information with FlightMap

Addon created and maintained by Dhask

Let's face it: You spend a lot of time traveling in World of Warcraft. The network of flight points can be difficult to navigate, let alone discover. Blizzard's recent change to the flight system allowing automated multi-hop flights was a huge improvement, but there's still a lot of flight data to keep track of. FlightMap provides pretty much everything you need to get around efficiently. It also optionally allows you to see the locations of flight points you haven't discovered yet.

Using FlightMap

FlightMap adds useful flight information to the game in several different places:

- **Individual zone maps:** Found in the World Map, these have green icons that mark the locations of flight points. If the Show Destination option is enabled, the tooltip for each of these icons will list each place you can fly to from the selected point, as well as the cost and duration.

■ **Continent maps:** Also found in the World Map, these display lines to indicate the flight network. Place your mouse over a zone to visually see which other zones you can fly to from there. A box in the lower-left corner of the World Map also details which flight points exist and what their coordinates are. Again, you can optionally view which points they connect to, as well as each flight's cost and duration (see Figure 3-16).

FIGURE 3-16: FlightMap gives you detailed information about flight points in each zone.

■ **Flight maps:** Also known as the window you see when speaking to a flight master, this can be enhanced to display the network itself via connecting lines. You can also add duration and location information to each destination's tooltip. Furthermore, you can view this window anywhere with a key binding or the slash-command /fmap open (see Figure 3-17), but of course you can't charter a flight from anywhere.

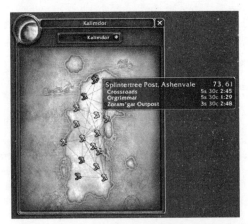

FIGURE 3-17: You can check out the complete flight point network from anywhere.

■ **In-flight progress bar:** While in flight, a progress bar slowly fills, showing how much of the flight has passed. A numerical timer on the bar also counts down the amount of time left until you reach your destination (see Figure 3-18).

FIGURE 3-18: A progress bar shows how long you have left on your flight.

Configuring FlightMap

FlightMap has an options panel that's used to configure how the addon behaves and what information is displayed. You can bring it up with either of the slash-commands /flightmap or /fmap. By default, FlightMap will not show any information about flight points you haven't discovered yet, but this can be changed with the Show Unknown Flights option. Some nice utility features are thrown in such as automatically dismounting at a flight master or an extra confirmation box before accepting a flight. All the other options simply toggle what information appears where.

FlightMap has only a few slash-command options, which are outlined in Table 3-4.

Table 3-4   FlightMap Command-Line Options

Option	Description
help	Show this text.
open	Open flight map window.
reset	Reset timer bar position.
lock	Prevent FlightMap from learning any more flight times.

Source: documentation by Dhask

Tracking the Next Departure with ZeppelinMaster

Addon created by Sammysnake, maintained by Drool

CURSE-GAMING   WORLDOFWAR   WOWINTERFACE

How often do you find yourself running to catch a zeppelin, only to have it take off ten seconds before you get there? ZeppelinMaster is a simple addon that gives you an estimate of where each zeppelin (or boat) is on its route. You can select which route to monitor, and are then presented with how long a wait there is until the next arrival or departure at each station. This isn't exactly a map addon, but it seemed appropriate to put it right after FlightMap.

ZeppelinMaster is not perfect. Because it can't just poll the server for the information it needs, it relies on two sources for its data: your own trips and a global channel. When you enter the world, ZeppelinMaster joins a hidden global channel and checks to see if anyone else is running the addon. If so, you might start getting arrival and departure times immediately.

In practice, data from other players can sometimes be inaccurate. The most accurate data comes from your own trips. Once you take a ride, the addon synchronizes itself to the route and can give you good times for quite a while. The addon's author, Sammysnake, has this advice: "For best results in tracking Zeppelins, stand at the front; for ships, stand at the back."

Using ZeppelinMaster

Upon entering the world you'll see the red ZeppelinMaster window (see Figure 3-19). Initially no route will be selected, so you'll need to select one from the drop-down menu. Routes listed in white don't have any data yet, so you'll have to ride that route before getting any times, at which point it will turn green in the list. If any routes are initially green, it means the addon has collected data from another player.

FIGURE 3-19: The ZeppelinMaster main window and its options panel.

You can hide the window with the X button and get it back by typing /zm or /zsm. The little arrow button next to it will collapse or expand the window. The exclamation mark button opens up the configuration panel (see Figure 3-19).

Configuring ZeppelinMaster

ZeppelinMaster has four self-explanatory options that change when the window appears, which routes are displayed, and how they're named. There are only two additional slash-command options:

- /zm reset: Resets all the data from the current session. Use this command when the arrival and departure times you're getting don't match with reality. This means another player has given you out-of-date data.

- /zm channel <name>: Sets the channel that the addon uses to communicate with other players. The default channel is ZeppelinMaster, which is a great choice unless you and your friends all agree to use a different one.

Exploring the World

With the pressure of leveling up, grinding rep, keeping up with guild members, destroying the opposing faction, and participating in raids, it's easy to forget that Blizzard has created a beautiful, expansive world for you to experience, relax in, and explore. Some of my most memorable experiences in WoW are from when I entered a new area for the first time and scouted around (the giant shrooms in Zangarmarsh come to mind). The tools covered in this chapter can help you navigate the world more effectively; visualize the land and dungeons in new, interesting ways; and remember where important (or simply cool) locations are.

In the next chapter, you'll examine the broadest category of addons: those that modify the structure of the basic interface in subtle or fundamental ways. The ease with which you can control your character's actions and absorb important information will directly affect the amount of fun you have and your ability to win battles. The world created by Blizzard is a wonderful place to explore, and the interface you create is the window to that world. The addons you read about next will help you craft an interface that suits your character perfectly.

Miscellaneous Addons

E ven though this is a catchall chapter of sorts, it contains some of the most important addons out there, which range from tiny tweaks to massive overhauls of your entire interface. A number of them allow you to reconfigure your action bars. In addition, they change your fonts, modify your quest window, allow you to click-cast, and analyze the population of your server, among many other things. Two of them provide modular operating-system-like info-bars at the top or bottom of your screen. In most cases, they give you an extra level of control over your interface or improve upon Blizzard's default offering.

Rearranging Elements of the Default Interface

A few addon packages are available that offer similar overall features: They break up the bar at the bottom of the screen, offer great flexibility in terms of rearranging its elements, and give you more action bars to work with. Each package differs in the details though, and ultimately what's right for you comes down to personal preference.

Bongos

Addon created and maintained by Tuller

WORLDOFWAR   CURSE-GAMING   WOWINTERFACE

The Bongos package provides a complete replacement for the menu bar that's normally at the bottom of the default user interface. In addition, you can place up to 120 action buttons (divided into bars of variable amounts) anywhere you want onscreen, adjust their layout, and rescale them individually. You can also move around the minimap, casting bar, and a number of other built-in frames. Bongos has an intuitive, friendly interface in which each frame has its own right-click options panel for adjusting settings. It's also completely modular, so you only have to load the specific modules that you need (see Table 4-1).

Table 4-1   Bongos Modules

Module	Description
Bongos	The core bongos addon
Bongos_ActionBar	Breaks up the main action bar into movable components
Bongos_CastBar	Replaces the casting bar with a movable one that includes a timer
Bongos_MapBar	Allows you to reposition the minimap, as well as toggle its components
Bongos_Options	A load on demand options menu for Bongos triggered by /bob or /bongos
Bongos_RollBar	Replaces the original frame for rolling on loot with a movable one
Bongos_Stats and latency	A replacement for the default FPS display that shows FPS, memory usage,
Bongos_XP	A movable experience bar

Source: original addon documentation

Using Bongos

Your interface might look a little cluttered right after installing Bongos (see Figure 4-1), so you will need to invest some time to set things up the way you want them.

First of all, if the options panel isn't already open, bring it up with /bob or /bongos. Then, on the General tab, there's an option to Lock Bar Positions. This master control (when disabled) allows you to select and drag any of the Bongos frames, as well as right-click on them for further options (like scaling, alpha, and spacing).

If the Sticky Bars option is enabled (a great feature, by the way) the frame you're moving will latch on to another frame, if you drop it close enough. Using Sticky Bars means that when one frame latches on to another, its name will turn from yellow to blue. The color change means it's parented to the yellow frame it's touching, so if you move the yellow one, the blue one will follow along. You can chain multiple frames together like this and move whole groups of them as a single block. Don't forget to lock the frames when you're done.

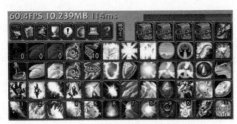

FIGURE 4-1: Bongos gives you the freedom to reposition almost everything.

Make sure to check out the remaining tabs on the Bongos control panel (Profiles, Visibility, ActionBars, Paging, Stances, and Bindings). You can save and load profiles, toggle the visibility of individual bars, tweak what information shows up on the action buttons, adjust paging (scrolling through action bars), and set up self-casting. The Bindings tab allows you to set key bindings directly by clicking on individual action buttons. Also make sure you right-click on each frame at least once, because they all have a different assortment of settings.

Bartender3

Addon created and maintained by Nevcairiel

CURSE-GAMING   WOWINTERFACE

Bartender3 is for the minimalists and perfectionists out there. Also, if your interface is primarily built around the Ace2 library, you'll naturally want to use this mod to reconfigure your bars. Bartender3 has all the controls you'd expect: movement, scaling, toggling, horizontal and vertical layouts, and transparency. A notable feature is borderless bars, giving your interface a more modern, squared-off look.

Bartender3's slash-command system (use /bartender3, /bar, or /bt3) isn't too bad actually, following the in tradition of Ace2 mods. If you use any of the commands alone you'll get the help, which provides a useful list of which bar is which. However, you don't need to use the slash-command system to accomplish everything. When you unlock the bars (type /bar lock), they turn green and you can drag them around with your mouse. Once they've been unlocked, you can right-click on them to bring up a contextual menu which allows you to control every option individually for each bar (see Figure 4-2). Once you have everything set up the way you want, type /bar lock again to lock everything in place.

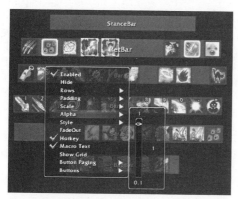

FIGURE 4-2: Configuring one of your action bars with Bartender3.

TrinityBars

Addon created and maintained by Maul

CURSE-GAMING   WOWINTERFACE

TrinityBars goes a little above and beyond Bongos and Bartender3. It has the same basic functionality; you can move, rescale, and reconfigure all your actions bars and menus. Its controls are slightly different though. Right after installing the mod, all your bars will be stacked neatly in the center of the screen and unlocked. When you click on a bar, controls for it will appear on the right and left, and the value for each control will appear in the tooltip when you hover your cursor over it, as well as a description of what it does.

I'm not going to cover all of TrinityBars' features here, but there are a few visual settings that might sell you on the mod. First of all, there are four styles of buttons you can choose from for each bar, some of which are very unique and flashy. When you have a bar selected, you can click on the small, round recycle button to the left of it to cycle between styles. Figure 4-3 compares all four of the available styles.

FIGURE 4-3: Each of the four button styles available
to you with TrinityBars.

Furthermore, there are a number of pre-made layouts as well. In addition to the basic horizontal and vertical configurations, there's a circular arrangement and arcs in various orientations. These predefined layouts are unique to the mod (see Figure 4-4). To switch between layouts, use the curved arrow buttons on the left side. Each layout supports a variable number of buttons.

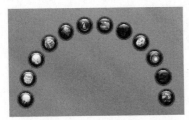

FIGURE 4-4: One of TrinityBars' built-in
arc layouts.

The hub of TrinityBars' options and settings is its minimap icon; left-click on it and seven additional buttons will swivel into place surrounding it. They'll disappear if you click on the center button again. You can also right-click on it to open a large options panel directly.

 A comprehensive document with all of TrinityBars' instructions is available online. The address is www.wowinterface.com/forums/showthread.php?p=36284.

Analyzing Your Server's Population with CensusPlus

Addon created by Ian Pieragostini, maintained by Rollie

Blizzard doesn't advertise the population of its World of Warcraft servers, other than giving them the less-than-precise rankings of High, Medium, and Low. Furthermore, there's no way to find out the breakdown of levels, classes, or races on a server. While you can't access Blizzard's server data directly, you're given a decent tool for locating and browsing through the other members of your little world: the /who command. This command returns the level, race, class, guild, and location of any player matching its arguments. If more than a few results are returned, the /who interface is opened, which provides a scrollable list of up to 50 characters. Still not satisfied? CensusPlus takes the /who command one step further.

By selectively narrowing the parameters of consecutive, automated /who queries, CensusPlus effectively collects information about everyone on your server. Since the /who command has a cooldown of a few seconds, queries are automatically executed on a timer, and an entire scan takes only two or three minutes. Granted, a character has to be playing in order to be counted—CensusPlus doesn't take into account the thousands of dormant characters—but despite this, the addon is still a significant statistical tool. Plus, you can rescan whenever you want, picking up new characters and updating existing ones.

 On WarcraftRealms (www.warcraftrealms.com), which is affiliated with the CensusPlus addon, you can browse collected census information from the Horde and Alliance sides of every realm, as well as submit the data you've already collected. Their database is large, and is a good way to find out if one faction outnumbers another on a particular server. This is also the only place to download the most recent version of the addon.

Using CensusPlus

CensusPlus is simple and straightforward to use. The addon adds a button to the minimap with a large yellow C on it, which you can click to open or close the main interface. Once open, the first thing you'll want to do is take a census with the button at the bottom-left corner. Note that unless the Verbose option is enabled, you won't get any feedback about the task's progress until it's finished. With Verbose on, you'll see each automatic /who query as it's made.

When the scan is finished, the areas of the frame for race, class, guild, and level are populated (see Figure 4-5). The race, class, and level area are presented as bar graphs, showing how each element compares to the others. Guilds are sorted by experience (the combined level of all characters). You can select up to one element in each category in order to filter the information that's displayed. For example, click the Orc button and the bar graphs for class and level adjust to reflect only Orcs. The Show Chars button opens a list of characters that satisfy the currently selected set of filters. The other buttons at the bottom of the window stop an active scan, Prune the database of characters that haven't been seen in a while, or Purge the database entirely.

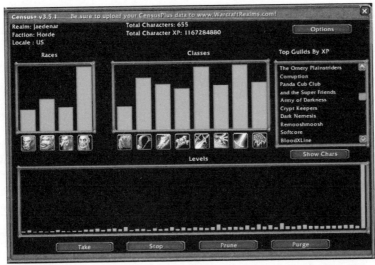

FIGURE 4-5: The CensusPlus interface displays a statistical breakdown of your server.

Configuring CensusPlus

The CensusPlus configuration panel can be opened with the button on the upper-right corner of the main interface. Each option is simple enough, and the defaults will serve you just fine. If you turn the Verbose mode on, you can monitor the progress of a scan, but if you have the addon set up to run in the background, you should probably leave it off. You can also control most of the options with slash commands; use /census, /census+, or /censusplus and refer to the following list of options (see Table 4-2).

Table 4-2   CensusPlus Command-Line Options

Option	Description
verbose	Toggles verbose mode on/off
options	Brings up the Options window
take	Starts a Census snapshot
stop	Stops a Census snapshot
prune #	Prunes the database by removing characters not seen in the number of days specified
serverprune	Prunes the database by removing data from all servers other than the one you are currently on
who <name>	Displays info that matches names or guilds
who unguilded #	Lists unguilded characters of that level
timer #	Sets the autocensus timer (in minutes)

Source: original addon documentation

 On the Web Shortly after the launch of The Burning Crusade, Blizzard created "The Armory," a section of their website that allows you to search for and view character profiles, guild rosters, and arena rankings. While you can't get the same realm-specific breakdowns that CensusPlus provides, it's still an interesting and useful service for examining individual characters. See http://armory.worldofwarcraft.com/.

Changing the Default Fonts with ClearFont2

Addon created and maintained by Kirkburn

WORLDOFWAR	CURSE-GAMING	WOWINTERFACE

ClearFont2 gives you a convenient means of replacing the game's default user-interface fonts. The default settings definitely provide increased readability over the standard fonts (see Figure 4-6). Furthermore, ClearFont2 comes with a number of additional fonts, which can be cycled-through in-game with a very simple options interface.

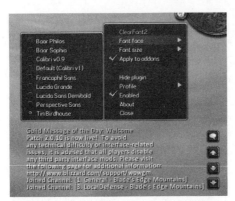

FIGURE 4-6: ClearFont2 replaces the standard interface fonts.

Visit the ClearFont website (www.clearfont.co.uk) for the latest updates. As of this writing, it's the only place to get ClearFont2 (as opposed to ClearFont).

To switch between fonts and adjust the addon's other settings (including the default font size and whether or not the new fonts should be applied to addons), right-click on the CF button that's been added to the minimap. A small drop-down menu opens. Settings can alternately be controlled via slash commands; use /cf, /clearfont, /cf2, or /clearfont2. ClearFont2 is an Ace2 addon.

Tracking All Your Cooldowns in One Place with Cooldown Timer Bars

Addon created and maintained by astraycat

WORLDOFWAR   CURSE-GAMING

Cooldown Timer Bars (abbreviated CDT, not CTB) is a simple addon for monitoring all of your cooldowns in the same place, and in status bar form (see Figure 4-7). The addon was completely rewritten in its second version in order to utilize Ace2 and CandyBar (a status bar library). Basically, whenever you have a spell that's cooling down, a status bar appears for it and slowly drains. You can configure the appearance of the bars, and there's also an alert feature (off by default), which will flash the name of a spell onscreen whenever it's ready to be used again. The addon has very little necessary setup, although you can tweak it to your heart's content. You might want to use the /cdt anchor command when you first install the addon so you can position it where you want onscreen.

FIGURE 4-7: CDT's status
bars in action.

Configuring CDT

All slash-command options are issued using /cdt. Typing the command alone will print a list
of commands to the default chat window. They're also outlined in Tables 4-3, 4-4, and 4-5.

Table 4-3   CDT Command-Line Options

Option	Description
alert	Settings for alert frame
anchor	Toggles the Anchor
bar	Settings for the cooldown bars
ignore	Adds a spell to the ignore list
test	Runs a test bar under each anchor
profile	Sets profile for this addon
standby	Suspends/resumes this addon
debug	Enables/disables debugging
about	Prints out addon info

Table 4-4   /cdt alert Command-Line Options

Option	Description
delay	How long an alert stays visible
fontsize	Changes the font size
frame	Where the alert messages are shown
toggle	Enables/disables alerts

Table 4-5 **/cdt bar Command-Line Options**

Option	Description
bgalpha	The transparency of a bar's background
bgcolor	The background color of the bars
color	The color of the timer bars
growth	The direction the bars will grow in
height	The height of the bars
maxtime	Max time in seconds a cooldown can be to show a bar
mintime	Min time in seconds a cooldown has to be to show a bar
scale	The scale of the bars
textcolor	The color of the text
textsize	Changes the font size
texture	Which texture to use on the bars
width	The width of the bars

Source for all three tables: original addon documentation

Expanding Your Quest Window with Extended QuestLog

Addon created and maintained by Daniel Rehn

WORLDOFWAR

The size of the default quest window can be frustrating. Once you leave the newbie zones and venture out into the larger world, you quickly approach the quest limit. With only six lines of text to display all of your quests, things can feel a bit cramped. Fortunately, Extended QuestLog (EQL) splits the frame and places the list and descriptions side-by-side, giving you a whole lot more room to view both (see Figure 4-8). With the addon enabled, you'll almost never need to scroll the list. In addition, EQL comes with a configurable tracker that lets you track as many quests as you want (compared to the default interface's limit of five).

Using EQL

EQL completely replaces the default quest frame. Trust me, you won't miss it. When you first open the quest log you'll be presented with a list of your quests that is much larger than before. When you click on one of them, the panel will expand to display the quest's description on the right. You can minimize or maximize the window (show or hide the description) with a button in the upper-right corner next to the close button. If you click the Options button, the control panel will open, allowing you to configure much of the addon's behavior and appearance, including its location and tracker (see Figure 4-9).

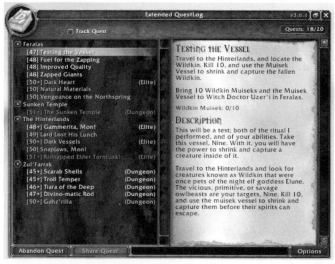

FIGURE 4-8: Extended QuestLog takes up twice the space, but it's worth it.

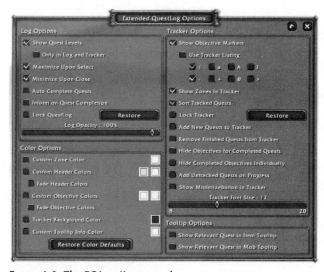

FIGURE 4-9: The EQL options panel.

Using the EQL Quest Tracker

The EQL tracker functions identically to the default one (see Figure 4-10); Shift+click on a quest to track it, and then Shift+click again to remove it. You can Ctrl+Shift+click a quest to add it to the EQL tracker and remove all other tracked quests at the same time. The tracker itself starts off in the center of the screen, so you'll probably want to click and drag it out of the way and into a more permanent position. Beyond that, you can configure the tracker in the options panel; its colors and symbols can be changed, quests can be automatically added to it, and it can be locked in place, among a few other things.

FIGURE 4-10: Thankfully, the EQL tracker can track more than five quests at a time.

Keeping Your Group Members Informed While Questing with FastQuest

Addon created and maintained by Vashen

CURSE-GAMING

FastQuest adds a number of small, toggleable features related to questing and the built-in quest tracker. Primarily, the addon allows you to automatically notify the people you're questing with about your progress. This is useful when doing collection quests with a group, so you don't have to keep asking each other how many skulls (or feathers or widgets) everyone has. Additionally, FastQuest increases the number of colors used to indicate quest difficulty, allows you to relocate the quest tracker, and displays quest levels in the quest log. Each option is controlled by a slash command (see Table 4-6); use /fastquest or /fq.

Table 4-6   FastQuest Command-Line Options

Option	Description
tag	Toggles display of quest tags (elite, raid, and so on).
lock|unlock	Locks/Unlocks quest tracker window.
nodrag	Toggles dragging of quest tracker; you must reload UI to apply.
autoadd	Toggles automatic addition of changed quests to QuestTracker.
autonotify	Toggles automatic notification of party members.
autocomplete	Toggles automatic completion of quests when turning them in.
allowguild	Toggles automatic notification of guild members.
allowraid	Toggles automatic notification of raid members.
alwaysnotify	Toggle automatic notification for non-party channel.
detail	Toggles quest notification in brief or in detail.
reset	Resets FastQuest moving components; dragging must be enabled.
status	Displays the FastQuest configuration status.
clear	Clears QuestTracker window from all quests.
format	Toggles quest notification output format.
color	Toggles colorful quest title in QuestTracker window.

Source: original addon documentation

Managing and Tracking Quests with MonkeyMods

Addons created and maintained by Trentin

WORLDOFWAR   CURSE-GAMING

MonkeyMods is a small collection of addons that have all been developed by the same author, but there aren't quite enough of them to consider it a full-blown compilation. The two most comprehensive components are MonkeyQuest, a highly tweakable quest tracker replacement, and MonkeyBuddy, which is used to configure all the MonkeyMods. The package comes with six components in total (see Table 4-7).

Table 4-7   MonkeyMods Modules

Module	Description
MonkeyBuddy	Provides a visual configuration panel for all MonkeyMods
MonkeyClock	A simple clock window
MonkeyLibrary	Main library required by all the MonkeyMods addons
MonkeyQuest	A comprehensive quest tracker
MonkeyQuestLog	Displays quest details when an entry in MonkeyQuest is clicked
MonkeySpeed	Displays the player's speed as a percentage of run speed

Using MonkeyQuest

MonkeyQuest is sort of a quest tracker/quest log hybrid that lists all of your quests, their objectives, their levels, and their zones. Everything is color-coded and organized (see Figure 4-11). Every zone listed has a little plus or minus next to it, which can be clicked to expand or contract the quests in that zone. Each quest listed also has a little checkbox next to it; if unchecked, the quest will disappear. In the upper-right corner of the frame is another little checkbox; if checked, all previously hidden items will be displayed.

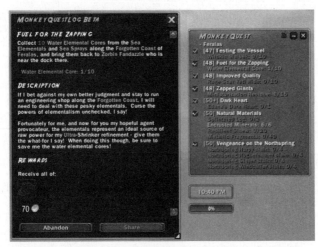

FIGURE **4-11**: MonkeyQuestLog, MonkeyQuest, MonkeyClock, and MonkeySpeed.F

If you mouse-over a quest, its details will be shown in the tooltip. Left-clicking on a quest will open MonkeyQuestLog, a detailed (and resizable) view of the quest's complete information (see Figure 4-11). Finally, MonkeyQuest can be dragged around by any of its empty space or by its border.

Note MonkeyClock and MonkeySpeed don't really need their own sections, because they're just about as simple as addons come. Drag them into place and lock them if you want to keep them around. MonkeyBuddy has a few useful options for each one.

Configuring MonkeyMods with MonkeyBuddy

Right under the minimap (next to the zoom buttons) there's a little monkey icon. Click on it to open MonkeyBuddy, the MonkeyMods configuration panel (see Figure 4-12). Alternatively, you can right-click on the MonkeyQuest, MonkeyClock, or MonkeySpeed frames. To remove the little monkey, type the command /mbdismiss. To get it back, type /mbcall.

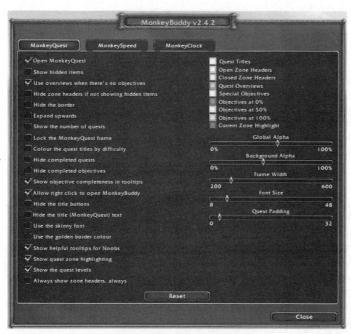

FIGURE 4-12: The MonkeyQuest tab of MonkeyBuddy.

MonkeyBuddy has three tabs that you can use to configure the three previously mentioned addons (MonkeyQuestLog has no configuration yet). All settings are spelled out expertly and are very straightforward (although MonkeyQuest sure does have a *lot* of them). You should also know that the default quest log and tracker are unaffected by this addon package.

On the Web MonkeyMods has its own website/blog called ".toctastic!" where you can download the latest versions of the mods and receive updates about them. See www.toctastic.net.

Placing Spell and Ability Statistics on the Tooltip with TheoryCraft

Addon created by Aelian, maintained by Sephyx

CURSE-GAMING   WOWINTERFACE

TheoryCraft does a few different things, notably the following:

- Allows you to add virtually any statistic pertaining to a spell to its tooltip. For example: damage / mana, resist rate, chance of critical hit, and so on.

- Allows you to place one of the aforementioned values directly on spell action buttons. For example, you could have each spell's button labeled with the average amount of damage that the spell causes, or its total cost in mana.

- Allows you to examine your vital statistics under several different conditions, including your current armor, no armor, your target's armor, or various endgame sets.

Each of these features is controlled by a jam-packed control panel.

Modifying Spell Tooltips

By default, the addon integrates each spell's damage per second (DPS) and crit chance into the tooltip. However, if it's raw numbers you're after, there's a whole lot more statistics that you can enable. Type /tc or /theorycraft to bring up the visual interface, and select the Tooltip tab for now. This panel allows you to enable/disable any of the listed statistics. If you're feeling confused, each setting has a decent mouse-over explanation to help you out. You probably don't want to enable everything (see Figure 4-13); simply enable the values that are useful to you and/or you understand.

FIGURE 4-13: TheoryCraft is capable of placing a huge amount of information in the tooltip.

Placing Statistics on Your Action Buttons

The default setting here is to place average damage or average heal values (whichever are available) on the action buttons, which you may have already noticed. However, you're welcome to select which values are displayed from a longish list of possible stats. This feature is controlled on the Button Text tab of the visual interface (see Figure 4-14). There are two stats to select; if the first one isn't available, then the second one will be used. Next to each is a drop-down menu to select the precision (for example, average damage is fine with a precision of 1, but damage per mana needs a much finer setting like 0.01). Below this is an intuitive interface for positioning the numbers on the buttons; just drag the large 1000 around and your action buttons will update immediately. Check one of the boxes next to the 1000 to justify it to the right or left. You can also set the size, font, and color.

FIGURE 4-14: You can place a statistic directly on each of your spells' buttons.

Checking Your Vitals While Wearing Various Kinds of Equipment

Finally, on the third tab (Vitals) you can view a rundown of your character's statistics and a list of talents that affect them. However, you can also modify this information by simulating wearing different equipment. There are a number of choices from the drop-down menu at the bottom of the frame. If you choose Custom, another frame will appear to the left, which allows you to define your hypothetical outfit (see Figure 4-15). It explains how to populate the list or overwrite a slot (by Alt+clicking items or links). You can also populate it with your current equipment or your target's (if they're close enough to you). Back in the main window, you can also select from a number of your class's endgame sets. We can all *dream*, can't we?

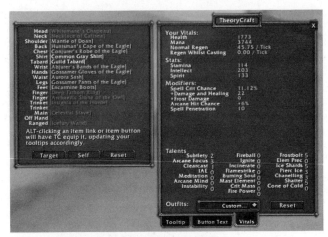

FIGURE 4-15: View your vitals with current armor, no armor, or
hypothetically awesome armor.

Adding a Modular Information Bar

In a similar style to the bars that adorn modern operating systems (Windows' taskbar and
Mac OS X's menubar), a couple of addon packages are available that add info-rich, highly
configurable bars to the WoW interface. Both offerings operate on a plug-in model, allowing
additional addons to expand the bars with more features than they ship with. Which should
you choose? It's a tough decision; try both. FuBar is built around the popular and speedy Ace2
system, whereas Titan Panel has been around for a longer amount of time. Both have a large
library of user-created plug-ins.

Titan Panel

Addon created and maintained by Adsertor

WORLDOFWAR   CURSE-GAMING   WOWINTERFACE

Titan panel's built-in features aren't exactly built-in; they're simply plug-ins that are distributed along with the core package. The Titan folder is the core of the addon, and all the rest
(TitanAmmo, TitanBag, TitanClock, and so on) are plug-in modules. The built-in modules'
directories actually contain little more than TOC files that point to files within the Titan folder
itself, enabling each module to be disabled or enabled from the Addon List.

When you first enter the game, you'll see two new Titan Panel bars, one on the top of your
screen and one on the bottom (see Figure 4-16). Several modules are enabled by default as
well. In general, modules are separated into two groups: Left Side modules, which are the main
informational plug-ins, and Right Side modules, which are utility features (like auto-hiding,

scaling, volume, and transparency). You can enable or disable modules on the fly by right-clicking one of the bars in an empty place to bring up the main menu. Built-in modules are listed in a special menu, and other plug-ins are sorted by category. When you enable a module, it will always appear on the bar from which the menu was opened.

FIGURE 4-16: A Titan Panel bar at the top of the screen, with a few modules active.

Modules consist of three parts: a display on the bar itself, a tooltip, and a menu. You can often get more information pertaining to a module's purpose by placing your mouse over its display on the bar. By right-clicking its display, you can access its options menu, and from there you can toggle its main settings, tweak how it's displayed on the bar, or hide it altogether. You cannot rearrange modules once they're shown; instead, you need to re-enable them in the order you wish them to appear.

The main menu (found by right-clicking in an empty spot) is also used to configure the core Titan Panel options (see Figure 4-17). Here, you can choose whether you want to enable the top bar, bottom bar, or both. You can also toggle a number of other settings relating to the addon's appearance.

FIGURE 4-17: The Titan Panel options menu.

Using additional Titan Panel plug-ins is as simple as downloading and installing them just like any other addon. A search for Titan on the addon websites will return more results than you can handle. Most plug-ins are named in the form:

```
Titan Panel [Plugin Name]
```

You may have to enable new Titan Panel plug-ins in-game before they show up on the bar. If installed properly, they should appear in Titan Panel's main menu under one of the categories. Simply toggle them on to start using them.

FuBar

Addon created and maintained by ckknight

`CURSE-GAMING`   `WOWINTERFACE`

Unlike Titan Panel, FuBar doesn't come with any modules by default. You can load the addon up, but it won't do anything interesting. However, a simple search for FuBar will return numerous plug-ins. Most FuBar plug-ins are named in the form:

```
FuBar - PluginName
```

There's also a download called the FuBar Starter Pack, which contains many popular FuBar plug-ins to get you started; I recommend installing this pack just to get the hang of the addon.

When you load up the game, you'll see two bars, one on top and one on the bottom (just like Titan Panel); however FuBar's bars are thinner and less embellished (see Figure 4-18). Unlike Titan Panel, you can drag various elements around; similarly-aligned modules can be rearranged on the bar by dragging them. You can also drag modules from one bar to another. Finally, you can drag entire bars from either top to bottom or bottom to top.

`128 ● 41 ● 24 ●   ● 22/72   ● Valley of Strength (54, 65)   ● 69.9% R: 150.0%   ● 55 fps 76 ms 10.9 MiB 0.6 KiB/s   ● 85%   ● 0 Honor | 0-0   6:49 PM`

FIGURE 4-18: A FuBar panel with several modules loaded from the Starter Pack.

The FuBar main menu is no surprise (see Figure 4-19); open it by right-clicking in an empty space. It controls which modules are visible, overall options (such as creating and destroying bars), and profiles. There's also no limit to the number of bars you can have, because they will simply stack with each other on the top or bottom of the screen when there's more than one of them. Bars can also be detached and dragged anywhere in between the top and bottom. Because anything can be dragged (though perhaps accidentally), you can also lock panels to prevent movement. You also have control over spacing, thickness, font size, and transparency.

FIGURE 4-19: The FuBar options menu.

Like Titan Panel, modules have bar displays, tooltips, and menus, all of which operate comparably. However, FuBar has two rather unique additional features. First, tooltips can be detached, which means they persist onscreen and can be moved around or locked in place (see Figure 4-20). Second, modules can be moved to the minimap, which means they no longer show up on a FuBar panel, but instead appear as minimap buttons. Each new button will have the same tooltip, respond to the same clicks, have the same right-click menu, and can be dragged around the border of the minimap by left-clicking.

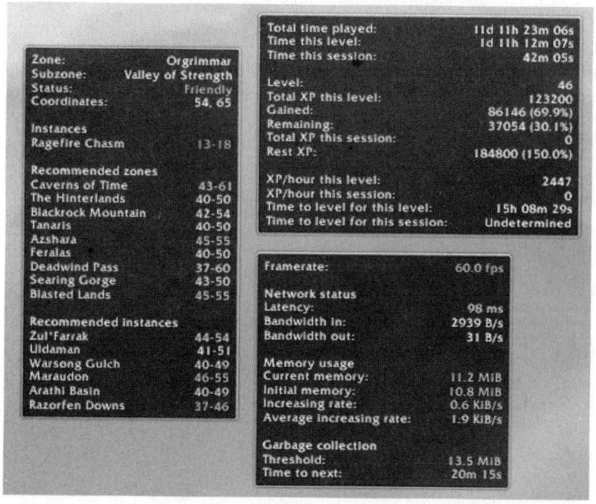

FIGURE 4-20: Three different FuBar module tooltips that have been detached.

FuBar is currently in its second version. It ships with an additional addon (called FuBar-compat-1.2), which allows modules designed for older versions of FuBar to function. This compatibility module requires the original Ace library (www.wowace.com).

Putting Spell Information on Your Action Buttons with ABInfo

Addon created by Ombres, maintained by FinalCast

CURSE-GAMING

ABInfo has a few simple features, each of which affects your action buttons. In all, it adds several helpful features:

- Colored cooldown counters (very similar to OmniCC)
- A large flash whenever a spell's cooldown ends

- A flash when certain abilities can be used (such as Overpower, Revenge, and Riposte)

- Red tinting over buttons when the target is out of range

- Display of how many times a spell can be cast, based on current mana

The addon ships with a few modules that support various action-bar packages, including the default Blizzard bars, Discord Action Bars, and FlexBar (a few other packages are supported by third parties as well). When installing the addon, simply select the appropriate module for your setup. You can see an example of the cooldown counters and spell counts in Figure 4-21.

FIGURE 4-21: ABInfo adds casting counters to the bottom-left corner of action buttons.

All of the ABInfo settings are controlled with slash-command options (see Table 4-8). Use the command /abinfo or just /abi. Either command on its own will print the help.

Table 4-8   ABInfo Command-Line Options

Option	Description
cooldown	Toggles the display of the cooldown
flash	Toggles the display of the flash effect
extraflash	Toggles the display of the extra flash for Overpower/Revenge/Riposte
red	Toggles the range display
count	Toggles the display of the count of spell/mana
countsize	Changes the size of the spell count (default: 11)
flashsize	Changes the size of the flash (default: 256)

Source: original addon documentation

Tweaking Your Unit and Party Frames with Archaeologist

Addon created and maintained by AnduinLothar

CURSE-GAMING   WOWINTERFACE

If you're interested in modifying the way information is displayed on the player frame, target frame, or party frames, the Archeologist addon is for you. Basically, it gives you a ridiculous number of options that you can tweak to your heart's content. There isn't enough room in this book to list all of the options (there are literally hundreds), but I'll give you a rundown of the various categories they fall into:

- Presets
- Experience and Reputation Bars
- Player Status Bars
- Party Status Bars
- Pet Status Bars
- Target Status Bars
- Alternate Options
- Font Options
- Party Buff Settings
- Pet Buff Settings
- Party Pet Buff Settings
- Target Buff Settings

Thankfully, you don't need to look up a slash command for each option (although each one *does* have a slash command). The addon uses the MCom library to display a long list of these commands, which you can interact with directly. Click on a command to insert it into the chat box, or you can often click on a value in green to adjust it directly. On/Off values toggle and a drop-down menu is used if there are more than two values to choose from. While it's still going to take you a long time to navigate through the entire list, it sure beats typing commands in one by one from scratch. Type /arch to open up the interface, and tweak away!

Note Archaeologist comes with the popular Cosmos compilation and has built-in support for the Khaos configuration system that ships with it. You can use Khaos to have an even easier time tweaking all of Archaeologist's settings.

Updating Your Casting Bar with eCastingBar

Addon created by elvendawn, updated by Repent, maintained by Neuro_Medivh

| WORLDOFWAR | CURSE-GAMING | WOWINTERFACE |

The default casting bar has absolutely *no* settings; and where's the fun in that? The eCastingBar addon (which sounds vaguely like an Apple product) is an excellent, modern-looking replacement. In addition, it has an attractive options panel sporting user-friendly settings. The sleek casting bar itself can be resized, recolored, and repositioned (see Figure 4-22).

FIGURE 4-22: The casting bar replacement, eCastingBar, does its thing.

When you first enable the addon, you'll see four frames hovering around: the Mirror Bar Outline, the eCasting Bar Outline, the Target Bar Outline, and the Focus Bar Outline. These frames allow you to move the bars around, and place them wherever you want. Because it's not altogether clear, you may be wondering what the Mirror bar is in the first place! Well, easy enough: It's used for monitoring your breath and exhaustion levels, while the casting bar is used for everything else (such as casting spells). The Target and Focus bars display spells cast by your enemies.

Open the options panel with the slash command /ecastingbar or /ecb, and you'll see that all of eCastingBar's settings are controlled from the panel. The appearance settings are pretty basic, but you'll want to make sure to turn on Hide Outline (for each bar) when you have them in the right place. Happy casting!

Managing Your Addons In-Game with myAddOns

Addon created and maintained by Scheid

Typically, you're at the whim of the Addon List when it comes to managing your addons, and unfortunately, you can't access the Addon List in-game. There are good reasons for this. You can't enable or disable most addons while the game is loaded. Also, you need to restart the entire WoW client in order to install a new addon. However, there's no reason you shouldn't be able to do *some* addon-related tasks from within the game, such as the following:

- View all your currently enabled addons
- View metadata about addons that are enabled
- Load addons that support load-on-demand functionality
- Define circumstances under which load-on-demand addons should be loaded automatically

Well, myAddOns does all this plus a little more, and has a nice interface too. In fact, it fits in with the default UI so well you might forget that it's not a part of it. The "plus a little more" depends on the addons you're using, because these extra features depend on addon authors to implement them. Some do and some don't. In order to create a myAddOns-enhanced addon, an author simply needs to add extra information to her TOC file. This information may include a multi-paged help document that myAddOns can display as well as an options frame, which myAddOns can launch directly from its interface.

Using myAddOns

Using myAddOns is very simple. Open the main menu (press Escape) and you'll see a new entry halfway down that says AddOns. Click this button to open the myAddOns interface (see Figure 4-23). The interface is divided up: On the left is a list of your currently enabled addons, and on the right is information on three tabs. The list of addons is sorted by category; so if an addon's author decides to specify a category, then it will appear appropriately; otherwise it will be sorted as Unknown. Addons in the list are yellow if they're loaded or gray if they're not. You can click on a gray entry, and then on the Load button to load it right away.

FIGURE 4-23: The myAddOns addition to the main menu and its interface.

If you select an addon, any available information about it is displayed to the right. You can write your own notes about the addon as well. These notes will be saved between sessions. If it's highlighted, you can click the Options button to load that particular addon's configuration panel. If a help variable is present, it can be viewed on the Help tab. If the addon is load-on-demand capable, you can configure whether or not to load it automatically on the Load tab. Options for this are included to load it conditionally based on class or character name.

Note It's not hard to modify an addon to support myAddOns' additional features. All the necessary information can be pulled directly from the TOC file. That said, you might wish to handcraft a help variable which will need to be inserted into your addon's code. Also, there are Lua methods for overriding the TOC information. See the `Readme.txt` file for details about this method and for the list of specific TOC codes that myAddOns understands.

On the Web Scheid has written several small, useful addons in addition to myAddOns. See `http://scheid.free.fr`.

Viewing Every Quest You've Completed with QuestHistory

Addon created by Jasters, updated by Dsanai, maintained by Aod_Knight

`CURSE-GAMING`

One of the biggest omissions in World of Warcraft is the lack of your character's questing history: what you've done, when you did it, and so on. Clearly, the game keeps track of these things; if you've done a quest, the game knows not to give it to you again. Unfortunately, *none* of this data is reported to the client. Once you've completed a quest, it's as if it never existed in the first place. With QuestHistory, you can track all the details of the quests you're working on or have ever completed. However, there's one big caveat: It only *records* information, meaning its database goes back to the point at which you installed it, and no further.

Using QuestHistory

The QuestHistory interface can be opened up with the commands `/questhistory` or `/qh`, or you can bind a key to do it. The frame itself shows a nice big list of everything in the addon's database (see Figure 4-24). You can sort the list by clicking on column headers or by using the drop-down menu in the upper-left corner, which gives you a few extra sorting options. You can also perform a text search by clicking the Search button in the lower-left corner. Submit a blank search to reset the filtered list. If you click on a quest in the list, a modified quest frame will appear to the left, providing you with the original quest text and more details than you could possibly want.

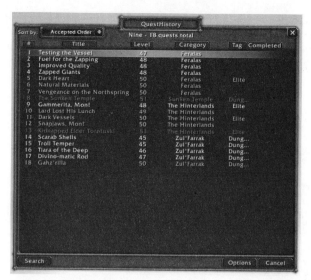

FIGURE 4-24: The not-so-large QuestHistory database belonging to a character.

Click the Options button to open up the options panel, which will appear on the left side of the frame. Here you can filter the list and choose colors for abandoned and completed quests (current quests are shown in the normal green-to-red difficulty scheme based on level). You can also view the quest history for any of your other characters. Below this, the mod gives you the option to toggle off any pieces of information you don't want it to collect. Why? In order to save some space; if you care about space, you can turn off any bits you don't care about. You can also clean up the database, removing duplicate entries and such. Finally, you have the option of modifying the database directly by adding, changing, or deleting entries if ever the need arises. I recommend leaving these features turned off for the time being. Enable them only if and when you need them.

Note You may want to check out the QuestHistoryMap addon, which extends the functionality of QuestHistory by placing important quest locations directly onto your maps, much like Gatherer does for ores and herbs.

Working with Heads-Up-Display (HUD) Mods

In the midst of a fight, the most important information is your stats and your enemy's stats. Why, then, is this information tucked way up in the *upper-left corner* of your screen? Since you can't concentrate on the center of your screen, you can't pay attention to the impressive-looking attacks that your character is deftly performing!

For a more cinematic and exciting experience, consider using a heads-up-display, or HUD. These addons replace the target and player frames with sets of rings placed squarely in the middle of your interface. With this kind of setup, you can monitor your and your target's vitals *and* watch the action at the same time.

ArcHUD

Addon created and maintained by Nenie

| WORLDOFWAR | CURSE-GAMING |

ArcHUD is a responsive, ring-based HUD based on the Ace2 library, which sports some very clean graphics and smooth animation. It's highly configurable in terms of layout and appearance, and it includes some unique features, such as the ability to see a small three-dimensional model of your target directly below (or above) the rings. (See Figure 4-25 for details.)

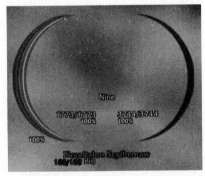

FIGURE 4-25: ArcHUD's rings make an attractive replacement for the player and target frames.

The addon sports the typical Ace2 slash command system, but is easier to configure with a hierarchical drop-down menu system; type /archud config to bring it up. Some people prefer static configuration panels, but this system gets the job done well enough, and fortunately most (but not all) settings take effect immediately without forcing you to reopen the menu.

Note ArcHUD plays nicely with MobHealth (for mob hit-points estimation) and FlightMap (for flight durations). It also replaces the default Blizzard casting bar.

Check out Moog HUD (created by Tivoli, maintained by Rezalas) for a visually comparable addon without nearly the same degree of configurability. It has an options panel, opened with /moog. It's not nearly as versatile, but sometimes *fewer* options can be more appealing.

MetaHUD

Addon created by Drathal, maintained by MetaHawk

WORLDOFWAR   CURSE-GAMING   WOWINTERFACE

MetaHUD also sports a ring-based display with unique graphics (see Figure 4-26). It provides a complete replacement for the player, target, and casting frames, and goes as far as to hide them automatically. Overall, MetaHUD provides an attractive heads-up display with an extremely easy-to-use yet feature-rich options panel.

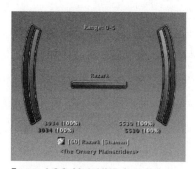

FIGURE 4-26: MetaHUD in action.

By default, health bars are placed on the left; mana bars on the right. Some prefer to set it up so that their stats are on the left and their target's stats are on the right (which is one of the two available layout options). A target's target bar is located in the middle of the ring and text-based information concerning your target adorns the bottom. To access the drop-down menu you'd normally get by right-clicking on the target frame, just right-click on your target's name.

MetaHUD adds a red button (with white marks) to the minimap, which you can left-click to effectively target yourself (bringing up the HUD) or right-click to open the options panel. You can also left-click and drag the button around the border of the map. The options panel is divided into six logical tabs. You can toggle most of the addon's elements (in case there's just too *much* information) as well as tweak the colors, fonts, formatting, and layout. Many adjustments are at your disposal; if you spend a little while looking through everything, you should be able to get the addon set up pretty comfortably. The Unit Text tab uses a considerably elaborate tag system, although there are plenty of presets built-in so you don't have to get your hands dirty unless you want to (and if you do, you have plenty of examples to work from). As for slash-command options (used with /metahud), there aren't many (see Table 4-9).

Table 4-9 MetaHUD Command-Line Options

Option	Description
menu	Opens the MetaHUD options panel
hud	Brings up the HUD (select yourself)
square	Sets the minimap button for a circular outline
circle	Sets the minimap button for a square outline

Source: original addon documentation

Handling More Than One Script Error with ImprovedErrorFrame

Addon created by Vjeux, maintained by AnduinLothar

CURSE-GAMING

Under default circumstances, if an addon, macro, or script you're running generates an error, it'll pop up in a dialog box (see Figure 4-27). Unfortunately, if *multiple* errors are generated (for example, maybe two addons each have a problem), you'll know about only one of them because only the first error that's generated will be displayed. For most people this is manageable, but not exactly ideal. If you're developing an addon, it's even worse; you want to know exactly which errors are popping up, especially if there's more than one of them.

FIGURE 4-27: The WoW client's default error dialog box.

ImprovedErrorFrame takes over the handling of errors entirely. It displays them in the chat window when they occur, and then queues them up (*all* of them), so you can examine each one at your leisure. Whenever errors occur, a minimap button appears and pulsates. You can click on the button at any point to view the script errors that have accumulated (see Figure 4-28). Once open, you can select and copy the error messages displayed as well.

To illustrate the benefit of ImprovedErrorFrame, suppose there are two tiny (error-prone) addons called Bob and Joe. With both of them enabled (and nothing else), the previous dialog box appears when the player enters the world. However, with the ImprovedErrorFrame addon enabled in addition, nothing pops up. Instead, there are two errors in the chat frame and a blinking minimap button. When you click the button, the (much more useful) dialog box shown in Figure 4-28 appears.

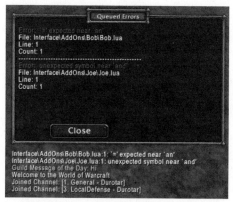

FIGURE 4-28: ImprovedErrorFrame handling the unruly Bob and Joe addons.

There are a number of options (see Table 4-10), which you use with the slash command /ief. You can follow commands with on or off to set their states explicitly or use them alone to toggle them.

Table 4-10   ImprovedErrorFrame Command-Line Options

Option	Description
notify	Determines whether errors are queued or shown immediately.
blink	Minimap button will blink when errors are pending.
count	Displays error count on the minimap button.
always	Always shows the minimap button.
sound	Sound plays when an error occurs (even during loading).
empty	Minimap button graphic will clear when blinking.
debug	FrameXML.log will be output in verbose mode (requires UI reload).
stack	Displays the stack trace along with the error message.

Source: original addon documentation

Reducing Minimap Clutter with CleanMinimap

Addon created by joev, maintained by s0urc3x

CURSE-GAMING

The minimap has a lot of extra information and little buttons surrounding it. CleanMinimap helps you reduce this mess down to the bare essentials, while giving you some extra tools to tweak the main minimap frame (and its child frames) at the same time.

First of all, you'll notice a new black minimap button with a yellow triangle on it. Click this to open the options panel. From here you can enable or disable the mod, adjust its own button, toggle all of the default minimap components, change the map's opacity and scaling, or adjust the positions of the built-in buttons (see Figure 4-29). You can also turn on cardinal direction markers. If you enable a modifier key, you can hold that button down and click on the minimap to turn it into a gray square with four handles. While it's a square, the minimap can be dragged around and the handles can be dragged to resize it. The OneKey feature allows you to quickly toggle between two minimap sizes at the push of a button.

The mod's minimal slash-command options can be used with /cleanminimap or simply /cmm (see Table 4-11); use the command alone to print the help.

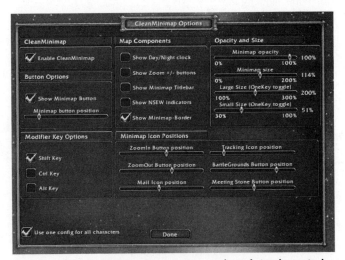

FIGURE 4-29: CleanMinimap gives you a number of simple controls for tweaking the minimap.

Table 4-11   CleanMinimap Command-Line Options

Option	Description
on	Turns the CleanMinimap functionality on
off	Turns all the CleanMinimap functionality off
config	Sets minimap options with a visual control panel
help	Displays help text

Source: original addon documentation

Setting Up Click-Casting with Clique

Addon created and maintained by Cladhaire

WOWINTERFACE

If you don't know what click-casting is, you're missing out. Essentially, click-casting allows you to click on a target's frame to cast spells on it. The target can be anything; dead, alive, hostile, or friendly. By using combinations of modifier keys (Ctrl, Alt, and Shift) and different mouse buttons (Left, Right, Middle, Button4, or Button5), you can cast different spells with different kinds of clicks. Furthermore, click-casting definitions are context sensitive, so Ctrl+left-clicking on a hostile mob could cast a damage spell while Ctrl+left-clicking on a friendly player could cast a buff. You're free to set things up exactly how you want. Click-casting isn't just for healers and spell casters; it can be used by anyone! Hunters can control their pets; Rogues can enter stealth; anything you can do in a macro can be assigned to a click-cast.

Clique is the premiere click-casting interface thanks to its intuitive approach in integrating itself with the default Spellbook. After installing the addon and opening the Spellbook, you'll see an additional tab-button on the right depicting a little mouse wearing a wizard's hat. This button toggles the Clique interface. In the upper-right corner of the Clique interface, there's a drop-down menu, which is used to switch between different click-sets. These associate click-bindings to certain situations such as a friendly target, an enemy, or casting spells out of combat. You can assign each binding (such as Shift+right-click) once per click-set.

Once you've chosen a click-set, it's time to assign some bindings. This is where Clique really shines. To assign a binding, simply click on a spell in your Spellbook using the button and modifiers you wish to associate with it. For example, left-clicking on Frost Shock, Rank 4 while holding down the Shift key creates a binding for it in the Clique interface associated with the action Shift+left-click (see Figure 4-30). You can create as many bindings per context as there are combinations of clicks and buttons (there are 35 in total).

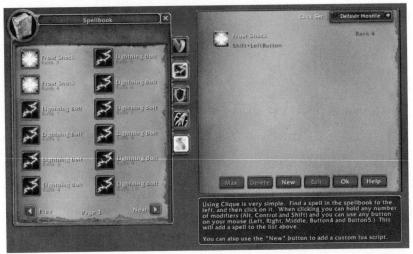

FIGURE 4-30: The Clique interface with a binding for Frost Shock defined and selected.

Once a binding has been created, you can click on it in the list to select it, at which point several options become available. First, the Max button will disassociate the binding from a particular rank of the selected spell, instead causing it to cast the highest rank you know. If the target of the spell is too low-level for the highest rank you know, the highest possible level will be used. You can also delete the binding or edit it. When editing a binding, you can change its name, icon, and reassign its button/click combo as well. If you click the Custom button, you can create a binding that does any of the actions available to addons, such as executing a macro, targeting a unit, opening a unit menu, even clicking another button.

Once you've set yourself up and used click-casting for any length of time, you'll wonder how you ever lived without it!

Repositioning, Scaling, and Hiding Frames with MoveAnything

Addon created by Skrag; modified by Jason, Kaitlin, and Scorpia; maintained by Vincent

`CURSE-GAMING` `WOWINTERFACE`

MoveAnything is a general-purpose tool for moving, hiding, and rescaling virtually any object onscreen. You can literally *move anything*. This mod provides a good contingency plan when you just can't find a way to reconfigure some aspect of another addon or interface element. In addition to tweaking entire windows, MoveAnything can target *pieces* of windows. Because buttons, sliders, and checkboxes are all derived from frames, they're fair game.

Use the command /move to open the addon's control panel, or you can use the button that says "MoveAnything!" on the main (Escape) menu. Two windows will appear when the mod is opened. The larger one contains a listing of known frames. The smaller one contains buttons to give you a finer degree of control over the currently selected frame (see Figure 4-31). Next to each entry in the list are two boxes; use them to enable modification of a frame or to hide it. Once you've enabled either one of them, a Reset button will appear to the left. Click it to take the frame back to its original state.

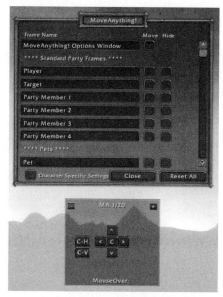

FIGURE 4-31: The MoveAnything interface.

While a frame is unlocked, a gray box will appear on top of it. You can now left-click and drag to move the frame (and box) around. Alternatively, you can use the arrow buttons on the smaller control panel to move it one unit at a time in any direction. You can also click on the C button to center the frame in the middle of the screen. The C-H and C-V buttons, respectively, center the frame only horizontally or vertically.

The display at the top of the small window (MA #/20) refers to the currently active frame; if you're moving more than one frame at once with MoveAnything, you can switch between them with the plus and minus buttons. While a frame is unlocked, you can Shift+right-click on it to toggle the gray box and name; the tiny handles will remain. Right-click to lock it in place; the box and handles will disappear.

Note Text that's displayed onscreen is a kind of object called a FontString. The FontString object type doesn't scale too well, especially if it's being scaled up. It *will* get larger, but it might also wrap or become cut off in the process. If you're scaling things up, be aware of this problem.

Using MoveAnything with Unlisted Frames

As mentioned previously, MoveAnything can move *anything*, not just the frames in its list. When the interface is open, the small window will display the names of any frames that are under your mouse. This is a good way to figure out what an object's name is, because you need to know it in order to move the object. For example, let's assume the Atlas addon is installed (see Chapter 3 for more info on Atlas). When Atlas is open, it has an Options button in the upper-right corner. If you have MoveAnything open and you place your mouse over the Options button, you can see that its name is AtlasFrameOptionsButton. To modify this button, type the following command:

```
/move AtlasFrameOptionsButton
```

The same gray box and handles will appear around the button, which can now be moved anywhere and scaled. An entry for the button is also added to MoveAnything's larger list window, providing the means to hide or reset the button. When you reset a frame that's been added to the list in this way, its entry is immediately removed from the list.

Adding an Action Bar for Usable Items with AutoBar

Addon created by Saien, maintained by Toadkiller

CURSE-GAMING   WOWINTERFACE

As you level up in WoW, your inventory begins to get more and more cluttered up with usable items that you've got to carry around, such as food, water, bandages, potions, your Hearthstone, and eventually your mount. All of these items can be dragged to action bars, and then clicked on to be used (or hot-key assigned). However, what if you have three different kinds of health potions? Well, in that case you'd need to have three action slots, or you'd have to choose only one size potion to have easily accessible. AutoBar's aim is to solve this problem by assigning a set of context-specific rules to each of the 24 new action buttons it provides (see Figure 4-32). Because AutoBar only supports items, it doesn't take up any of your built-in 120 action slots.

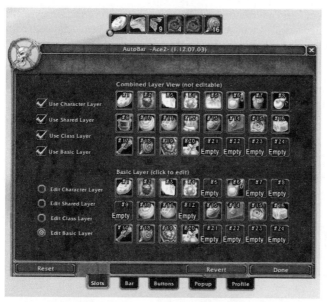

FIGURE 4-32: AutoBar provides intelligently updated buttons for your usable items.

Tweak the Tooltip

The tooltip is the context-sensitive info-box that pops up when you place your mouse over certain things, like spells, items, other players, signs, and objects. There are *very few* default options for tweaking this frame. One of the most common things you'll want to do is re-anchor (move) it once you've rearranged your whole interface. The two addons discussed next allow you to do this, as well as to perform many other modifications.

TinyTip

Addon created and maintained by Thrae

WORLDOFWAR **CURSE-GAMING** **WOWINTERFACE**

TinyTip is an attractive upgrade for the default tooltip, which subtly improves it while keeping it very recognizable. Built around the Ace2 system, TinyTip comes in three parts: the TinyTip core addon itself, an options framework called TinyTipOptions, and finally TinyTipExtras, which provides some additional options (like raid icon, PvP icon, and buff displays).

The default changes to the tooltip are subtle and the layout remains very similar. One of the main differences is coloring: class, level, name, backdrop, and border are all color-coded, and adjustable. Guild names can be displayed, as well as (the now obsolete) honor ranks. There's even an option to spell-out reaction (Hostile or Friendly) if you're color-blind. Another big difference (that you'll notice immediately) is the anchoring options. By default, the TinyTip anchors the tooltip for units to your mouse (see Figure 4-33), although you have the option to set it back to the typical spot, or any corner of the screen. Combined with offsets, you can position it anywhere you want.

FIGURE 4-33: A TinyTip modified tooltip and its options menu

Configuration is modified via a loaded-on-demand, hierarchical drop-down menu. This is not the easiest thing in the world to use, but a wonderful alternative to configuring everything with slash commands. The menu is opened with a slash command, however; type /tinytip or /ttip to bring it up. The menu's options are dependent on which modules are loaded (you can remove any of the addon's Lua files if you don't need them, except TinyTip.lua of course).

TipBuddy

Addon created by Chester, updated by bluskale, maintained by aezay

CURSE-GAMING

TipBuddy does pretty much the same thing as TinyTip, but it has slightly different settings. Furthermore, instead of menu-based configuration, TipBuddy employs an options panel. It's jam-packed, but usable, although it might take you a few minutes to get your bearings.

TipBuddy's other big noteworthy feature is something called Compact Mode. When enabled for a particular kind of tooltip, Compact Mode causes it to appear much smaller onscreen — not by scaling it down, but by condensing and reformatting the information. The result is quite attractive (see Figure 4-34).

FIGURE 4-34: Compact tooltips are one of TipBuddy's nicest features.

Settings are configured separately for players, NPCs, and pets, and are then even further divided with tabs (between friendly, neutral, and hostile NPCs, for example). TipBuddy also employs a draggable anchor frame, making it a breeze to reposition the tooltip anywhere you want it.

Summary

In this chapter you learned about a whole variety of addons, many of which involved bars: action bars, info bars, and progress bars. You also explored many other random addons that modified your quest log, casting bars, tooltip, and unit frames. When combined, the mods discussed in this chapter allow you to reconfigure the entire layout of your interface.

In the next chapter, you are introduced to addons that have everything to do with items.

Loot Addons

Loot is the nuts and bolts of World of Warcraft and it's the reason that many of us are so addicted to the game; better loot is something to aspire toward, as well as something to fight for. Loot drives the game's economy, causes endless drama, and separates the weak from the strong.

There are tens of thousands of items in the game. Thousands of items appear on the auction house each and every day. Players collect gold, hoard it, farm it, spend it, buy it online, and waste it, but they never quite have enough of it. Then there's all the equipment: armor, weapons, sets, and trinkets. If you raid, you need special resistance gear and you need to *manage* your arsenal. Finally, there's all the rest: reagents, food, potions, water, ingredients, recipes, snowballs, quest items, and vendor trash. It's enough to keep you busy and enough to make you crazy.

The addons in this chapter all deal with loot. They help you acquire it, buy it, use it, sort it, equip it, sell it, and in one case, destroy it. They help you create outfits out of your equipment, make wise financial decisions, and dream of the gear you wish you had.

Scanning and Analyzing the Auction House with Auctioneer

Addon created and maintained by Norganna and the Auctioneer Team

WORLDOFWAR   CURSE-GAMING

Auctioneer is the premiere auction house addon, allowing you to scan all the items for sale, check out their prices, and do interesting things with the data. If you play your cards right, you can use Auctioneer to make money. It can suggest what price you should set your minimum bid and buyout when posting an item, as well as which items to buy if you want to resell them for a profit. You can easily determine the market price of an item, which auctions are rip-offs, which are steals, and how much items will sell for (or cost) at a vendor. The only trade-off is that you have to spend a good deal of time (10 minutes per day, more or less) scanning all the auctions; and you can't do this from just anywhere either, you have to be at an auction house.

Auctioneer has grown over time into the Auctioneer Complete package (see Table 5-1). While you can use the Auctioneer addon alone if you want to, the supplemental addons are probably worth your time, especially Enchantrix, which helps you predict what you'll get when an item is disenchanted (including the percentage chance of getting each possibility). This is useful not only for enchanters, but also for anyone who *knows* an enchanter.

Table 5-1   Addons in the Auctioneer Complete Package

Addon	Description
!Swatter	Debugging tool for handling and displaying error messages in a useful way
Auctioneer	Displays item info and analyzes auction data
BeanCounter	Maintains an auction house transaction database
BtmScan	Allows you to monitor new auctions for bargains
Enchantrix	Displays information in item tooltips pertaining to the results of disenchanting said item
EnhTooltip	Used to display enhanced tooltips under the original tooltip or in the original tooltip; contains hooking functions for almost all major in-game item tooltips
Informant	Displays detailed item information in tooltips, and can produce item reports by binding an information window to a keypress
Stubby	Allows on-demand addons to load automatically based upon simple event notification hooks

Source: original addon documentation

Scanning the Auction House

Once you have auctioneer up and running, the most common thing you'll be doing with it is scanning the auction house in order to refresh your pricing database. Because the maximum length for an auction is 24 hours, you'll want to do this at least once each day before you sell anything. To perform a full scan, follow these steps:

1. Go to an auction house and talk to one of the auctioneers.

2. Press the Scan button, which is found on the Browse tab.

3. You can follow along with the progress of the scan. In the center of the auction window you can see how many pages have been scanned out of the total number of pages, as well as how fast the scan is progressing in terms of auctions per second. Don't leave the auction house while the scan is taking place. Go make a snack if you get bored.

4. When it's all done, the database will update itself, and you'll get a little report in the chat window. Item tooltips will now display detailed up-to-date pricing information (see Figure 5-1).

FIGURE 5-1: Once you've scanned the auction house at least once, Auctioneer provides extensive pricing data in the tooltip for each item it's encountered previously.

Selling an Item

Once you've performed a scan, Auctioneer usually has enough information to suggest a minimum bid and buyout price for your items, as long as they're common enough that other people have been selling them too. To post an item, click on the Post Auctions tab on the bottom of the auction house window, and then drag the item from your bag into the single slot. Auctioneer will populate the price fields for you and display a message indicating how the price was calculated (see Table 5-2). Of course, you can always overwrite the selected values.

Table 5-2   Auctioneer Pricing Models

Message	Explanation
Marking up vendor by 300%	This item has not been seen at auction. We are estimating that it will be worth three times more than what you could sell it to the vendor for.
Undercutting by x%	This item has competition on the market, but it's not so bad that we'd be cutting our throats by matching them. The default amount is 5%.
No competition	This item is not on the market; you have a monopoly on this item at this time.
Competition above market	The prices for this item are no threat to you because they are all over-priced (you could bump your prices up a little, too, if you feel like it).
Cannot match lowest price	The lowest price is too far below the market value. Selling at this time is not recommended. Bide your time until this item is gone, risk it and put your item up anyway at a higher price, manually reduce your price to match it, or buy out the cheap items, and relist them and your items for proper market value.
Using my current price	You have the most competitive price on the market, so we are re-listing at your current price.
No data for HSP	No data exists to work out what the highest sellable price for this item is.

Source: original addon documentation

Searching for Deals

One fun thing you can do with Auctioneer is search for items whose current minimum bids are lower than their market value. If you do this a lot, you can attempt to make some cash by buying items and turning them around for a profit. Here's how to search for the best deals:

1. Perform a full auction house scan.

2. Switch to the Search Auctions tab at the bottom of the auction house window.

3. Leave the settings alone and click the Search button. A bunch of results should appear. If nothing shows up, there might not be any good deals. You can try lowering the Minimum Profit or Minimum Pct Less values and clicking the Search button again.

4. I suggest sorting the list by the percent profit you stand to make. Click on the Pct column header twice to get the highest percents at the top (see Figure 5-2).

FIGURE 5-2: Auctioneer adds a pane to auction house window allowing you to search for the best deals currently on the market.

5. The items listed at the top of the list represent the best deals. By default, all the results in the list end within two hours. You can hover your cursor over items to get a better idea of how well you might be able to resell them.

6. To bid on an item, click on it to select it, and then press the Bid button.

Auctioneer has a huge number of well-documented slash commands. Type /auctioneer for a complete list. You'll never need to touch the vast majority of them, because Auctioneer works so well right out of the box, but they're there if you need something to tweak.

Note The full Auctioneer pack provides a whole lot of functionality beyond what I've described here. For more information and links to extensive documentation (in a wiki format), check out the official Auctioneer website at http://auctioneeraddon.com/.

Consolidating Your Bags with vBagnon

Addon created and maintained by Tuller

WORLDOFWAR   CURSE-GAMING   WOWINTERFACE

It's a personal preference, but some people dislike dealing with five different bags separately. It can be a pain moving items around from bag to bag and keeping track of which bags are full. The current state-of-the-art bag management software is vBagnon (formerly just Bagnon; the v was introduced with the rewritten post–WoW 2.0 version), which takes all of your bags' slots and arranges them together. It's like having one giant bag. If you try to open *any* of your bags, only the one big one will be displayed.

The vBagnon package (there are three addons in all; see Table 5-3) does quite a bit more than that as well. In addition to consolidating your bags into a single, configurable window, it does the same thing for your bank. In fact, it allows you to view the contents of your bank from anywhere, which is handy, though of course you can only modify it when dealing directly with a banker. Furthermore, the latest version of the package includes a category system that you can use to filter certain kinds of items together. There's also a built-in text-based search.

Table 5-3   vBagnon Modules

Module	Description
vBagnon	Displays your inventory and bank in single frames.
vBagnon_Forever	Optional; lets you view your bank from anywhere.
vBagnon_Options	Provides a load on demand options menu.

Source: original addon documentation

Using vBagnon

There's no setup required to use vBagnon, as the default options serve pretty well. When you press B to open your backpack (or Shift+B to open all your bags) the vBagnon inventory window will open instead (see Figure 5-3) and display every slot in every bag arranged together in a grid. Alternatively, you can type /bgn bags (or /bagnon bags). You can move the window around by left-clicking and dragging its title bar. Directly below the title there are several small item icons, which represent the various pre-configured categories.

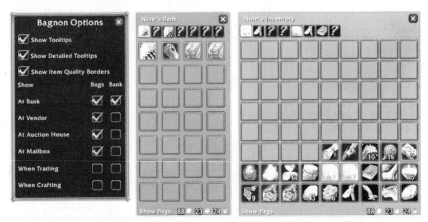

FIGURE 5-3: The vBagnon options, bank, and inventory windows (from left to right).

You can think of categories as filters for different types of items. The default category is All, which simply displays all your items, but others can include quest items, armor, weapons, and so on. Each tiny icon at the top can be enabled (it will glow) or disabled. The category's icon is set to the icon for the first item that's in it; a question mark is used for empty categories. Each enabled category will add another grid (with only the filtered items) to the bottom of the inventory window. If you mouse-over a category, its contents will be highlighted. You can drag the category icons around to swap the order of them, or you can drag one of them into an empty part of the screen to break off a separate window, displaying the contents of that category only. As you rearrange the icons, the grids below will reorder themselves to match.

At the very bottom of the window is clickable text that says Show Bags. Click it, and your bags will appear in a grid, too. Mouse-over each bag to highlight its contents or click on one to toggle whether its contents are shown in the grid above.

The bank window works in exactly the same way, both in terms of categories and bags. To open your bank window bind a key or type /bgn bank. You can open this window from anywhere in the game, but you must visit a banker once before you'll see any of your items.

To search for items, use the command /find <name>. For example, /find potion will open up a new little window with all the matching results, based on the item names. You can also search for types of items with /findr <rule>. Rules can be anything listed in the category configuration window, which will be covered a bit later. For example, you could type /findr quest to return all quest items. Dragging the Quest category icon into an empty spot would achieve the same result.

Configuring vBagnon

A few overall vBagnon options can be controlled via a central options panel; type /bagnon or /bgn to bring it up. You can control tooltips, border coloring (by default, the borders of item slots are colored based on the occupying item's rarity), and under what circumstances the bank or inventory windows should be automatically opened.

In order to open either one of vBagnon's individual display options, right-click on the title bar of either the bank or inventory window. From here you can adjust the number of columns, spacing, scale, background color, and a few other things. You can also tweak the categories; click on the Categories entry in the menu to bring up yet another panel from which you can create or delete categories (you can also right-click on the category icons to arrive here). If you don't like the little category icons at all, and don't plan to use the features they provide, delete all of them except the All category; you'll see that the strip of small icons will disappear.

Keeping a Local Item Database with LootLink

Addon created and maintained by Telo

CURSE-GAMING

There's no way to interface with Blizzard's item database. This means you can't search or browse through all the items in the game, just the ones you own or the ones people you inspect have equipped. LootLink is an item database that's stored locally on your computer, to which every single item you encounter is added. Why is this useful? There are many reasons. For starters, you can browse and search the database. With LootLink, you can sort the list of items according to many statistics, as well as create targeted search queries to narrow down the list. The interface itself is very simple, and can be picked up in a few minutes. Item acquisition happens completely behind the scenes.

Note The latest versions of Telo's mods are available from his thread on the official WoW forums at http://forums.worldofwarcraft.com/thread.html?topicId=71580196.

Note Several websites provide item databases. Many of them also include quests, mobs, locations, and skills. Despite the fact that you can't access them from within WoW, they're still incredibly useful. See the next section for more information about them.

The other use of having a local item database is this: Querying the server for information about an item that you don't have is a little risky. Granted, this isn't something you'd do very often, but some addons (like AtlasLoot) give you the opportunity to do so. If an item has never been seen on your server before, and you query for its information, the server will disconnect you immediately. However, if you instruct addons to query your LootLink database instead (which gets really big, really fast) there's no danger of getting disconnected. If an addon can interface with LootLink like this, it will either do so automatically or provide you with an option.

Using LootLink

Unless you're using an addon that requires (or optionally depends on) LootLink, you're probably more interested in its core features. Once you've installed the addon, it will automatically start collecting information about every item it can; it does this by hooking many of the actions taking place in the interface already and silently copying each item's information when it becomes available. You can think of it as a legal wiretap. If you want to browse the database, type /lootlink or /ll to open its window (see Figure 5-4).

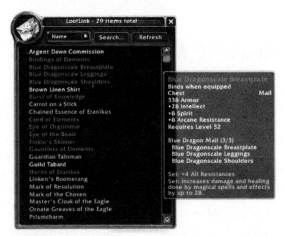

FIGURE 5-4: The main LootLink interface displays all items or the results of a search.

By default, the list of items is sorted by name, but you can change this with the drop-down menu at the top of the frame; you'll find there are a lot of properties you can sort by. If you mouse-over any item in the list, you'll be presented with its tooltip. Click the Refresh button to update the list with any items that have been added since you opened the window. You can narrow down the list by clicking on the Search button, which opens a new frame.

Note You can Ctrl+click on an item to see how it looks on you in the dressing room.

The LootLink Search window allows you to specify the parameters of your search with a straightforward form. You don't have to fill out every field, only those of which you want to use to narrow the search. Depending on what you select in the Type drop-down menu, context-specific fields and settings will appear below it, allowing further specification. Click Okay when you're done to see the results in the LookLink window. Your search parameters are saved, so you can always reopen the Search window and tweak them a little bit. If you want to go back to the entire database, just click Search ⇨ Reset ⇨ Okay.

Using Saeris's Alternate Version of LootLink

`WOWINTERFACE`

An addon author named Saeris has created an alternate version of LootLink (called, quite appropriately, Saeris's LootLink), which does basically the same thing as Telo's version, but provides a number of additional features as well. It comes with one core addon and four more load-on-demand modules. The extra features provided by this version include:

- Conversion of typed item names into real item links.
- You can reparse your database, refreshing all data from the server.
- Optional display of vendor price, basic IDs, socket IDs, and time last parsed.
- Automatic combing of your `itemcache.wdb` file.
- Scan of all pages of the auction house for new item data (`/lootlink scan`).
- A QuickSearch edit box for quickly performing a search by name.
- The ability to manually add items to the database.

Source: original addon documentation

Note "Load-on-demand" means that certain modules in a package of addons aren't loaded unless the functionality provided by them is actually needed. This keeps the load on your memory lighter, and results in improved performance. Load-on-demand is a feature that must be programmed into an addon specifically by its author.

Note There are various pre-made databases consisting of tens of thousands of items available for both versions of LootLink. Follow the installation instructions that come with them to successfully merge the new items into your current database.

Note You can maintain a lightweight item database with the Ludwig addon, which is created and maintained by Tuller. Ludwig uses your local item cache to find items that you can safely get the data for. This allows you to quickly search without needing large saved variable files or a huge memory footprint. Ludwig is based on the GetLink addon by Kremonte.

`CURSE-GAMING`   `WOWINTERFACE`

Web-Based World of Warcraft Databases

As I mentioned earlier, several websites give you access to databases full of the game's items, quests, mobs, spells, and locations. Typically they're cross-referenced, so an entry for a quest might tell you which mob starts it, where that mob is located, and what items are offered as rewards. These references can be clicked, so you can "chain" your way through the piles of information. Furthermore, most databases allow you to perform very advanced queries, so you can search for upgrades easily, among other things.

The data in these databases doesn't come from Blizzard directly. Instead, it's entirely *mined*, which means that it comes from the users who are playing the game. However, it isn't collected by hand. Each site offers a collection tool, which usually consists of two parts:

- An addon, which records information about everything the player encounters.

- An uploader, which sends all the recorded data off to the appropriate site.

Because these tools never interact with the game's memory (they use the game's approved addon interface instead) they're completely legal. However, because the data isn't official, you'll sometimes encounter anomalies. For example, if the level of a mob changes, you might see two entries for it in a database: one for the old level and one for the new. Some sites are more vigilant than others when it comes to cleaning up these anomalies.

The last huge benefit provided by these sites is the ability for visitors to add comments. These comments range from obnoxious to mature, so most sites have a way of making sure that the useful ones filter to the top of the heap. When you're looking for more than cold, hard data, these comments can really save the day.

Here are brief overviews of four of the WoW database sites:

Thottbot

www.thottbot.com

Thottbot was the first of its kind, and managed to obtain a critical mass of users. With its extremely simple Google-like front page, it allows you to quickly perform a search or select which category to browse from a myriad of drop-down menus. For a long time, Thottbot had the most complete database, because it was first on the scene and its collection tool was bundled with the Cosmos UI compilation. At this point, some other sites have caught up sufficiently.

Thottbot's simple interface is no great shakes, but it gets the job done. You'll routinely encounter extremely long pages of search results or comments. The server speed is OK, but nothing to write home about. As far as database anomalies go, Thottbot seems to suffer more than other sites, but finding the info you need is never too hard. When searching for a specific mob, you should almost always select the entry with the highest kill count, as it's usually the

Web-Based World of Warcraft Databases *Continued*

best. On the plus side, Thottbot has the most user comments by a long shot, so it's a good place to go if you're looking for advice from humans. Many of the comments are completely useless, but the best ones are highlighted in yellow so they're easy to find.

By default, Thottbot has two graphical banner ads adorning the top and right side of every page, however they can be hidden with a simple click on the "Close Ads" link beneath the top banner. This applies to the current page only, so the next page you visit will display them again. There are also some small text-based ads on the right that can't be hidden.

Allakhazam

`http://wow.allakhazam.com`

World of Warcraft isn't the only game Allakhazam provides databases for, and as such it generates traffic from its long-standing reputation as an online-gaming database site. Allakhazam provided *the* definitive database for EverQuest, and the site includes sections for many other games, too, including DAoC, EQ2, FFXI, and SWG. Because its services are broad, it feels slightly less tailored to WoW than some of the other sites. In addition, its front page provides news and updates; there's no Google-inspired Zen-simplicity to be found here.

That being said, the site is fairly fast and complete. There's a simple search box on the front-page, and a list of categories you can browse through on the left. Elegant isn't quite the word I'd use to describe the interface, but it feels a little bit cleaner than Thottbot. The comments are much more forum-like than Thottbot's and tend to be slightly more mature as well. In general, the site is more feature-laden than most.

Allakhazam has one large banner ad at the top of every page, and another vertical one on the left, beneath the menu. In addition to advertising, the site makes money by selling premium memberships for a monthly fee. Premium members don't see the ads, and have access to a large number of unique features and additional searches.

Wowhead

`www.wowhead.com`

Wowhead is one of the more recent arrivals on the scene, and is one of the finest offerings currently available. Its sleek and simple interface combines both speed and aesthetics. The front page is another Google rip-off, though very well executed. Like Thottbot, Wowhead exists to serve only the WoW community, and has been built from the ground up with that fact in mind. The database is quite complete, well cross-referenced, and anomalies are rare. Features are still being added to the site on a regular basis. Also, Wowhead has hosted (and presumably will continue to host) regular contests.

continued

Web-Based World of Warcraft Databases *Continued*

Despite having fewer comments than some of the other database sites, the comments on Wowhead tend to be of extremely high quality. As their user base grows, the volume of comments is increasing rapidly, especially for Burning Crusade–related content. By default, useless comments are filtered out entirely. In addition, the site is *blazing* fast now that IGN Entertainment hosts it. Wowhead has very few additional features, except for a very handy talent calculator.

Like most sites, Wowhead is supported by advertising, and has two large graphical banners on every page: one on the top and one on the left. There's also a smaller box advertisement below the left-hand banner.

Wowpeek

www.wowpeek.com

Wowpeek is a very recent addition to the myriad of database sites. Unlike many of the other offerings, Wowpeek was initially built as a hobby, not as a business venture. As such, it has a slightly more interesting interface and a little bit more of a human touch. Graphically, the site is very slick, employing the most WoW-like look and feel out of all the database sites. Their database is growing daily, and the site has a few unique features including human-written quest guides and a library of instance maps.

At the time of this writing, Wowpeek has no advertisements.

Other database sites

Believe it or not, that's not nearly all of them! Here are some others to check out. Some offer the complete assortment of items, mobs, and quests, while some are more limited. Most are associated with large gaming networks, and are only small parts of much larger websites.

- **MMO DB:** http://wow.mmodb.com
- **WarCry:** http://wow.warcry.com/db
- **WoWGuru:** www.wowguru.com/db
- **WWN Data:** http://wwndata.worldofwar.net
- **TenTonHammer:** http://wow.tentonhammer.com
- **Curse:** http://wow-en.curse-gaming.com/database
- **The Goblin Workshop:** www.goblinworkshop.com

Counting Your Empty Bag Slots with BagStatusMeters

Addon created by Madorin, updated by Romualdo, maintained by Throndorin

WORLDOFWAR   CURSE-GAMING

BagStatusMeters (or BSM for short) is a nice little addon that's been around for a long time. Quite simply, it displays the remaining (or alternately, full) slots in each of your bags. Unlike real-life bags, you normally can't tell how much is in them without opening them up and looking inside. BSM places small, text-based meters on each bag, as well as a color-changing progress bar (see Figure 5-5). In addition, it provides an overall meter for totaling the values from all bags.

FIGURE 5-5: BagStatusMeters adds counts to your bags as well as an overall meter.

No setup is necessary, although you'll want to find a nice place for the overall meter to live if you decide to keep it around. Left-click on the status bar itself and drag to move it. By default, the text values (like 4/16) represent the number of empty slots over the total number of slots, although this can be switched to represent filled slots in the options. To open the (very long) options panel, click on the minimap-looking icon. It's actually tied to the overall meter, not the minimap, but you can place it on the minimap if you want it to feel at home. Alternatively, you can type /bsm.

Don't be intimidated by the long list of settings; there isn't anything confusing here. Basically, you have the option to toggle every aspect of the addon: the individual meters, the overall meter, the round icon, the color display, the bag slot totals, the labels, and the bars. Be aware that some of the checkboxes are exclusive and should probably be radio buttons instead, because that's how they behave. Just go through the list one by one to get BSM set up just the way you like.

Checking the Vendor Value of Items with SellValue

Addon created and maintained by CapnBry

WORLDOFWAR   CURSE-GAMING

You're out hunting, your bags are completely full of gray items to vend, and then you get a big drop: a BOE blue. What do you destroy to make room for it? The buzzard wings or the raptor hides? Whichever stack is worth less, right? You've probably been in this situation, and you've probably just guessed — but you don't have to if you have SellValue.

SellValue simply keeps track of the vendor price for all your items, and displays this price in the tooltip, as shown in Figure 5-6. For stacks of items, it displays the value of just one of them. The primary limitation of the addon is that it doesn't ship with a pre-populated database. This is probably a good thing since vendor prices could change at any time and new items are always being added to the game, but it means that you won't know the value of an item until you've been to a vendor with it at least once.

FIGURE 5-6: SellValue attaches the vendor value of an item to the tooltip.

An additional feature of the mod is a sortable list of all your items and their values (see Figure 5-7). Type /inventorylist or /il (or set a key binding) to open the window. By default, values are shown for the entire stack of each item, and items with no value are hidden. Click the column headers to re-sort the list. You can also prevent specific items from showing up in case you're never planning to sell them. Type /il hide <itemname> to ignore the specified item. The name is case sensitive. An easier way to do this is to use a chat link. To do this, type /il hide, a space, and then Shift+left-click on the item you want to ignore. There are just a few other SellValue slash commands, all of which are covered in Table 5-4.

FIGURE 5-7: SellValue's inventory list window.

Table 5-4   SellValue Command-Line Options

Option	Description
hide <itemname>	Hides the specified item from the value list.
show <itemname>	Removes the specified item from the hide list.
list	Displays a list of which items are being hidden.
tooltipmode <mode>	0 = Do not show sell value on tooltips. 1 = Show only for things not on the hidden list. 2 = Show for all items.

Source: original addon documentation

Improving the Inspect Frame with SuperInspect

Addon created and maintained by smurfy

CURSE-GAMING   WOWINTERFACE

The default inspect window leaves a lot to be desired. Just when you're starting to look through someone else's equipment, they might run away and cut your inspection short. SuperInspect does away with this limitation by storing a cache of your target's equipment so you can browse through it for as long as you want. You can even pull up a list of cached targets to inspect long after the players themselves are gone. Beyond this under-the-hood improvement, SuperInspect provides numerous aesthetic and informational enhancements.

SuperInspect (SI) comes with two modules, but both are required; one of them simply loads the other on first use (this decreases the initial loading time). The first thing I suggest you do after installing the addon is bind a key to toggle the inspect frame. This way you can target a player and simply press the bound key to open the window. One of SuperInspect's coolest features is that you can inspect *any* targetable unit in this way; including NPCs, monsters, and pets. Granted, you can't see what items they're wearing (because they don't have any) but you can inspect their model in detail, with complete control (and a nice background image). The model viewer is a step up from the typical display, allowing three full ranges of movement:

- Left-click and drag to rotate the model.
- Right-click and drag to pan it around.
- Use the mouse wheel to zoom in and out.

If inspecting a player, you still need to be within 10 units of them at first. After all of their equipment has been cached, you (or they) can move around freely. In addition to their equipment, SuperInspect also allows you to query for their honor information. Click on the small triangle button in the upper-right corner of the frame to open a list of cached characters. Click on a character to inspect them, but note that you're only browsing their saved data, so it might be out of date if they've changed or upgraded equipment since they were last in range. There's also a nice little item bonuses summary card you can pop up, which can be shuttled off to the side of the window for comparisons between targets. Finally, there's a button to hide or show the ring of items around the player's model, in case you want an unencumbered view.

SuperInspect has a few options that can be configured with slash commands; use /superinspect or /si to toggle them (see Table 5-5).

Table 5-5   SuperInspect Command-Line Options

Option	Description
reset	Resets the frame to the center of your screen.
scale <number>	Changes the scale of the frame (0.25-2.0).
defaulttoggle	Toggles default mode on/off. When on, SI acts like the default inspect window. When off, you can drag and scale the window.
itembgtoggle	Toggles the art used to display quality color of items.
durabilitytoggle	Toggles durability info that is shown when inspecting yourself.
sound	Toggles the open and close window sound.
playercache	Enables and disables player cache.

Source: original addon documentation

Managing Your Many Trinkets with TrinketMenu

Addon created and maintained by Gello

| WORLDOFWAR | CURSE-GAMING | WOWINTERFACE |

By the time you're reasonably high level, chances are you've accumulated a healthy number of trinkets, some of which are no doubt collecting dust in your bank. There are a lot of useful ones out there, but except for a few, they tend to have pretty specialized purposes. You only want to wear your Carrot on a Stick while traveling, of course; likewise, your Argent Dawn Commission isn't so useful unless you're hunting in the Plaguelands. TrinketMenu gives you a quick and easy way to swap your active trinkets around. Furthermore, it provides an advanced auto-queuing system for swapping trinkets automatically based on a custom set order.

The TrinketMenu frame itself is simple: two action buttons represent your top and bottom trinket slots, as shown in Figure 5-8. If either of the equipped trinkets is usable, you can (right or left) click on them to activate their ability. When you mouse-over either of them, a menu displaying all of your other available trinkets is displayed. To generate this menu the addon searched through your bags, which means that any trinkets in your bank won't be displayed. Left-click on a trinket in the pop-up menu to equip it in your top slot, or right-click to equip it in the bottom slot.

FIGURE 5-8: TrinketMenu shows your two trinket slots and a pop-up menu of available trinkets.

Several configuration options are at your disposal for both the frame and the menu. To begin with, you can left-click on either one's border to drag it around. The menu (if docked, see options panel) will highlight in one corner when dragged near a corner of the buttons; this allows you to re-dock it in a different configuration. Right-click on either frame's border to reorient it vertically or horizontally. Click and drag the little handle in the lower-right corner to rescale either frame; or alternatively you can use /trinket scale main <number> or /trinket scale menu <number> to respectively (and precisely) scale the frame or its menu. There's also a little gear minimap icon, which can be left-clicked to toggle the buttons or right-clicked to toggle the options panel (or you can use /trinket opt).

The options panel provides a bunch of display and notification settings. You can toggle and lock the frame, enable cooldown counts, enable out-of-range tinting, and set key bindings directly, among a few other things. At the top of the window there are two buttons labeled Top and Bottom with checkboxes next to them; these tabs are used to set up the auto-queues.

Queuing Trinkets with TrinketMenu

Enable an auto-queue by checking the box on its button. A golden gear will appear on the appropriate TrinketMenu slot. Then click the Top or Bottom button (on the options panel) to configure the queue itself. All of your trinkets are listed. You can select one and then use the buttons to the left to rearrange the order of the list. The auto-queue follows a specific set of rules. See the readme file for the details, but in general it works like this: When a usable trinket is used, the next trinket in the queue will be equipped. Therefore a passive trinket will effectively end the queue. If a trinket is marked as Priority (select an item in the list and you'll see checkboxes below) and it's listed above the current one, then it will be automatically reequipped when its cooldown is over. For the purposes of TrinketMenu, a trinket's cooldown is considered over once it becomes less than 30 seconds.

There are subtleties to the queue system that you should learn in order to use it most effectively. For example, certain trinkets need to remain equipped for some time after they're used. For this, you can set a delay value. You can also mark certain trinkets to pause the queue when they're equipped. See the readme for more information about these features.

Note You can't swap trinkets while you're in combat or dead. If you attempt to, TrinketMenu will queue up the request and perform the swap as soon as possible. If you do a manual swap, then a small icon for the queued trinket will appear over the slot. If the auto-queue makes the attempt, then the golden gear will turn gray. A paused auto-queue displays a red gear.

Comparing Items Side By Side with EquipCompare

Addon created and maintained by Legorol

> CURSE-GAMING   WOWINTERFACE

You're probably already used to the comparison tooltips presented when you mouse-over an item while at a vendor or in the auction house: The item you're looking at will have its tooltip displayed, and next to that will appear tooltips for the items you currently have equipped. Unfortunately, these are typically the only places you see them. The EquipCompare addon enables them just about *everywhere*, including in your bags or when you click on an item link posted to chat (see Figure 5-9), making it much easier to figure out when an item is actually good for your character or not.

FIGURE 5-9: The item's tooltip is expanded to show you a side by side comparison.

There's virtually nothing to configure. You can type /eqc (or /equipcompare) to turn the basic functionality on or off. Type /eqc control to prevent the item comparisons from appearing unless you're holding down the control key. For a full list of slash-command options, see Table 5-6.

Table 5-6   EquipCompare Command-Line Options

Option	Description
on|off	Turns EquipCompare on/off
control	Toggles Ctrl key mode on/off
cv	Toggles integration with CharactersViewer (another addon)
alt	Toggles Alt key mode on/off (with CharactersViewer only)
shift	Toggles shifting tooltips up when they're too tall
help	Prints a list of commands in chat

Source: original addon documentation

Viewing the Contents of Your Bank Anywhere with BankItems

Addon created by Merphle, updated by JASlaughter and Galmok, maintained by Xinhuan

WORLDOFWAR

BankItems is one of the rare addons that do one thing well and don't attempt to do much else. It was an oversight on Blizzard's part to let you examine the contents of your bank *only* while actually *at* the bank. BankItems corrects this oversight, allowing you to open the bank window whenever and wherever you want (see Figure 5-10). You can't move items around or purchase new bank slots, but you can examine everything, including anything in bags. Furthermore, you can examine your *other characters'* banks as well.

FIGURE 5-10: Checking out the bank contents far away from a banker.

You need to visit the bank once before you can view it from anywhere. However, because the contents of the bank can never change while you're away from it, there's no danger of the snapshot becoming out of date once you have it. Whenever you want to open the BankItems window type /bi, /bankitems, or bind a key. There's also a key binding to open the bank and all your bank bags at the same time. In the bottom section of the window you can select which character's bank snapshot you'd like to view. BankItems has just a few simple slash-command options (see Table 5-7).

Table 5-7   BankItems Command-Line Options

Option	Description
all	Opens BankItems and all bank bags
list	Lists bank contents in chat
clear	Clears currently selected player's info
clearall	Clears all players' info
help	Displays a list of commands in chat

Source: original addon documentation

Keeping Track of the Fish You Catch with Fishing Buddy

Addon created and maintained by Sutorix

WORLDOFWAR   CURSE-GAMING   WOWINTERFACE

The core of Fishing Buddy (as is the case with many addons) is a local database. In a (virtual) world so full of discrete, quantifiable events and numbers, no wonder there are a million tools for tracking, calculating, and analyzing the reams of data. If you're an angler, this addon's quite useful, for a few main reasons:

- Fishing Buddy keeps a database of all your catches, and it records the type of fish (or item) reeled in as well as the location in which it was caught. An interface is provided to browse this database, which you can sort either by location or by item.

- A heads-up fishing display is provided, showing your location, skill, and history of catches in this spot, broken down by quantity and percentage.

- Several options are provided to make fishing easier.

Type /fishingbuddy or /fb to open the main window, or click the fishy minimap icon. The Locations tab provides the database browser, which can be toggled between its two modes (area vs. fish) with the big button at the top. Use the Options tab to configure the addon; you can tweak the heads-up display, auto-apply lures, and enhance the sound made by the lure (when a fish bites).

Creating and Swapping Sets of Equipment

Are you a packrat? If so, you probably have every trinket you've ever found in the bank, as well as a few complete sets lying around for nostalgic reasons. If you're a raider, you might also have a few sets of resist gear. You probably also have a tuxedo, a spyglass, a funny hat, and ten badass-looking weapons. Keeping multiple sets of equipment around can be both fun and useful. As such, there are a few addons that help you organize and equip any variation of your equipment you can imagine.

ItemRack

Addon created and maintained by Gello

WORLDOFWAR	CURSE-GAMING	WOWINTERFACE

With ItemRack you can build sets of equipment and then equip them with the click of a button. These aren't specifically set items, but rather arbitrary groupings of equipment that you define. This is an incredibly useful feature. You can have different sets of equipment for soloing, raiding, fire resistance, cold resistance, PvP, traveling, and dueling (to name a few), all of which you can switch between rapidly. Of course, this means that the equipment has to be available in your bags, and you can't swap armor during combat.

Swapping Individual Pieces of Equipment

Forgetting sets for a minute, the first feature ItemRack provides is the ability to quickly swap between individual pieces of equipment. Open up the character window, hold down the Alt key, and mouse-over any of your equipment slots. You'll be presented with a pop-up menu displaying every available piece of equipment in your bags that you can use in that slot (as well as an empty slot, representing no item at all). If you click anything in the menu, it will be equipped (if you click the empty icon, then the slot will be emptied). This alone is a fine way to switch between weapons, but not the most accessible.

If you Alt+click on the *slot itself* (instead of on a pop-up menu item), then the slot will be added to the main (formerly empty and invisible) ItemRack bar (see Figure 5-11), where it will behave exactly in the same way, except that it's always onscreen (you can also Alt+click a slot on the bar to remove it). This bar can be dragged around, reoriented, scaled, and locked in place. If locked, hold down Alt and mouse-over it to make the controls reappear.

FIGURE 5-11: The ItemRack bar.

Creating and Swapping Entire Sets

To create and set-up a set:

1. Equip the items you want included in the set. (You don't need to unequip slots that you don't care about. For example, if your riding gear consists of just a trinket and a pair of gloves, you don't need to take all your other armor off to create this two-item set.)

2. Right-click the ItemRack minimap icon to open the control panel (see Figure 5-12).

FIGURE 5-12: The ItemRack
control panel.

3. Click on the Sets tab at the top of the window.

4. Name your set in the field near the top; something like Riding Gear, for example.

5. Select an icon from the (huge) list to represent this set.

6. Now select the slots that the set should affect by clicking on the appropriate buttons surrounding the control panel (they mirror the character window precisely). When you click them, they'll light up, and you can toggle them on and off. Only highlighted items will be associated with the set, while other slots will remain unaffected.

7. Click the Save button. You should see a little confirmation message.

8. Open the character window and Alt+click your character's model. This will add a button to the ItemRack bar that allows you to quickly swap between sets. It starts off as a brown icon.

9. Mouse-over the icon and a menu with your new set will appear. Select the new set, which will be instantly equipped. The brown icon will no longer be accessible.

At this point, you may want to create another default set that contains all your regular gear and affects every single inventory slot. That way you can always get back to baseline with one action. Note that you can always Shift+click a set's icon in the ItemRack bar to unequip the set, returning you to the exact state you were in when you last equipped it. If you don't want to use the ItemRack bar to swap sets, you can alternatively left-click on the minimap button to produce the same menu. You can also bind a key to the set with the Bind Key button.

Swapping Set Automatically with Events

So, let's say you have a set with all your riding gear in it. How do you automatically equip the set when you mount and automatically unequip it when you dismount? ItemRack has a built-in event system that you can use to achieve this kind of functionality. The addon comes with several pre-built event handlers (Mount, Skinning, and Swimming, among others) so you don't have to get your hands dirty with Lua code. However, if you dare to, you can create your own event handlers from within the framework of the addon, as well as tweak the existing presets. A relatively advanced knowledge of Lua and the WoW API is required, however.

For starters, here's how to connect a set with an already existing event:

1. Create a set that you want to hook up to an event (see the previous steps).

2. Click the Events tab on the ItemRack control panel.

3. Locate the appropriate event (Mount, for example) in the list.

4. Click the question mark icon to the left of the event's name. A list of sets appears.

5. Select the appropriate set.

6. You'll be returned to the event list, and the event you selected earlier will have the set's icon next to it as well as a small checkbox. Make sure this checkbox is checked.

7. Make sure the checkbox above labeled Enable Events is checked.

Now whenever you get on your mount, the associated set will be equipped, and whenever you dismount it will be removed. Read the notes that go along with each event carefully (just mouse-over the event in the list) for a description of how that event functions. A few of them have specific caveats you should be aware of before using them.

Click the Options tab for a whole bunch of toggleable settings. Almost every control related to ItemRack is well documented in the tooltip. There's even an in-game help write-up; just click the tab labeled with a question mark. There are also two good out-of-game documentation files that come along with the addon:

- `readme.txt`: General documentation, usage, and a FAQ

- `events manual.txt`: How to use and create your own events

ItemRack has a few basic slash-command options; use them with `/itemrack` (see Table 5-8).

Table 5-8   ItemRack Command-Line Options

Option	Description
reset	Resets the ItemRack bar. Use `reset events` to reset all the events. Use `reset everything` to wipe all settings/sets and start from default.
lock	Locks the bar.
unlock	Unlocks the bar.
scale	Sets the bar's scale precisely.
equip	Equips a set.
toggle	Equips/unequips a set.

Source: original addon documentation

Note If all you're looking for is a way to auto-equip items when you're mounted, then there are (at least) two addons made specifically for this purpose: Check out QuickMountEquip (by Merrem) and Baud Mount (by Baudzila).

Outfitter

Addon created and maintained by mundocani

WORLDOFWAR   CURSE-GAMING   WOWINTERFACE

Outfitter is a complete alternative to ItemRack, providing many of the same features. Of course, there are many minor differences, both functional and aesthetic. With Outfitter, you're unable to tweak the custom event-driven sets yourself, but there are slightly more built-in ones to choose from. There's also no independent bar for switching item slots or sets; everything is controlled via the character window or the minimap button. Some of the more prominent features of outfitter include the following:

- You can easily swap individual pieces of equipment. With the character window open you can left-click on an item slot to bring up a menu of possible replacements, including an empty slot. Left-click a slot in the menu to swap items (or unequip them). In Outfitter terminology these are called QuickSlots.

- You can open a menu to quickly swap between outfits by clicking on the minimap button. Here, you can select which set to wear. Many Outfitter sets are pre-built. For example, +frost resist items will automatically be placed in the Frost Resist set, and +riding speed items will be placed in the Riding set. You can rebuild these sets whenever you wish. Certain sets (such as the Riding set) are automatically equipped when appropriate.

- Sets are managed via a pop-out on the character window (there's a toggle button in the upper-right corner). On the Outfitter tab, select a set to equip/edit it. While a set is selected, each equipment slot gains a little checkbox. Check or uncheck boxes to indicate which slots should be associated with the set. If all slots are checked, the set will be considered a complete wardrobe. In addition, there are three other types:

- **Mix-n-match:** These sets override the base wardrobe; only one can be used at a time.

- **Accessory:** These sets are the same, but can be combined.

- **Special occasion:** These sets are automatically equipped at the appropriate time.

■ Next to each set (on the right) is a small button; click it for a drop-down list of options pertaining to that set. You can rebuild it (if applicable), assign a key binding, disable it, or quickly move it in and out of the bank (if you're at a bank).

■ The New Outfit button guides you through the creation of a new set. You can optionally start it off with your current equipment, nothing, or optimize it for a certain statistic or skill.

Outfitter has an excellent manual, which you should use to supplement this brief guide. The file is called `UserManual.html` and is located in the Documentation folder.

Automatically Deleting Certain Items with Loot Filter

Addon created and maintained by Meter

WORLDOFWAR   CURSE-GAMING

Caution

This section starts off with a warning, and there are two more in the paragraphs ahead. This addon (Loot Filter) deletes items automatically, with no confirmation. With the wrong setting enabled, your next epic drop is history. It's not difficult to configure. In fact, it's painfully simple. However, use it at your own risk.

Now that you've had the hell scared out of you, let's talk about why you might actually *want* to use Loot Filter. Based on a huge number of radio buttons and two explicit lists, Loot Filter can automatically delete items as you acquire them. Still: Why? Well, some loot is downright annoying, and this addon can save you the time it takes to deal with it. Some gray items are worth next to nothing. Even some whites are tossups when it comes to lugging them back to town. Why the addon has an option to filter legendary loot (or *anything* besides gray and white, for that matter) is absolutely beyond me; perhaps it's just to satisfy the masochists out there.

Initially, Loot Filter will (thankfully) delete nothing. Its behavior is controlled via a control panel with five tabs. To bring up the panel, type `/lf`, `/lfr`, or `/lootfilter`. First of all, there's a small round button in the upper-left corner that enables or disables the mod; if it's unchecked, nothing will be deleted. The three small buttons to the right control the status of notification. You should leave them on, so that a chat message will be displayed whenever an item is deleted.

The Quality and Type tabs allow you to specify which items should be filtered. Each entry has three radio buttons next to it. If the leftmost button is selected (the default for everything) no action is taken at all. If the middle button is selected, that type of item will *never* be deleted, despite any other settings. If the rightmost button is checked, the item will be deleted when looted, unless it also matches a "keep" setting somewhere else (see Figure 5-13).

Caution

For god's sake, please don't mark anything above Uncommon (Green) for deletion unless you seriously know what you're doing! Better yet, mark none of them, and stick to only using the blacklist feature (discussed next).

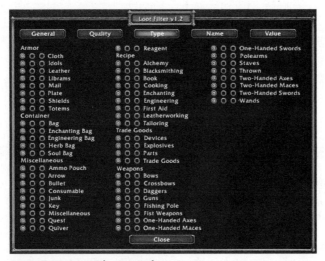

FIGURE 5-13: Loot Filter's interface.

The slightly saner side of Loot Filter is found in its explicit whitelist and blacklist. It doesn't use these exact terms in the interface; in fact, it spells out their purposes even more clearly. On the Name tab are two multiline text entry boxes:

- The left box is the whitelist. This is for specific items that you want to keep, no matter what. If you have filtering of Common (White) Items enabled and you enter Light Leather into this list, then *all* white items *except* Light Leathers will be deleted.

- The right box is the blacklist. This is for specific items that should be deleted. If you have none of the filters enabled and you enter Light Leather into the bottom list, then *only* Light Leathers will be destroyed, everything else will be saved.

Clearly, the safest way to use Loot Filter is via the blacklist only. Simply enter the specific names of items you want to delete into the box, each one on its own line. Names should be complete and are case sensitive. However, you can also use patterns in the lists to match groups of items; see the documentation for details.

It could be argued that this addon should *only* provide blacklist functionality, in order to eradicate any possible mistakes, but that's not the way it's been programmed. If you're careful, you won't lose anything by accident.

The final tab (Value) allows you to automatically delete loot based on its value to a vendor. This feature requires the Informant addon, which is part of the Auctioneer package.

Caution   If you already have a partial stack of a particular item in your inventory, and the same item is looted and subsequently destroyed (filtered), the entire stack will be destroyed.

Looting Mobs Faster with QuickLoot

Addon created and maintained by Telo

CURSE-GAMING

Telo's addons have been a staple of the WoW interface community from the very beginning, with QuickLoot being one of the six or so that he actively maintains. QuickLoot is a very simple addon that provides a very popular feature, which will save you time and effort in the long run. Simply put, QuickLoot moves the loot window precisely underneath your mouse, so your cursor is always directly over the next item to loot. Sounds a little trivial, I know, but after looting hundreds and hundreds of items, it adds up.

QuickLoot has no slash commands and no options. Just install it and forget about it. Note that if there's more than one item to loot on a corpse, QuickLoot will move the window *between* items; all you have to do is click once for each item.

Note   If you're not already aware of it, auto-looting is a feature that's built right into the World of Warcraft client. By default, if you Shift+right-click on a corpse you'll automatically loot everything on it (rendering QuickLoot moot, although some people prefer it that way). You can set auto-loot to function without a modifier (or a different one) on the interface options panel.

Adding an Item's Uses to the Tooltip with Reagent Info

Addon created by Jerigord, maintained by Pelion

CURSE-GAMING

Reagent Info is a tooltip front-end of sorts for an otherwise interface-less library called Reagent Data. Hence, you'll be installing two addons here. By referencing this library whenever necessary, Reagent Info is able to place a healthy dose of extra information on the tooltip (see Figure 5-14) including which professions, classes, and recipes can use the particular item being examined.

Figure 5-14: Reagent Info lets you see the various uses for this Rugged Hide at a glance.

Reagent Info has a modest control panel, which you can bring up with the `/ri config` command. The settings almost entirely consist of various toggles, which determine what information is potentially displayed on the tooltip (you can exclude various professions, for instance). You can also adjust a few colors and tweak a few controls related to the display of recipes. Reagent Info has a few slash-command options (see Table 5-9), executed with `/ri` or `/reagentinfo`.

Note You must open a profession window once before data related to that profession can be displayed. The addon informs you of this the first time you log in. Don't worry, it's not an error even though it sort of looks like one.

Table 5-9   Reagent Info Command-Line Options

Option	Description
enable	Enables tooltip information
disable	Disables tooltip information
clear	Clears the current character's settings, returning them to default
clearall	Clears all Reagent Info settings (for all characters)
config	Displays the Reagent Info configuration screen

Source: original addon documentation

Summary

In this chapter, you learned about a number of addons at your disposal that help you view, manage, and get rid of (either sell or destroy) your items. You read about tools that enhance your experience when you visit the auction house or inspect other players. You also learned how to consolidate your bags, switch equipment rapidly, and compare items side by side anywhere. Finally, you were introduced to several web-based WoW database sites. The addons in this chapter will hopefully help you save time, make money, and achieve happiness!

Because communication is such a huge part of WoW, the next chapter focuses entirely on addons that help you when you're chatting or role-playing with other people.

Chat Addons

Despite the fact that World of Warcraft is a visual environment, much of the communication between players, as well as most of the information you send and receive from the game's servers, is in the form of text. You spend a lot of time staring at the chat window, scrolling through it, and typing commands and messages into it. Fortunately, several addons are available that allow you to tweak and configure the way you interact with this window, as well as with other players.

A number of these addons are simply collections of many smaller tweaks and improvements that have been made to the chat window. Also, because so much player communication happens one-on-one via whispers, many addons aim to improve your capability to handle multiple tell conversations at the same time. A couple of these add ons are modeled after instant messaging clients.

Finally, because role-playing has so much to do with the way players interact with each other, a bunch of role-playing related addons fall into this category, including Eloquence and Lore. Even if you're not a role-player, some of the features in these addons might appeal to you, such as the capability to correct everyone's grammar (including your own) or the option to create and speak in your own custom languages. You can find more information about them at the end of this chapter.

WoW is a social game that requires more and more teamwork as your characters progress, so it's important that you're comfortable following conversations in general chat, guild chat, raid chat, and whispers, often all at the same time. The capability to quickly and easily navigate through your chat history and communicate articulately when it counts is key to successfully completing content, making friends, and having fun!

Using the Wheel to Scroll Chat Frames with ChatScroll

Addon created and maintained by AnduinLothar

CURSE-GAMING

Note This addon is included in the Cosmos compilation. The latest version of it can be downloaded from `http://cosmosui.org/addons.php`.

ChatScroll adds a few simple, useful features to the chat interface, the main one being that while your cursor is hovering over any chat window, you can use your mouse wheel to scroll through it.

Why not use key bindings in this situation? Well, if you used the default key bindings interface to accomplish this, the mouse wheel would only scroll the selected chat window, and you wouldn't be able to use it to zoom the camera in and out anymore. ChatScroll is context sensitive, so you can continue to zoom the camera normally with the wheel as long as your cursor isn't over a chat window.

ChatScroll also adds a few other simple features:

- You can hold down the Shift key while scrolling to immediately jump to the top or bottom of the chat window you're hovering over.

- You can bind a key (via the key bindings interface) to jump immediately to the top of the chat window (Blizzard already provides a key binding to jump to the bottom, which is Shift+Page Down by default).

ChatScroll has no other options or slash-commands.

Adding Chat-Related Features with ChatMOD

Addon created and maintained by solariz

In a sense, ChatMOD is a compilation. Because it's distributed and developed as a single package by a single author, it's included here instead of in the compilations chapter. ChatMOD provides a huge collection of (mostly) chat-related features, most of which you can simply toggle through. The benefit here is that you don't need to manage 10 or more obscure addons for each individual feature, nor do you need to worry about possible conflicts between them.

The first time you enter the world after installing ChatMOD, an info box pops up to get you started. It points you to the addon's documentation file (`README.html`), which outlines its basic use and covers the settings that aren't available via the options panel. You open the options panel with the slash-command:

```
/chatmod
```

The following list is taken from the ChatMOD documentation by solariz and provides a good rundown of the addon's numerous features. While you browse the ChatMOD options panel, you'll see that most settings have their equivalent slash-command option conveniently listed right next to them. A few of ChatMOD's features aren't chat-related; they're simply thrown in for their extra utility.

- Colors the chatters' nicknames in their class color.
- Option to hide Channel names ([Guild], [Party]) from chat.
  - Option to shorten the Channel names [Guild] = [G].
- Mouse wheel scrolls in chat window.
  - Mouse wheel jumps to top/bottom.
  - Mouse wheel scrolls five lines up/down.
- Option to relocate Chat editbox to top of the chat frame.
- Clickable hyperlinks, ready for copy and paste (URL, IP, TS2, e-mails).
- Colors raid members' map pins in their class color on Map.
  - Colors raid members' map pins in their class color on BG minimap.
- Fully customizable time stamps with HTML color codes.
- Option to highlight your own nickname in chat messages.
  - Specifies up to three custom highlight words.
  - Brings highlighted sentences to the center of the screen.
- Whisper Target Function. Whispers your current target (/wt).
- Key bindings for /say, /raid, /g, /party, /yell, /6, /7, /8, /o, and /wt.
- Option to hide Chat buttons.
- Makes invite calls in chat clickable [invite] (invites on click).
- Option to increase the Editbox scrollback (history) buffer.
- Option to use arrow keys without pressing ALT in chat editbox.
- Auto Skip Gossip Pages at NPCs (can be temporarily disabled by holding key while talking to an NPC, or switched off).
- Auto Dismount on Flightmaster (Taxi).
- Chat notifications by sound.

Coloring Names (and More) with CleanChat

Addon created and maintained by wbb

WORLDOFWAR

CleanChat is a lot like ChatMOD in that it provides a ton of useful features in one easy-to-install package. CleanChat isn't quite as comprehensive though, and might be a good choice if ChatMOD is just a little too feature-rich for you. CleanChat's specialty is giving each person a different color name in the chat window, and it gives you several options to accomplish this, including basing the colors on the player's class or just picking them randomly (random colors are based on a hash of the name, so a player will always get the same color).

CleanChat's other features tend to focus on saving space by abbreviating (or removing) the channel prefixes (such as [Guild] and [Party]) that are placed before chat messages. CleanChat's options panel, from which all of its settings are configured, is opened with the slash-command:

/cleanchat

In the end, if you're looking for an addon with many chat tweaks, I suggest trying out both ChatMOD and CleanChat to see which one appeals to you. They both have a number of unique features as well as many overlapping ones.

Following is a list of CleanChat features from documentation by wbb. You can compare it to the ChatMOD feature list in the preceding section.

- Removes [Guild], [Party], [Raid] and [Officer] prefix from chat.
- Abbreviates [Raid Leader] and [Raid Warning].
- Removes channel names (like General and Trade) or replaces them with a short prefix.
- Removes custom channel names.
- Colorizes chat names.
- Option to activate cursor keys while typing a message (instead of pressing Alt+Cursor keys).
- Option to hide scroll buttons.
- Option to use the mouse wheel to scroll. Hold the Shift key while scrolling up or down and it scrolls immediately to the top or bottom of the chat window.
- Option to collect class and level information from random chat people (people not in party/raid/guild/friends list).
- Option to save this information between sessions.
- Option to pop up messages that contain your name.
- Highlights custom text in chat message (requires editing a text file; advanced users only).

Tweaking the Chat Window Editbox with Confab

Addon created and maintained by Kulyeh

WORLDOFWAR   **CURSE-GAMING**

The editbox is the long, thin frame that you use to type in chat messages and commands. Typically, it appears only when you press Enter or the slash key before inputting a message. Confab gives you a whole bunch of options for tweaking this frame, allowing you to move it around, prevent it from auto-hiding, or make it bigger or smaller. Another nice feature of Confab is the ability to use the cursor keys when entering text — without holding down the Alt key at the same time. There are a ton of features, all in the form of slash-commands, which are listed in Table 6-1. Use the following syntax to control the various options:

```
/confab <option>
```

You can type /confab by itself to print a daunting list of all these options in-game.

Table 6-1   Confab Command-Line Options

Option	Description
style1	Default WoW placement of the editbox (the very bottom of the docked frame).
style2	Places the editbox at the bottom (but inside) the docked frame.
style3	Places the editbox at the top (but inside) the docked frame.
style4	Places the editbox on top of the docked frame.
autohide on|off.	Editbox is hidden when text is not being typed or editbox is always shown, yet empty.
undock	Allows the editbox to be resized and/or moved anywhere on the screen.
dock	Re-docks the editbox to the last frame it was docked to. Optionally a frame name can be given to specify the frame that you want it to dock to (careful, your mileage may vary using this optional parameter).
autodock on|off.	The editbox is automatically docked with the Chat Frame the mouse cursor is in. This feature has limited uses and may be removed in future releases.
lock	Locks the editbox. When editbox is locked, it is not movable.
unlock	Unlocks the editbox. This feature is usable only when editbox is in undocked mode.

continued

Table 6-1 *Continued*

Option	Description
chatsticky	Used to lock (or unlock) the editbox to a chat channel. You can use off, default, confab, party, guild, raid, officer, say, or 1-10. See the Confab documentation for more information.
enableArrowKeys	Allows the arrow keys to be used to edit entered text without having to hold down the Alt key (Alt+arrows will still work however).
disableArrowKeys	This is a default Blizzard setting, which allows arrow keys to be used for movement and Alt+arrows for editing entered text.
texture	Specifies the name of a .tga file that will be used as the editbox artwork.
alpha	Sets the alpha of the editbox to n where n is a number between 0 and 1 (0 being fully transparent, 1 being fully opaque — well, as opaque as the texture will allow).

Source: documentation by Kulyeh

In addition to the /confab slash-command options, Confab comes with a few extra commands that can be used on their own or in your macros; they're described in the following list documented by Kulyeh. Take a look at the documentation that comes with Confab (readme.txt) for some additional explanation of these commands, as well as a few examples of how you might use them.

- /tt: Does a tell-target or target-tell, depending on whether you have a friendly player targeted. There's an important distinction between these two actions. If you have a friendly player targeted, this command executes a tell-target, which sends a tell to the targeted player. If you don't have a friendly player targeted, it executes a target-tell, which attempts to target the last player that sent you a tell.

- /retell, /rt: Send another tell to the most recent person you whispered, regardless of whether he or she has responded. Any tells sent via macros (using /tt or /telltarget) do not update the target of a message sent with this command.

- /targettell: An explicit version of /tt. This attempts to target the person who last sent you a tell message. Mostly provided for completeness and for macro use (although /tt works just fine in macros).

- /telltarget: A dumb version of /tt (it doesn't change the editbox header to reflect your target). Mostly provided for completeness and for macro use (although /tt works fine in macros).

- /targetsave, /tsave: Saves your current target for later retrieval.

- /targetrestore, /trestore: Restores a previously saved target.

Keeping Track of Multiple Conversations with TellTrack

Addon created by Sarf, maintained by AnduinLothar

CURSE-GAMING

Note Like ChatScroll, this addon is included in Cosmos. You can download the latest version at `http://cosmosui.org/addons.php`.

It can easily get really annoying (and confusing) to carry on multiple whisper conversations at once. Personally, I send tells to the wrong person all the time. TellTrack attempts to make it easier to stay on top of a number of different tell conversations without utilizing its own complex windowing system (like ForgottenChat or WIM). Instead, it utilizes a chat tab to display all of your tells, one conversation at a time, and a separate window where each user you're chatting with is listed. This window allows you to switch between conversations.

Using TellTrack

It might sound a little complicated, but you'll catch on quickly. TellTrack is disabled by default when you install it, so you first need to enable it with the slash-command:

`/telltrack enabled`

A window immediately appears with a bunch of slots that say Empty. This is the main TellTrack window (see Figure 6-1). Whenever someone whispers you (or you whisper them), their name will appear in one of the slots. Before we move on, you should know that the window can be dragged around. You can also resize it by dragging the lower-right corner. If you click the little question mark in the upper-left corner, the help will be displayed (you can also type `/telltrack` for the help). Use the arrows at the top and bottom of the frame to scroll the list.

FIGURE 6-1: The main TellTrack window lets you switch between multiple conversations.

Players' names appear in either red or green. Green means you're the last person to send a message, while red means the other person was the last to speak. The next step is to right-click on a name (it doesn't matter which) and select Create Whisper Frame from the drop-down menu. This opens a new chat tab that will house all future conversations. All new tells will appear there.

Now, as you receive tells from different people, you can click on a name in the main TellTrack window to view only their conversation in the Whisper Frame. A little number will appear next to a name if you have unread tells from that person. If you click on someone's name while his or her conversation is selected, TellTrack sets you up to send them a tell. In this way you can switch back and forth between multiple conversations with different people. If you're still a little confused, try it out for yourself; everything will make sense when you see the addon in action.

Note   Unfortunately, if you drag the Whisper Frame out into a separate chat window, the General chat tab is hidden whenever you switch between conversations. This is an annoying problem that will hopefully be fixed in a future version of the addon.

Configuring TellTrack

TellTrack has several settings, all of which are configurable via slash-commands. If you're planning to use TellTrack for the long haul, it's a good idea to enable the `hidewhispers` option so that tells no longer appear anywhere besides the Whisper Frame. The rest of the options are covered in Table 6-2, and are used in the following format:

```
/telltrack <option>
```

Table 6-2   TellTrack Command-Line Options

Option	Description
enabled	Enables/disables TellTrack
dontsavelist	Stops the TellTrack list from being saved between sessions
hidewhispers	Hides whispers in all chat frames except the TellTrack whisper frame
timestamps	Prints time stamps on messages in the TellTrack whisper frame
autowhisperframe	Auto-creates Whisper Frame
whisperfirst	First TellTrack name click opens a whisper, second reveals their chat log
invert	Inverts/Normalizes TellTrack list
clearall	Clears all TellTrack entries

Source: documentation by AnduinLothar

Viewing Whispers in an Instant Message Format

If you think about it, tells are no different from instant messages. Why then does WoW lack an advanced interface for managing tells coming from many different people at once? We've already seen how TellTrack attacks the problem using the built-in chat windows; however, there are more comprehensive solutions, namely ForgottenChat and WoW Instant Messenger (WIM). Both of these addons create special windows for managing your whisper conversations, much like AIM, MSN, or Google Chat. Both addons are quite usable and are somewhat similar; the main differences are mostly aesthetic.

ForgottenChat

Addon created and maintained by ForgottenLords

WORLDOFWAR   CURSE-GAMING   WOWINTERFACE

After installing ForgottenChat, a small window pops up for each tell conversation you're involved in (see Figure 6-2). By default, your messages appear in light blue and the other person's appear in purple. To send a message back to someone, just click anywhere in the window and a new editbox will appear, or you can continue sending whispers via the general chat window. Each conversation will open a new floating window; this makes it much easier to keep track of everyone you're talking to.

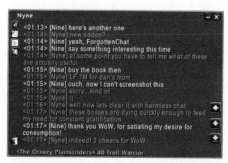

FIGURE 6-2: A whisper conversation displayed in a ForgottenChat window.

One of the nicest features of ForgottenChat is the collapsible frames. Click the little bar button next to the X in the upper-right, and the window reduces itself to only a bar. If you receive a tell while the window is minimized, the name turns red and the number of missed messages is displayed.

ForgottenChat has several options, all of which are configurable via the options panel, which is opened with the /fc slash-command (you can also use /forgottenchat). All the settings are nicely categorized, and descriptions are available via mouse-over. If you check Save History, you can see past conversations with people the next time you talk to them. Old messages appear in gray by default. The remaining slash-commands are:

- /fc log: Opens the Message History window where you can browse through all logged conversations and optionally delete them.

- `/fc disable`: Disables most of the addon's features, closes any open windows, and sends whispers back to the default chat window.

- `/fc enable`: Reenables the addon if it's been disabled. If installed, ForgottenChat is always enabled when you enter the world.

- `/fc <name>`: Opens a ForgottenChat window for talking to the specified character.

ForgottenChat has many other features including aliases, profiles, and blacklisting. For more information about them and the addon in general, take a look at the comprehensive documentation that comes with it. From within ForgottenChat's main folder, go inside the Documentation folder, and then open the `Readme.html` file in a web browser.

WoW Instant Messenger (WIM)

Addon created and maintained by Pazza

WORLDOFWAR   CURSE-GAMING   WOWINTERFACE

WIM is a much newer addon to hit the scene, and it provides much of the same functionality as ForgottenChat. In my opinion, it does so slightly more aesthetically than the other addons (see Figure 6-3). WIM will open a new window whenever you send or receive a tell, and you can continue using this window for the rest of the conversation. There's no way to minimize WIM windows, but they're easy to reopen using the minimap button's drop-down menu.

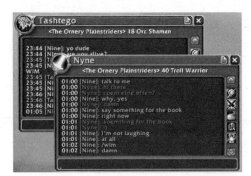

FIGURE 6-3: Two WIM conversation windows.

One nice feature of WIM is that it recognizes web addresses and displays them in blue. If you click on a web address, it'll open a floating editbox with the address selected so you can immediately copy it, tab out of the game, and paste it into a web browser.

WIM also comes with a nicely organized options panel, which you can open with the `/wim` slash-command. WIM has a history feature as well, which records conversations with friends and guild members by default, but can be enabled for everyone or disabled altogether. Past whispers are displayed grayed-out in the conversation windows themselves, or you can type /wim history to open the History Viewer. You can also access the History Viewer by clicking the little page icon next to the X on any conversation window.

Finally, WIM includes in-game documentation. Use the command /wim help (or click the ? icon in the upper-right corner of the options frame) to open a frame where you can read about the addon, a few additional slash-commands, and some helpful hints.

Sending Item Links in Private Channels with ChatLink

Addon created and maintained by Yrys

```
WORLDOFWAR    CURSE-GAMING
```

Just as a refresher, the term *item link* refers to when the name of an item appears in chat surrounded by square brackets. This allows other players to click on the item's name to display its stats. Item links can be posted most of the time, but not in private channels; you can still link the name of an item by Shift+clicking on it, but the text isn't clickable. It isn't an item link.

ChatLink enables you to send item links (and enchant links) to private channels by inserting a special code into the message that the addon also knows how to decode. If anyone who receives the message is running ChatLink, they'll see the item link as normal. If they're not running the addon, they'll see a plain text code like the following:

```
{CLINK:item:ff0070dd:6463:0:0:0:Deep Fathom Ring}
```

Notice how the name of the item is still in there, just surrounded by some other data that tells ChatLink how to turn the code into a link. Non-ChatLink users may be a little confused, but the necessary information remains readable. Clearly, the downside to ChatLink is that it requires other people in the channel to be using it. Even so, you might find it worthwhile, especially if you often use private channels with your friends. The addon is also tiny and has no slash-commands and nothing to configure.

Logging Your Conversations with ChatLog

Addon created and maintained by pb_ee1

```
WORLDOFWAR    CURSE-GAMING    WOWINTERFACE
```

ChatLog does exactly what it sounds like: It logs pretty much all communication that goes through the chat window, channel by channel. It can be very frustrating to scroll up in the chat window, only to discover that the message you're looking for is too old and has been discarded. ChatLog records the last thousand lines of each type of message (compared to 161 lines for everything, by default), and can also output the chat window or combat log to a text file. Best of all, logs are preserved between sessions.

ChatLog adds a button next to your chat window that fits in so well with the default interface that you might miss it at first; it has a little triangle on it (see Figure 6-4). This button opens the main ChatLog window, which is used for browsing all the logs and configuring most settings. You can right-click and drag the button to move it around; otherwise it'll stick to the chat window frame.

— ChatLog button

FIGURE 6-4: ChatLog adds a new button next to the chat window.

When you first open the main ChatLog window (see Figure 6-5), it displays a log of your recent whispers, but you can select a category of messages to browse from a drop-down menu (click the curved arrow button in the upper-left or right-click anywhere on the window).

FIGURE 6-5: The main ChatLog window displays your chat history by type.

The rest of the options and buttons are pretty straightforward. Some highlights are as follows:

- Enable logging to file with the buttons in the upper-right corner. Note that these files will only be updated when you leave the world. The two files created will be:

```
World of Warcraft\Logs\WoWChatLog.txt
World of Warcraft\Logs\WoWCombatLog.txt
```

- You can copy text with the Copy button at the bottom of the frame. It will open the entire log in a window in which you can select text to copy. Note that even though it might look like long logs are cut off, you can still copy the invisible text.

- The arrow buttons on the right side of the window work the same way as the buttons next to the chat window. The arrow button at the top jumps you all the way to the top.

- You can click on player names and item links in the log just the same as you would in the chat window.

ChatLog has a few simple slash-command options (shown in Table 6-3) that are used in the following format:

```
/chatlog <option>
```

Use the command alone to toggle the main ChatLog window.

Table 6-3   ChatLog Command-Line Options

Option	Description
reset	Resets all window positions
resetbutton	Resets the ChatLog button position
clear	Clears the specified log
clearall	Clears all the logs
help	Displays the help

Source: documentation by pb_ee1

Automatically Ignoring Spammers with Spam Guard Plus

Addon created and maintained by Ryan Hamshire

CURSE-GAMING

Spam Guard Plus (SGP) is an addon that automatically ignores spammers (chat text, emotes, mail, duels, rolls, and speech bubbles will all be blocked) based on their behavior in chat. SGP looks for multiple messages rapidly coming from the same person. When this happens, that person is automatically ignored for the rest of your session. SGP has no configuration and has only one slash-command.

Following are several additional features:

- **Unlimited Ignores:** Your default ignore list is limited to 25 names. With SGP installed, you can ignore as many people as you need to.
- **Shared Lists:** Your ignore and friends lists will be shared between all of your characters on the same server.
- **Right-click Menu:** If you right-click on someone's name in the chat window you can choose to temporarily or permanently ignore him.
- **Temp Ignore:** Use the slash-command /tempignore <name> to add a player to the temporary ignore list, which means he or she will only be ignored for the rest of the session.

You can continue using the /ignore command normally, as well as the Ignore interface in the Social window. Friends, guild members, party members, and raid members will never be automatically ignored.

Adding a Pop-Up List of Emotes with EmoteMenu

Addon created and maintained by Shervin

CURSE-GAMING

EmoteMenu is a simple addon that gives you a huge drop-down menu full of emotes. By default you'll find it to the left of your portrait; a round button with a big "E" on it. You can Shift+click and drag to move the button anywhere. The menu is opened with a left-click, and the options panel brought up with a right-click. Besides offering an easy way to tons of emotes, EmoteMenu is nicely configurable and can even be used to execute non-emote commands.

Note After you install EmoteMenu, the drop-down may be cut off by the edge of the screen. If you experience this, there's a Horizontal Position setting on the options panel that can be used to push the menu fully onscreen without moving the button itself.

The first method of configuration is the options panel. From here you can tweak the general appearance of EmoteMenu as well as the color filters, which specify which entries appear in green, red, blue, or yellow instead of the default white. Each color filter consists of a list of comma-separated emote names. Each filter list must also begin and end with a comma.

The second method of configuration consists of editing the EmoteList.lua file outside of the game. Open the file with a text editor. The filters can be edited here as well, at the beginning of the file. Below them is the list for the menu entries themselves. You can add, remove, or modify the emote list to your heart's content. Each entry is in the form of:

```
{"Name", "/slash-command"},
```

The wonderful thing about this is that you're not limited to just emotes! Take a look at the included Water entry for a good example. You can use any slash-command you can think of (because emotes are really just slash-commands anyway), including /played, /camp, or the following:

```
/script if(PlayerFrame:IsVisible()) then PlayerFrame:Hide(); else
PlayerFrame:Show(); end
```

This script will toggle the Player window on or off each time it's executed. Also, remember that you need to reload the interface each time you make any changes to this file. Use the following command in-game:

```
/script ReloadUI()
```

Improving Everyone's Speaking Ability with Eloquence

Addon created and maintained by Marr

CURSE-GAMING

World of Warcraft players don't exactly have the best grammar. They also love to use acronyms, which can both simplify and confuse your life (depending on whether you know what the heck they all mean). Also, if you're into role-playing, I can understand how someone shouting "LF2M UBRS" might kill the suspension of disbelief a little bit. Eloquence aims to fix all of this by simply changing what it looks like people are saying.

Eloquence, at its heart, is a filter. It can filter both incoming and outgoing chat messages based on a system of levels that affect how much the speech is modified. For example, with Eloquence running and active, the above shout of "LF2M UBRS" would show up in your chat window as "Seeking two more for Upper Blackrock Spire." Eloquence actually works surprisingly well in practice.

Using Eloquence

Eloquence works from the moment you install it, and you'll notice its effects right away. By default, only incoming messages are modified; anything you say will be seen by other people exactly the way you typed it. You'll also notice that channel names are abbreviated. The party and guild channel markings are reduced to one letter and numbered channels no longer display their names. All of this is configurable.

Configuring Eloquence

You can open the Eloquence configuration panel with the /elo slash-command (/eloquence also works). The first thing you'll see is the Filters tab, where you can control what is and isn't filtered (see Figure 6-6).

FIGURE 6-6: The Eloquence options panel displaying the Filters tab.

The left column is for messages you type, the right column is for messages typed by others. At first, everything is set to Level 1. Here's a rundown of the different filter levels taken from the Eloquence documentation by Marr (each level builds on the functionality of previous levels):

- **Level 1 - Grammar Nazi:** Corrects spelling, punctuation, capitalization, d00dspeak, and elongates many WoW and Internet chat abbreviations. This filter style makes chat more readable without making drastic changes to what the speaker said.

- **Level 2 - Sanitizer:** Includes Grammar Nazi. This level replaces nasty words with more pleasant sayings of similar meaning. Important: WoW's internal profanity filter changes offensive words to %*!#@ before this addon can process them, so please turn off the WoW profanity filter to properly use this filter.

- **Level 3 - Acting Coach:** Includes both Grammar Nazi and Sanitizer and also replaces modern slang and other out-of-character expressions with RP phrases consistent with Warcraft lore. This style automatically detects whether the player belongs to the Horde or the Alliance and prepares faction-specific sayings. It also detects the current server time and adjusts greetings accordingly.

- **Level 4 - Dialectician:** Adds a layer of personality to chat through accents and dialects based on the speaker's race. Players of an unknown race are filtered using Level 3.

Below the left column of filter settings is an important checkbox: Filter Outgoing Messages. If checked, Eloquence modifies your messages before sending them to the server, so other people (whether they're running Eloquence or not) will see them "cleaned up" and not the way you originally typed them.

Following are other settings not to miss while configuring Eloquence:

- One of the first things I wanted to see after installing the addon was the original messages before they were filtered (so I could compare them to the filtered results). On the Chat Links tab, toggle the Output Mode to Debug. You can then click on chat messages to have the unfiltered originals appear in a frame.

- Adjust the way channel headers are displayed under the Headers tab. There's also a setting here to color player names according to class and to display their level.

- The Display Options tab contains many anti-spam settings (in this case spam refers to unnecessary game messages as opposed to annoying messages from other players).

- A unique feature on the Display Options tab checks prices in Trade Channel and limits what you see based on how much money you have.

Eloquence includes a comprehensive slash-command system, which isn't covered here because it would take many pages (and many of the commands simply duplicate options that are already available on the panel). Nevertheless, you can familiarize yourself with it by reading the Text Commands tab on the options panel or by typing any of the following:

```
/elo help
/elo misc
/elo display
```

Creating Custom Languages with Lore

Addon created by Rook, maintained by Liise

CURSE-GAMING

The language system in World of Warcraft is not as full-featured as it could have been, and in some ways feels like an afterthought. The Lore addon ambitiously attempts to give role-players the tools they need to speak in all sorts of languages not implemented by Blizzard. It does this via its own translation system that modifies text before it's passed to the game's built-in language functions. Lore isn't the most user-friendly of addons, but once you familiarize yourself with it, it has the potential to enrich your role-playing experience.

Installing Lore

Besides downloading the latest version of Lore, you also need to download the `dialects.lua` file, which should be available as a separate download wherever Lore is available. On the curse-gaming site the dialects file appears right below the addon itself in the list of downloadable files. After you install Lore, simply extract the `dialects.lua` file into Lore's folder.

Caution If you don't install the `dialects.lua` file, Lore will generate an error when you enter the world, and you won't be able to use the addon properly.

Setting Up and Using Lore

Once you enter the world, you'll see a new button onscreen called the Tablet. Simply click and drag if you want to move the tablet around. Pick a spot for it now, because you need to lock it in place before it successfully registers left-clicks. Once you've got it where you want it, type the following:

`/lore lock`

You start off not knowing any languages (as far as Lore knows), so you need to learn some. Start out by adding the base language that everyone in your faction speaks:

- If you're Alliance, type `/lore tablet` Common
- If you're Horde, type `/lore tablet` Orcish

Next, pick another language to play with, for example Dark Iron. Type the following command to add the Dark Iron language to your Tablet:

`/lore tablet Dark Iron`

Now you can click the tablet to cycle between your base language and Dark Iron. Next, turn on self-translation. This enables you to see translated versions of messages that you type in languages other than your base language. To turn on self-translation, enter the following command:

`/lore self on`

Now select Dark Iron and speak! You'll see something like this (my character's name is Nine):

```
(Nine: Why am I talking to myself?)
[Nine] says: [Dark Iron] Nag ka I kharnos il dun-gar?
```

Other players certainly won't have any idea what you're saying, unless they have Lore installed and know the Dark Iron language, in which case your message is automatically translated into text they can read. This should be enough to get you started playing with Lore.

Lore comes with quite a few additional features, including the following:

- The capability to modify your language skill. If you set it to anything less than 100 percent, you'll only be able to partially understand messages spoken in that language.
- The capability to process your messages with voice effects, including stuttering, hissing, growling, lisping, and cutting off your words.
- The capability to designate another player as a translator. This player receives readable translations of your messages as whispers, so he can act as an interpreter to other players who don't speak the language.

Lore's configuration panel can be opened with the /lore slash-command, and a long list of slash-command options can be printed out by typing /lore help. If you plan to use Lore regularly, spend some quality time with the complete documentation, which is quite comprehensive; look for the ReadMe.txt file in Lore's base directory.

 Note If the languages that come in the default dialects.lua file aren't enough for you, you can download player-created language packs. At the time of this writing, two of them are available. Look for them wherever Lore is distributed, and follow the directions that come with them to install and use the additional languages. Very advanced players might want to try creating their own languages.

Auto-Responding to Events with Roleplaying Helper

Addon created and maintained by Syrsa

`WORLDOFWAR` `CURSE-GAMING`

Roleplaying Helper is one of the few addons that I discourage you from using right out of the box because its default settings are likely to annoy you and other players if you use them for any length of time. Despite this, it has some amazing potential if you personalize it to fit your character. Basically, Roleplaying Helper gives you a system in which your character has a chance of automatically reacting (saying something or emoting) to certain events such as entering combat, leveling up, dodging, and much, much more.

Configuring Roleplaying Helper

There's a configuration system in-game for changing two variables for each event: delay and chance. Delay is the amount of time before a reaction occurs, and chance is the probability that you'll react to that event at all. Take a look at the default settings (type /rp, and then choose the Events button); you can see that the chance for most events is pretty low. If you set it too high for certain events, such as combat, anyone nearby is going to get annoyed really fast.

Besides a few other settings, such as language, there isn't much more configuration that can be done in-game. The real beauty of this addon, though, is going into the files and creating your own personalized responses. All responses are stored within files inside the English directory of the RoleplayingHelper folder. You'll want to edit three files per character:

- ANY.lua: Used by all characters.
- <RACE>.lua: For example, the TROLL.lua file.
- <CLASS>.lua: For example, the MAGE.lua file.

You can choose which files are used by clicking the Phrase Lists button in-game; it defaults to the ones best suited for your current character (you could have some fun changing it around though). The `How to Customize.txt` file provides a detailed technical guide to customizing your responses. Also check out the general Roleplaying Helper documentation in `readme_RPHelper.txt`.

Using the Emotion Feature

Roleplaying Helper comes bundled with a pretty nice emote selector called Emotion, which isn't all that unlike EmoteMenu. In fact, Emotion includes more of Blizzard's built-in emotes (all of them, it claims) than EmoteMenu's default list does. The frame is disabled by default, but can be turned on easily by typing the command `/es`. When you enable it, you'll see a tall list of clickable emotes that you can drag around the screen or scroll through.

The menu is fully configurable via the Roleplaying Helper options dialog (type `/rp`, and then click the Emotion button). In addition to changing the display options, you can even hand-tweak your own lists (select Keyword Examples or New List from the drop-down menu) or stick with the default Blizzard list. If you do configure your own lists, you can take advantage of Emotion's keyword replacement system for creating your own emotes. Click the Custom Emote button to bring up the interface, which happens to do a good job documenting the various keywords you can use.

Adding Character Descriptions with FlagRSP2

Addon created by Flokru, maintained by Azxiana

[WORLDOFWAR] [CURSE-GAMING]

FlagRSP2 isn't exactly a chat addon, but because a few other role-playing addons have been covered in this chapter, it seemed appropriate to include it here alongside them. FlagRSP2 gives you the means to share character information with other interested role-players who are also running the addon. This information includes custom extra names, a title, and a physical description, as well as your role-playing status. FlagRSP2 also serves as a tooltip enhancement. It has no slash-commands.

Note   FlagRSP2 is backwards compatible with the original FlagRSP addon.

FlagRSP2 adds a minimap button with a little scroll on it. Clicking the button opens the main window, which is also the options panel (see Figure 6-7). The Character tab allows you to enter extended information about your character that will be available to other FlagRSP2 users. The

Options tab allows you to set your role-playing status as well as configure how other player's descriptions are displayed to you. Finally, the Tooltip tab lets you tweak how the modified tooltip information appears and what kind of information is displayed.

FIGURE 6-7: FlagRSP2 lets you share character information with other role-players.

When you encounter another player who's sharing information with FlagRSP2 you'll see his or her full name, title, and role-playing status in the tooltip. If he or she has a physical description entered, it also pops up in its own window when you mouse-over their body (depending on your settings). Figure 6-8 shows an example of this.

FIGURE 6-8: This is what it looks like to encounter another player running FlagRSP2.

Communication Is Key

Whether you're a role-player, a casual player, or a hardcore raider, you're constantly interacting with other players and entering chat commands into the game. This chapter provided some tools that can help you manage your interactions and improve your communications. Some of the changes these addons make are purely utilitarian, while some of them can be a whole lot of fun on their own (Eloquence, for example).

Unlike the real world, where you can use body language and other subtle forms of communication, your relationships in WoW are defined primarily through your words (and your actions, of course). Some of these addons (such as the IM-style whisper packages) help to make in-game conversations feel much more natural, especially if you're used to talking on AIM (or similar services) all the time.

In the next chapter, you examine addons that are specifically designed to benefit raids (groups of more than five players).

Raid Addons

Through the course of World of Warcraft, you'll find opportunities and quests that require a group of more than five people to complete. These encounters (such as quests labeled "Raid" in your quest log, or Player versus Player in the battlegrounds) are typically built around an organized group of players working together for a single objective.

This chapter introduces several addons that make raiding in World of Warcraft a more enjoyable experience, from organizational addons you can use before the raid starts, to those that attempt to provide information and strategy notifications mid-fight.

Organizing Your Group

Coordinating schedules with a large number of people to ensure that you have a full group for raiding or organized PvP can be a challenge. Several tools are designed to help your group communicate upcoming raids and events, so your members can prepare ahead of time. Out-of-game calendars accomplish the same task, but being able to view the raid schedule within the game can be quite helpful.

Group Calendar

Addon created by Mundocani

`CURSE-GAMING`   `WORLDOFWAR`   `WOWINTERFACE`

Group Calendar attaches itself as an analog clock to your time-of-day indicator on the minimap. Clicking the button opens the in-game calendar. Using the calendar is quite simple; selecting a date opens the right pane displaying detailed information. You can click the New Event button to open the event creation window.

You can specify the length of the group event, specify which dungeon or raid you are planning to run, and provide a description of the event, as shown in Figure 7-1. You can also specify (with a checkbox) that your character plans to attend, so that the addon can keep track of who is already signed up for your event.

FIGURE 7-1: Adding an event to Group Calendar.

Synchronization of events is handled through the Setup tab, where you define the channels to use for synchronization. If your guild has been set up for automatic configuration, you can use the Automatic setting. If you don't have a guild or it hasn't been properly configured, use the Manual setting to choose a method for synchronization. You can configure the system to use your guild's hidden channel, or specify a channel name and password (handy if you are working among multiple guilds). You can specify a list of people to ignore events from, and also denote a minimum guild rank necessary to have an event displayed.

Group Calendar is a great, easy way to coordinate events within a group of people. While the addon doesn't have a ton of configurable options, it just works right out of the box in most cases. Group Calendar has several advanced options only available from the command line. You can view these options (see Table 7-1) by typing /calendar help within the game.

Table 7-1   Group Calendar Slash-Command

Command	Description
/calendar help	Shows the list of commands.
/calendar versions	Displays the last known version of GroupCalendar each user was running.
/calendar kill playerName	Deletes all events for the player from the calendar (guild officers only).
/calendar mon	Sets the calendar to start the week on a Monday.
/calendar sun	Sets the calendar to start the week on a Sunday.
/calendar reset [all]	Resets your calendar for all characters on the current realm. Use the ALL switch to reset your calendars on all realms.
/calendar clock [off | local | server | auto]	Sets the display mode for the minimap clock.

Source: in-game documentation

GuildEventManager

Addon created by kiki

CURSE-GAMING

GuildEventManager offers a different set of features on top of those provided by Group Calendar. When you load up your game you'll find a new minimap button that looks like a little clock. Clicking this icon loads up the list view of all scheduled events. Click the checkbox in the upper-right corner to change to a calendar view. As you may know, many of the raid zones have lock-out timers on them, which means that they can be run only once within a certain time period. For example, Onyxia resets every five days. GuildEventManager can display these reset timers for you when in calendar mode, to help in scheduling your events (see Figure 7-2).

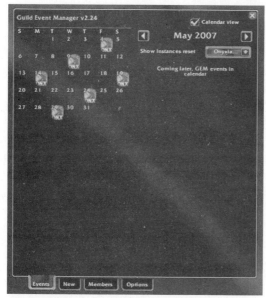

FIGURE 7-2: Calendar mode showing Onyxia raid timers.

Adding an event to the calendar is easy, and you get a few more options than with Group Calendar. You can specify the minimum and maximum number of each class you want to attend the event (see Figure 7-3). From the event editing screen you can add members to the group, and keep a list of substitutes. Having organized 40-man raids in Blackwing Lair and The Ruins of Ahn'Qiraj, I can tell you that having a place to keep a substitute list is an absolute timesaver. Players can subscribe to events even if the raid leader is offline.

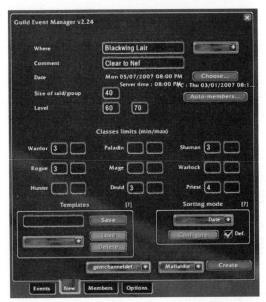

FIGURE 7-3: GuildEventManager's event creation screen.

GuildEventManager has many options you can change, including setting the channel for synchronization and the position and look of the minimap icon. Unlike Group Calendar, GEM doesn't allow you to synchronize events through the hidden guild channel, so you'll need to join a common channel for those features to work. You can access the advanced options for GEM by typing /gem at the command line.

By default, GEM joins a channel called gemdefaultchannel, which is used to synchronize events over an entire server, so you may see some events show up from people who aren't in your guild. You can change this default channel on the Options tab.

Tip If you uninstall GuildEventManager, you may find yourself getting messages on gemdefaultchannel (it should show a number before the channel name when messages are printed to your chat window). You can type /leave num to leave this channel and stop the spam.

Deciding Between the Two

Group Calendar is a fairly simple mod that has enough features for the average small guild, whereas larger guilds may opt for GuildEventManager. If you're trying to decide on one as a solution for your guild, you may want to load each one to explore the options, and ensure that it will suit your guild's needs.

Displaying Your Raid

When playing with 9 to 39 other people, it's often necessary to get information about each of those different players, such as their current health and mana, or buffs and debuffs. Finding a way to display that information and a place to put it on your screen can be a difficult task. This section examines several different addons meant to display your raid's unit frames.

Blizzard's Raid Frames

In Patch 1.6, Blizzard introduced a native version of raid unit frames in the default UI. You could use these frames by opening the Raid tab, and dragging any class or group from the panel, which creates a new frame showing that group of players. Since that initial introduction, the default raid frames have matured, gaining buff display options and the option to save frame positions in between raids.

To use the raid frames, open your social frame, and click the Raid tab. A panel displays your raid makeup, and a number of small icons on the right side of the frame. Each icon represents a specific class. You can either drag one of these icons or drag a group name from the Raid tab (see Figure 7-4) to create a new frame showing that group of players. The last icon attached to the frame is a special icon for Raid Pets. You can drag it to show all the raid's pets in a single easy-to-move frame. If you want to watch someone in particular, you can Shift+click his name on the Raid panel, and drag it to the game field. This creates an individual raid frame for that unit.

FIGURE 7-4: Blizzard's default Raid tab (left) and Blizzard's Raid frames in action (right).

You can right-click on any of the new raid frames to change the display, such as hiding the background or toggling display of buffs and debuffs. If you've created any individual raid frames, they will have an extra right-click option that enables you to show that player's target for easy healing and assisting. The Blizzard Raid UI lacks customization, but doesn't require the user to download any addons; it just works.

X-Perl Unit Frames

Addon created by Zeksie

X-Perl Unit Frames includes a set of raid frames that are a combination of CT_RaidAssist (see the "CT_RaidAssist Sets the Standard" sidebar a little later in the chapter) and Blizzard's Raid Frames visually, with a bit of flair thrown in. What sets X-Perl apart is its integration with other addons, and the amount of information it displays. You can use X-Perl as a simple set of frames based on class or group, or use it to assign and view main tank targets (see Figure 7-5).

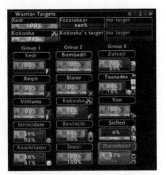

FIGURE 7-5: X-Perl Raid frames and main Tank frames.

You can open the configuration UI with the command /xperl. There are an immense number of options, which can be somewhat overwhelming, but almost every aspect of the mod is configurable. I won't try to detail each of the options here, but Table 7-2 describes some of the different modules that X-Perl provides. Each of these modules has several options that are configurable under the /xperl menu.

Table 7-2 Highlights of X-Perl's Modules

X-Perl Module	Description
Range Finder	Can be combined with a health check to dim any units that are out of range, or don't meet a certain health requirement. This gives you an easy way to display the units that are both in range and likely need healing. You can dim either the name of the frame or the status portion of the frame, along with the frame as a whole.
HoT Monitor	Highlights units that have your heal over time spells active on them.
Debuff Highlights	Colors frames by debuffs, with priority given to debuffs you can cure or remove.
Heal/Damage Indicators	Flashes a frame red when it takes damage, and green when it receives a heal.
MT Targets	Serves as main tank frames.

sRaidFrames

Addon created by Saroz

sRaidFrames was originally created as an alternative to CT_RaidAssist, offering a few more configurable visual options, but removing the bulk of the extra features from CT_RaidAssist. Plain and simple unit frames, they copy the visual style of CTRA, without the raid leader functionality.

sRaidFrames can optionally show buffs or debuffs, and sort frames by group or by name, in a number of different layouts. Frames can be highlighted when a unit has aggro, or when a special critical ability is used (such as Shield Wall or Innervate) and can be dimmed when a unit is out of range. Using the same basic underlying system as CT_RaidAssist, sRaidFrames offers a different set of visual styles (see Figure 7-6).

FIGURE 7-6: sRaidFrames using the default visual style.

PerfectRaid

Addon created by Cladhaire

WOWINTERFACE

PerfectRaid is a set of raid frames based on a conceptual mock-up that was circulated through closed beta by Shiver of <Forgotten Aspects> on the Hyjal server. The idea was to have a compact display that made it easy to get the overall state of a battle, as well as gather focused information. Initially, I created a small proof of concept mod that used a similar visual style, but the addon wasn't complete.

PerfectRaid uses the same visual style initially created by Shiver, and has added several features that make it geared toward healers in particular, although features are constantly being added to assist raid leaders. When you first load PerfectRaid and join a raid, you're greeted with a single frame set up to display your raid members. Your raid is sorted by class, and then by name within the classes. PerfectRaid displays one column of 25 members, and moves anyone else into a second column on the right side. All configuration options can be found using the /praid command, which activates the configuration UI.

One of PerfectRaid's best features is the custom buff editor (see Figure 7-7), and the way it displays those buff notifications. Rather than use the traditional icons, PerfectRaid displays colored text markers that the user can define. These notifications can be filtered based on several different conditions, such as the unit's class, group, or whether the unit is a mana user (handy for Innervate). Buffs can be configured to show only when the unit is missing the buff, making it quite useful for a class that can cast buff spells.

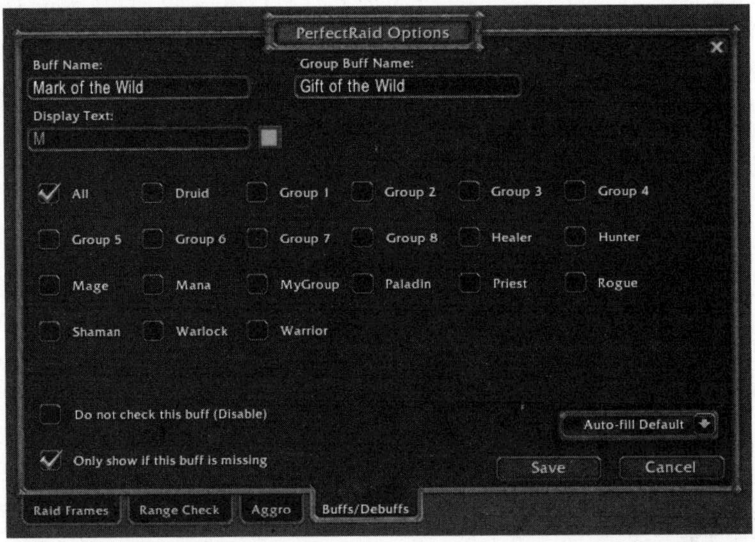

FIGURE 7-7: PerfectRaid's Buff Editor.

PerfectRaid was designed by a healer for a healer, so it offers many features that make healing easier (see Figure 7-8). Health bars are colored by deficit (green when health is full, changing to red as the unit loses health). Each frame displays numerically how much health a unit is missing, to aid in healing spell selection. If a unit has aggro, the word "Aggro" is displayed on the frame, or the health deficit is colored red to indicate active combat. PerfectRaid offers two levels of range checking, dimming any frames that indicate a unit is out of range of a spell you specify. Tailoring your PerfectRaid frames to work for you may take some time, but it can be extremely handy when raiding and learning new encounters.

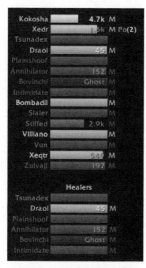

FIGURE 7-8: PerfectRaid during a PvP session.

RDX.Cid

Addon created by Shirik and Cidan, based on original code by Venificus

CURSE-GAMING   WOWINTERFACE

If you have been an active member of the user interface community, you may have heard of a raid addon called RDX. Originally created by Venificus for his guild <Scions of Destiny>, it has a long history. RDX was initially a private addon limited to a few guilds using activation codes and obfuscation cryptic code. These protections were cracked and bypassed version after version, and eventually Venificus released a public version of the code, with full comments, under a license that made the code open and free. After releasing the free version of the addon, Venificus began work on a new version, called RDX6. This addon is only available to paid subscribers, and that is the source of most of the controversy surrounding RDX.

RDX.Cid is a modified version of the open RDX5 version that has been updated and improved consistently. RDX.Cid has a style that is unique to the RDX series of addons, and comes with many themes and options to customize the layout of a frame. Each frame can be filtered based on several conditions, including class and group. You can add frame decorations based on certain conditions (such as a player being cursed or poisoned). I don't have the space here to detail all the options of RDX, so I leave you with the following screenshot and encourage you to explore this addon to see if it works for you. Most RDX.Cid features can be configured under the RDX control panel, displayed at the top of the screen when you first log in (see Figure 7-9).

FIGURE 7-9: RDX.Cid frames, with control panel.

CT_RaidAssist Sets the Standard

CURSE-GAMING   WOWINTERFACE

CT_RaidAssist is the gold standard for raid addons. When WoW was originally released, there was no way to view your raid members, so you had to download an addon for that purpose. CT_RaidAssist was the first major addon to meet this need, and it continues to offer a nice basic set of unit frames, coupled with several extremely useful tools for raid leaders.

CT_RaidAssist Sets the Standard *Continued*

Raid Frames

Once you have CT_RaidAssist installed, open your social window by pressing O, or clicking the gossip bubble in your menu bar. You should see the familiar Raid tab, with an extra tab labeled CTRaid. From the CTRaid tab, you can open the CT_RaidAssist options, and select the groups you'd like to display. An RA button is attached to your minimap that opens the options as well.

Each raid frame created by CT_RaidAssist can be dragged around and placed on the screen wherever you'd like. The frames themselves aren't very customizable, but you can change a number of options in the configuration GUI, such as displaying mana bars, hiding energy and rage bars, showing group titles, hiding borders, and sorting the frames in a specific way. Here's an example of the default CT_RaidAssist raid frames:

CT_RaidAssist showing a raid

CTRaid's frames can display buffs and debuffs, so the addon comes with a nice buff editor that lets you control buff display and priorities. You can choose to see when someone is missing a buff that you can cast (such as Mark of the Wild or Arcane Intellect). You can also choose to watch debuffs that you can cure, such as Poisons and Diseases. Filters come in handy to only watch for buffs and debuffs on a specific group or class.

continued

CT_RaidAssist Sets the Standard *Continued*

Leading a Raid

CT_RaidAssist provides several slash-commands, as described in the following table.

Slash-Command	Description
/radisband	Disbands the raid by uninviting everyone, and leaving the group.
/radur	Performs a durability check, showing the durability level of anyone using CT_RaidAssist or a compatible mod.
/rahide	Hides all groups currently being displayed.
/rainvite minlevel-maxlevel /rainvite level	Invites all members of your guild within a current level range.
/raitem <itemname> or <[Item Link]>	Queries all members using CT_RaidAssist to see if they are carrying the given item in their inventory.
/rakeyword <word>	Turns on keyword inviting. Anyone who whispers you with the given keyword will automatically be invited.
/ralog	Shows the changelog for this version of CT_RaidAssist.
/raloot	Sets the default loot method from the command line.
/raoptions	Opens the CT_RaidAssist options GUI.
/raquiet	Stops the raid from talking while the leaders talk.
/raready	Performs a ready check, asking all CT_RaidAssist users to see if they are ready.
/rareg	Performs a reagent check, showing how many of each spell reagent a player had.
/raresist	Shows the spell resistance of each member in the raid.
/rashow	Shows all selected frames.
/raversion	Performs a version check for CT_RaidAssist.
/ravote [question]	Polls the members of your raid, optionally asking a specific question.
/razone	Shows all members not in your current zone.
/razinvite minlevel-maxlevel/razinvite level	Same as /rainvite, but only invites people in the same zone as you.
/rs	Allows the raid leader to send a message to the entire raid, broadcast in the center of their screens.

Source: CT_RaidAssist documentation

CT_RaidAssist Sets the Standard *Continued*

These commands are extremely useful for raid leaders. Leaders can right-click on any member of the raid on the CTRaid tab to set him as a "main tank," which is then broadcast to all members. These tanks can be displayed along with their targets, and their targets' target using CT_RaidAssist. This makes it easy to see what each tank is currently targeting, and is helpful when assisting and healing during an encounter.

The combination of these commands and the visual display of your raid members makes CT_RaidAssist an incredibly helpful tool, which has set the standard for raid frames and communication in World of Warcraft.

Planning and Strategizing

Raiding in World of Warcraft is all about coordination. Both PvP and boss strategies require some manner of communication, and typing can be quite cumbersome and slow for the more difficult encounters. These addons are meant to improve your battle strategy and communication when working as a group.

Battle Planner

Addon created by Ituriel

CURSE-GAMING

Since World of Warcraft was released in 2004, guilds and players around the world have been asking for a way to draw plans on the in-game maps to help explain strategy to their group mates. Finally, there's an addon that does just that: Battle Planner. Battle Planner is a slick addon that lets you select any of the preset maps and then choose a specific portion to focus on (see Figure 7-10), and draw up battle plans. Open the addon by selecting the new button on your minimap, and clicking the Maps button to select a map.

Once you have a map section selected, you're presented with an editing window with a bunch of icons and other options. You can place group number, class types, bosses, adds, or any number of other directives to make the strategy clear to your group. You can add custom notes, as well as draw lines for movement (see Figure 7-11). Some strategies require a description of movement, so you can even draw lines, and have those lines recorded and played back by your group at any time. Essentially, Battle Planner acts as your clipboard for drawing up the big plays. Your battle plans can be shared with anyone who is listening to your client (that is, those in your guild/raid) or sent to specific individuals directly.

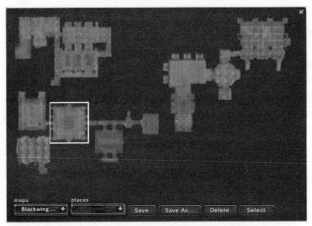

FIGURE 7-10: Selecting a map section with Battle Planner.

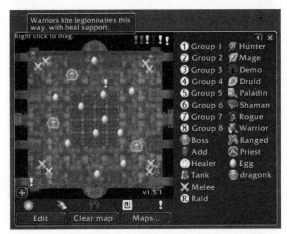

FIGURE 7-11: Showing the Razorgore tank kiting path.

If you've ever tried to draw up a strategy or pass a bad line drawing around your guild forums, you'll appreciate the time that Battle Planner will save you and your group. Draw up your strategies ahead of time, and discuss them when the time for the encounter comes.

CT_RABossMods

Addon created by Cide and Ts

CURSE-GAMING   WOWINTERFACE

The team that brings you CT_RaidAssist also creates an addon designed to help you in major boss fights. CT_RABossMods contains timers, scripts, and warnings that are triggered and played back during a boss fight. Some boss mods are as simple as making bosses yell or emotes display large in the center of your screen, whereas others are more specific, such as providing you with a timer until Ragnaros submerges. Each of these mods can be turned on or off individually, and they're all configured through the same options interface. Figure 7-12 shows the Boss Mods configuration screen, where you can enable or disable specific mods.

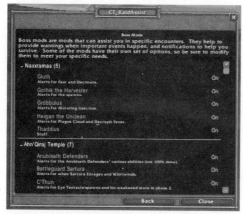

FIGURE 7-12: CT_BossMods configuration screen.

oRA2

Addon created by Haste, Ammo

CURSE-GAMING   WOWINTERFACE

oRA2 was written initially to provide the communication features (setting of main tanks, durability, ready checks, and so on) without requiring the whole CT_RaidAssist addon. Using the same communication methods as CT_RaidAssist, the addons work right alongside each other, without complaint. If you are looking for the extra features of CT_RaidAssist, but don't want to use the raid frames, oRA2 might be a good choice for you. Table 7-3 shows a comparison between CT_RaidAssist and oRA2 features.

Table 7-3   CT_RaidAssist Feature Comparison with oRA2

Feature	CT_RaidAssist	oRA2
Resurrection Monitor	Yes	Yes
Emergency Monitor	Yes	No
Raid Frames	Yes	No
Raid Status Frame	Yes	No
Boss Mods	Yes (with CT_BossMod)	No
Ready Check	Yes	Yes
Version Check	Yes	Yes
Vote System	Yes	Yes
Item Check	Yes	Yes
Main Tank Frames	Yes	Yes
Durability Check	Yes	Yes
Zone Check	Yes	Yes

Source: Ace Wiki (www.wowace.com/wiki/ORA2)

Deadly Boss Mods (La Vendetta)

Addon created by Tandanu

CURSE-GAMING

Deadly Boss Mods (La Vendetta) is another addon that provides lots of customizable options. You can access the configuration panel by running the /dbm slash-command. From there you can select your world (Burning Crusade or Classic World of Warcraft), and which zone addons you want to load (see Figure 7-13). Each zone has a number of boss mods that you can enable or disable, along with additional options specific to each mod.

Deadly Boss Mods has many configurable options — for example, you can change the style of the timer bars or enable full-screen effects such as an aggro warning (turns the border of your screen red) or screen shaking (another visual indication of some critical event). You can use the options panel to create custom timers (such as the suggested Pizza timer that comes by default, notifying you when your pizza is due).

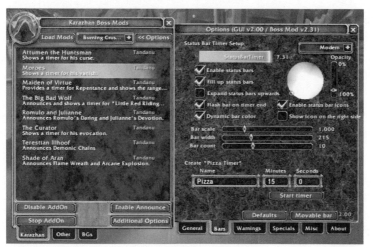

FIGURE 7-13: Deadly Boss Mods configuration panel.

KLHThreatMeter

Addon created by Kenco

CURSE-GAMING

KLHThreatMeter is a clever use of extensive user testing and a bit of math to create an addon that attempts to determine the formulas for aggro as it relates to mobs within the game. It assigns each spell a specific threat value, including attacks, spells, heals, anything that could potentially get you attacked. Each user running this mod keeps track of his current threat value, and broadcasts it to a special channel.

To use this addon, the raid leader sets a master target to be concerned with (the boss in a boss fight), which is sent down to all users in the raid. Any threat recorded against that target is broadcast and displayed on each member's threat meter. While this information isn't 100 percent accurate, it does give you a general picture of the fight. In a very aggro-sensitive encounter, this can be used to ensure no one causes more threat than the main tank, hopefully preventing a wipe of the entire raid. Figure 7-14 shows an example of this addon at work.

FIGURE 7-14: KLHThreatMeter showing relative threat meters.

While not everyone agrees with this addon's concept, it's certainly useful in specific situations. It can be used outside of a raid, such as in a small group of friends to help keep track of threat levels.

BigWigs Boss Mods

Addon created by Ammo, Tekkub

CURSE-GAMING

BigWigs is a modular boss mod system with a very active community, in a very simple package. Each specific boss addon is written with a trigger that activates that mod — for most fights this means as soon as you mouse-over or target a specific named boss. BigWigs provides two main methods of notification: messages sent to the center of your screen, and a series of timer bars to indicate a timed event. Figure 7-15 shows the BigWigs bar test along with a warning in the center of the screen.

FIGURE 7-15: Running BigWigs tests.

You can configure a few options, such as the colors of messages or the size and location of the timer bars. All options can be found by right-clicking the minimap icon that BigWigs places.

BigWigs is updated quickly because of the large number of people working on the individual boss fights. Users like you and me can submit transcripts of boss fights for the experts to scour and use to create new boss mods. This allows the addon to stay on the cutting edge of boss encounters, even if the mods can be somewhat buggy for new fights while the kinks are worked out.

Whispercast

Addon created by Valconeye

CURSE-GAMING   WOWINTERFACE

Whispercast is a simple mod that serves a simple need, but it provides immense utility to the user. Any class that is capable of casting spells on another player (such as Arcane Brilliance or Mark of the Wild) or curing an ailment (Abolish Poison, Remove Curse) will find Whispercast useful. Simply put, when someone whispers you a keyword for a spell, the spell is added to a queue and displayed (see Figure 7-16). Anytime out of combat, you can click the Whispercast button (or use a key binding) to cast the requested spell on whoever asked for it. You no longer have to remember to rebuff your party or wonder who asked for what spell because it will always be displayed in a simple window.

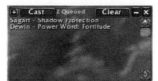

FIGURE 7-16: The Whispercast window.

Who Gets the Loot?

The goal of most raids is to march into dungeon *<mystical name here>*, find the evil beast *<some evil character>*, and kill it, claiming your *<item of doom>*. Unfortunately for all of us, most raid targets drop a finite number of items per kill, meaning someone, somewhere down the line needs to decide who should get what items. Many guilds solve this issue by just using the in-game loot system (rolling need or greed on any items above a certain threshold), but others use complex mathematical systems to determine loot order. The addons in this section try to make those systems a bit less complicated, or at least display the current status in-game.

Suicide Kings

Addon created by Joehunk

CURSE-GAMING

Suicide Kings is a unique system that takes a straightforward approach to loot ordering, attempting to make a friendlier atmosphere for loot competition. Essentially an ordered list is kept of the players in the guild, and the person at the top of the list gets first choice of whatever piece of loot he would like to have. This means when a new item drops, the process starts at the top of the list, and the first person who wants the item "commits suicide" and drops to the bottom of the list of players currently in the raid. As a result, a natural rotation of guild members is established, and the more often a player raids, the more often he can get loot.

Note The system is simple, but still rather complex. You can get more information about the loot system by visiting the official forums at `http://blackcompanywow.com`.

EPGP (Effort Points, Gear Points)

Addon created by disht

CURSE-GAMING

EPGP is a combination of older systems under a new name. Effort Points are rewarded for any number of things including potion making, herb collection, being present for a learning attempt on a new boss, or killing a boss that's already on farm status. Gear Points are accumulated with each item the individual is rewarded. Both Effort Points and Gear Points decay over time, which helps to prevent point hoarding and solve a number of other issues.

The loot priority is defined by (Effort Points) / (Gear Points). If a member has a large number of Effort Points compared to his Gear Points, he gets the opportunity to choose the next item he would like to loot. Members who take upgrades quickly, and then continue to accumulate points rise in the priority by having their Gear Points decay while the loot order continues. EPGP involves a lot of math, but as the user, you don't need to do any of it — it's all presented in-game.

EPGP uses an in-game addon to track and display all loot order information. As a matter of fact, it uses the guild and officer notes within your guild to store the point information, so you won't be able to store any notes there, but that's a minor price to pay for having a completely in-game system.

Note   You can find more information about EPGP at the Google Code hosted page, at `http://code.google.com/p/epgp`.

WebDKP

CURSE-GAMING   WORLDOFWAR

In the days of Everquest, a loot system called Dragon Kill Points (DKP) was designed. This system rewards members who help kill a dragon (or major boss) and assign a certain point cost to each item. WebDKP is a hosted DKP service that provides both a web-based system for controlling and displaying points, and an in-game addon that helps track point changes. The system is relatively straightforward and the resulting status pages can be placed within your own guild pages for easy display.

The in-game addon provides a simple way to award points and loot. This information is saved under your game directory, and the log can be uploaded using WebDKP's software directly to its website. More of a traditional DKP system, WebDKP offers several utilities for a guild that wants to use an established system, without needing to create an elaborate hosted web system.

Note   You can find more information about the WebDKP system at its website, `http://webdkp.com`.

Exploring Individual Roles

This chapter gave you a look at the addons that are available to help you better organize raids and develop and communicate strategies. In the next chapter, you explore several class-specific addons that serve the specific needs of classes.

Class-Specific Addons

Y ou've been introduced to several addons that are useful for a large
number of classes, but when it comes down to it, each class has
some very special needs. This chapter explores a number of addons
that are built for specific classes and play to the specific needs of those
players.

Warriors

As a warrior in World of Warcraft, your job is simple: Protect your party
members while helping them kill your enemy. Between rapidly changing
stances, moving equipment around, and managing your many cooldowns,
you have a difficult job. These addons try to give you enough information
to always be prepared in combat.

Satrina's CombatMonitor (CombatMonitor-PL)

Addon created by Satrina, maintained by shaten

CURSE-GAMING   WOWINTERFACE

CombatMonitor affords every warrior the opportunity to crunch numbers to increase their effectiveness. This addon provides a breakdown of all
the physical and elemental damage your character suffers, enabling you to
decide what equipment he or she should wear during the next encounter
with that type of mob. Understanding that a boss only puts out Fire-based
damage means you can skimp on your armor for more fire resistance, or
knowing that a boss only hits using physical attacks means you can plan
accordingly. This addon doesn't give you any hints or directives; it just
makes the information available in a very nice format so that you don't
need to parse your combat log after every single fight. CombatMonitor
provides a small window that displays your incoming DPS rate, and
another window that counts the overall incoming damage you've taken.
You can click the overall damage window to display the advanced view
(see Figure 8-1) and show detailed statistics.

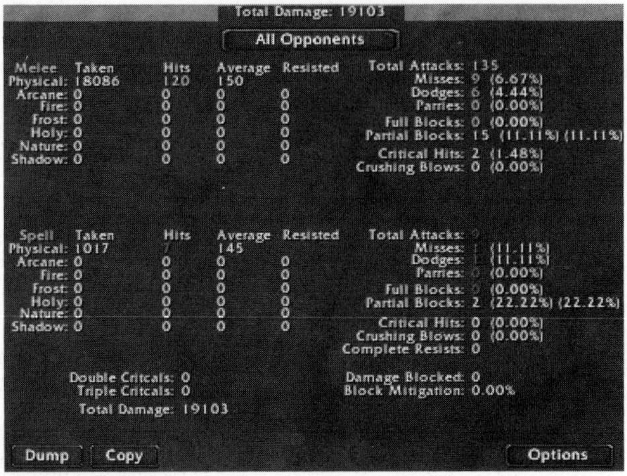

FIGURE 8-1: CombatMonitor's output frame.

Cirk's Ammocheck

Addon created by Cirk, maintained by Dridzt

WOWINTERFACE

As a warrior, the only way you can pull a mob from a distance is to have some other class help (you may not always find someone willing to help) or use your ranged weapon (bow, gun, and so on). Because you're not a hunter, you don't rely on ammo all the time and it's easy to forget that you've run out. Cirk's Ammocheck is a simple addon that notifies you (see Figure 8-2) anytime you're talking to a vendor or a flight master that your ammo has fallen below a predefined level. Ammocheck disables itself if you don't have a ranged weapon equipped or if you're playing a class that can't use ranged weapons. Ammocheck's messages are displayed in the center of your screen, so they're easy to see.

FIGURE 8-2: Ammocheck's warning message.

RedRange

Addon created by Iriel

WOWINTERFACE

The RedRange addon is extremely useful for anyone, but I'm putting it under Warriors because of the large number of abilities they have to be able to recognize at a glance. RedRange simply puts a red shade over any buttons that you can't use because you're too close or too far away from your target, and puts a blue shade on any buttons that you don't have enough rage to use. The default UI only changes the key binding to be red; this addon expands on that, making it clearly obvious which skills are currently usable — short, simple, and very effective.

WatchCombat

Addon created by Iriel

WOWINTERFACE

Another simple addon by Iriel, WatchCombat, notifies you when a party member has aggroed an enemy NPC (see Figure 8-3). If you're trying to sneak around some mobs, this is a nice way to check whether you need to fall back and help one of your squishy casters. While not useful all the time, it's nice to be notified when it does happen, so you can ride to the rescue!

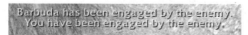

FIGURE 8-3: WatchCombat notifies you when someone in your party enters combat.

WatchCombat also lets you know when you're in the clear, as shown in Figure 8-4.

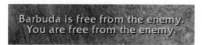

FIGURE 8-4: WatchCombat informs you when you and your party members leave combat.

StanceSets v3

Addon created by CapnBry, maintained by Tageshi

CURSE-GAMING   WOWINTERFACE

StanceSets enables you to preconfigure weapon sets (see Figure 8-5) based on stance or other conditions, and provides an easy way to cycle between these combinations (up to three per stance). Open the configuration GUI by typing /stancesets, and then simply drag the weapon combinations to the window under the correct stance.

Stancesets provides a slash command to cycle between sets (/stancesets next), and key bindings (see Figure 8-6) to change weapons. Optionally, you can use it to change weapons automatically when you change stances.

StanceSets 3
Default
Equip first on activate
Battle Stance
Equip first on activate
Defensive Stance
Equip first on activate
Alternative Sets 2
Alternative Sets 3
Close

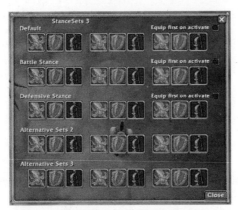

FIGURE 8-5: StanceSets configuration panel.

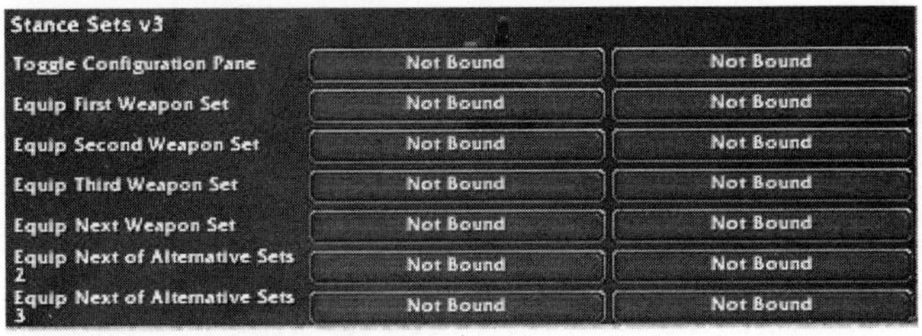

Stance Sets v3
Toggle Configuration Pane
Not Bound
Not Bound
Equip First Weapon Set
Not Bound
Not Bound
Equip Second Weapon Set
Not Bound
Not Bound
Equip Third Weapon Set
Not Bound
Not Bound
Equip Next Weapon Set
Not Bound
Not Bound
Equip Next of Alternative Sets 2
Not Bound
Not Bound
Equip Next of Alternative Sets 3
Not Bound
Not Bound

FIGURE 8-6: Key bindings for StanceSets.

Priests

"What do you mean you can't heal me while a big monster is stomping on your face?"

As a priest, you tend to be held responsible for your party's livelihood and are often the first one blamed when something goes wrong. Following is a collection of addons that work to protect you and make your healing job a bit easier.

ShadowOff

Addon created by romeocat

WOWINTERFACE

If you're a priest who dabbles into a bit of the shadow magic, you might have run into situations where you'd like to cast a holy spell, but forget to shift out of shadow form. The

ShadowOff addon helps to solve that problem by canceling your shadow form buff anytime you cast a spell that cannot be cast in shadow form. (If you have Scrolling Combat Text installed, it will show the shadow form buff being cancelled.)

SacredBuff

Addon created by Damon (jje), maintained by Eternally777

`WOWINTERFACE`   `CURSE-GAMING`

SacredBuff is the first of a series of "circle" or "sphere" addons being covered. Each of these addons takes a class's skills, and puts them around a small circle (see Figure 8-7). SacredBuff tries to make a priest's job easier by putting buff spells in a single, easy-to-use place. The center of the circle displays how many Sacred Candles you have in your inventory, and the addon can be configured to show your health and mana on the outside of the circle.

FIGURE 8-7: SacredBuff's circle.

You can click on the main circle to toggle between group buff and single buff mode. Right-clicking on a buff always casts the spell on you, whereas left-clicking casts it on your target. Right-clicking in the main circle activates your hearthstone. You can configure SacredBuff with the /sb command.

ShackleWatch

Addon created by mubari

`WOWINTERFACE`

ShackleWatch enables a priest to keep track of the undead unit he or she has shackled and be given an estimate of when the spell will wear off (see Figure 8-8). When you shackle an undead mob, a status bar appears over your target frame (the bar can be moved) counting down the spell's duration.

FIGURE 8-8: ShackleWatch counting down.

You can also use ShackleWatch to announce to your party (or raid, or guild) when you are casting the spell. Figure 8-9 shows such an announcement.

FIGURE 8-9: ShackleWatch announcements.

Open the configuration panel (see Figure 8-10) by typing /shw.

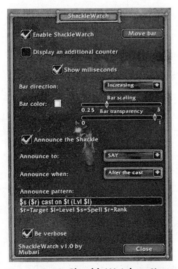

FIGURE 8-10: ShackleWatch options.

MendWatch

Addon created by Polima

WOWINTERFACE

At level 68, priests learn a new spell called Prayer of Mending. Using this ability places a spell on the target that heals them for 800 the next time they take damage. When the heal occurs, Prayer of Mending jumps to a raid member within 20 yards. It jumps up to five times and lasts 30 seconds after each jump. The spell can be placed on only one target at a time.

Once you've cast the spell it can be difficult to track where it is, how many charges are active, and how much it has healed for. The MendWatch addon displays several bars counting the spell down, and showing where it currently is. Figure 8-11 shows a Prayer of Mending in its travels. The first bar shows the buff has expired, the second shows that it was previously on Sai, but it healed for 992 and jumped (the bar is fading out). The third bar shows another heal, which has jumped to Nadialya.

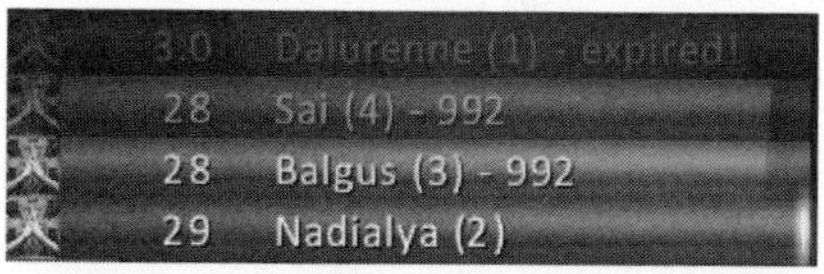

	3.0	Dalurenne (1) - expired!
	28	Sai (4) - 992
	28	Balgus (3) - 992
	29	Nadialya (2)

FIGURE 8-11: MendWatch showing a Prayer of Mending hopping around.

This addon doesn't have many configuration options, but you can access all options with the /mw or /mendwatch commands.

Druids

Druids, being a mix between warriors, priests, and rogues, can use many of the same addons. Still, there are some very specific druid addons that many consider indispensable when playing these shape-shifters. Three of them are described in the following sections.

Druid Bar

Addon by Saeris, SkaDemon

WOWINTERFACE   CURSE-GAMING

Have you ever been in cat form, but wondered how much mana you have? Maybe you're taking some time off to regen mana, and need to know when it's safe to pop back into caster form. Druid Bar gives you a small draggable frame (see Figure 8-12) that estimates the amount of mana you have at any given moment, so you can make intelligent decisions regarding your gameplay. When you are in cat form, the game only sees you as having energy, so this information isn't available directly from the game. The Druid Bar addon makes an educated guess by noting how much mana you gain each "tick" as well as your mana regen statistics in the game.

FIGURE 8-12: Druid Bar showing mana in bear form.

ShapeBind

Addon by JWoose

ShapeBind is designed to make shape-shifting a bit less painful by enabling you to do some simple two-press spellcasts. You can bind a key to each type of shape-shift, as well as define what happens when you press the key a second time. You can cast Enrage or Feral Charge after shifting into bear form, or cast Prowl on your second press in cat form, for example.

Open the configuration panel (see Figure 8-13) by running the /shapebind slash-command. Here you can set the preferences of your shapebind keys. Click the Bindings button to set the key bindings.

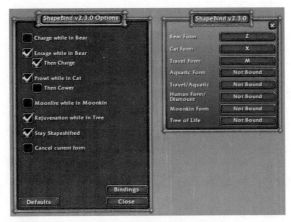

FIGURE 8-13: ShapeBind's configuration panel.

HotCandy

Addon created by Nevcariel

`WOWINTERFACE`

As a druid, you have many heal-over-time spells at your disposal. Keeping track of what you've already cast and how long each spell has left on it can be a difficult task. HotCandy is a simple addon that adds a countdown bar for each heal-over-time you cast, showing who you've cast on, and how long the spell will last (see Figure 8-14). HotCandy doesn't have many configuration options, but you can display the bar anchor (which enables you to move the bars) by using the /hotcandy anchor command.

FIGURE 8-14: HotCandy tracking heals over time.

Shaman

Totems, totems, totems! Shaman have quite a bit to pay attention to, including casting spell interrupts, dropping buffing totems, and keeping people healed while dealing damage. The following addons all try to make your totem hugger a bit easier to play.

Chaman (TotemManager)

Addon created by Lhooq

`CURSE-GAMING`

Chaman is a spectacular little shaman addon that not only provides totem timers, but also gives you pop-up bars (one for each element) to easily drop new totems. When you install this addon, you'll see a series of buttons in four different rows on your screen. Each row represents one of your four elements. Once you've selected a totem, a timer displays showing long until that totem expires, and how many people in your party are receiving the buff (if it's a buff totem). All but the selected box disappear, cleaning up your UI.

You're left with four buttons, each with a timer (see Figure 8-15). You can click these buttons to recast the totem, or right-click the button to reopen the selection menu. From this selection menu, you can right-click to select a new totem for your main slot, or left-click to cast that totem and select it. Chaman has several options available with the slash-command /chaman. Download this mod as soon as possible — you won't be disappointed, and you'll save a ton of space on your action bars.

FIGURE 8-15: Chaman's totem timers and selection buttons.

Totemus

Addon created by Poolpy

Totemus is yet another "sphere" mod that tries to put a bunch of functionality in a single little circle (see Figure 8-16) somewhere in your UI. Continuing with the separation of your elemental totems, there's a button for each of your elements that can be left-clicked to cast, or right-clicked to select a new totem. You also have a button to drink or eat, a button to use your mount, and a bunch of customizable buttons.

FIGURE 8-16: Totemus at work.

You can open the configuration GUI with the slash-command /totemus. This addon puts your mount, your hearthstone, your totems, and many other spells that you only use periodically in one place, freeing up your hotbars.

Paladins

Paladins belong to the brotherhood of the bubble, are the masters of the holy, and have one of the highest maintenance buffing jobs in the entire game. Healing with a paladin is similar to other healers, but Tank-a-dins (tanking paladins) and Ret-a-dins (DPS paladins) need entirely different sets of tools for their jobs.

PallyPower

Addon created by Aznamir

`CURSE-GAMING`   `WOWINTERFACE`

Coordinating paladin blessings in a group/raid environment is often a nightmare, and PallyPower tries to make that easier for everyone involved. It offers a buff assignment config screen (see Figure 8-17) that displays all paladins using the addon, and enables you to assign buffs to each individual. A series of buttons is displayed when you are in a group or raid that tells you how long is left on each type of buff, and how many people in your group need your assigned buff.

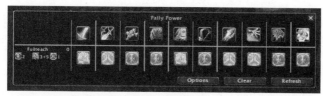

FIGURE 8-17: PallyPower configuration UI.

HolyHope

Addon created by Bonkler, maintained by Battochon

`CURSE-GAMING`   `WORLDOFWAR`

Because everyone knows about paladins and their bubbles, it makes sense to introduce the paladin version of the "sphere" addon — HolyHope. HolyHope actually comes with two separate spheres. One is the usual health, mana, hearthstone, and other common spells (see Figure 8-18).

FIGURE 8-18: HolyHope's main sphere.

The other sphere's main button is used to cast Judgement, and the outer rim of the circle has each of your seals (see Figure 8-19). This is a nice way to clean up a cluttered UI, and have all your spells still readily accessible.

FIGURE 8-19: A secondary sphere showing your seals, and Judgement.

Mages

Master of the elements, able to freeze targets and blast them with fire, all while falling with grace from incredible heights — mages can be a lot of fun to play, but with so many different manners of snaring, crowd control, and self buffing, there are many addons that any mage would find helpful.

Cryolysis

Addon created by Kaeldra, maintained by Paene

CURSE-GAMING

You can set up your mage's Cryolysis sphere (see Figure 8-20) to show a ton of information, but more importantly it helps consolidate a number of buttons into a single location. You can eat, drink, cast Evocation, Mount, open a portal, teleport, and conjure mana gems. If you click the food or water buttons while having someone else targeted, it makes the highest level of food or water that that player can eat or drink.

FIGURE 8-20: Cryolysis's sphere.

Cryolysis also provides an interesting timer frame (see Figure 8-21) for spells that have cooldowns, or those that have an effect on the target. This can be handy for both fire and frost mages.

FIGURE **8-21:** Spell timers and cooldowns.

Lukewarm MageTimers

Addon created by Widgetick

Keeping track of all of your cooldowns can be somewhat challenging, and Lukewarm is a system that displays them in a single frame (see Figure 8-22) that is draggable and resizable. Lukewarm MageTimers is an addon designed specifically to track a mage's cooldowns. When loading the mod for the first time, you will find a blank frame that you can drag and resize. MageTimers doesn't try to do a lot — it just does one thing very well.

FIGURE **8-22:** Lukewarm's cooldown timers.

Rogues

Rogues have many abilities with long cooldowns, along with the need to poison their weapons, manage different skills when stealthed versus unstealthed, and keep tabs on energy regain. Most of these addons won't give you any advantages in combat, but will help you make better decisions through the course of gameplay.

Atropine

Addon created by haste

Atropine provides an easy way to purchase materials for poisons, and even "refill" materials next time you visit a reagent vendor, or shady dealer. The Atropine window (see Figure 8-23) will appear whenever you are at a vendor who sells poison materials, and you can select the number of each poison to keep stocked.

FIGURE 8-23: Atropine's poison window.

WeaponRebuff (Redux2)

Addon maintained by VincentSDSH

CURSE-GAMING   WORLDOFWAR   WOWINTERFACE

Applying poisons to your weapons can be annoying — you have to open your bags, find the poison, right-click it to use it, and then open your character window to apply it to your weapon. WeaponRebuff shows you two icons — one for each of your weapons — and lists the poison currently applied to the right of the icon (see Figure 8-24). You can right-click either of these icons to select a poison to apply, and it is automatically cast on that weapon.

FIGURE 8-24: WeaponRebuff's poison window.

kEnergy

Addon created by Kergoth

WOWINTERFACE

Unlike mana regeneration or rage gain, energy is a constant cycle, gaining 20 every few seconds, typically referred to as a *tick*. Having a way to visualize energy gain can make it easier to plan an attack strategy. kEnergy displays a small bar that shows a count until the next energy tick (Figure 8-25). Right-click on the bar to open the configuration menu, from which you can change several options, such as font size, bar texture, and color.

FIGURE 8-25: kEnergy bar displaying combat points and energy.

ErrorMonster

Addon created by Rabbit

CURSE-GAMING	WOWINTERFACE	WORLDOFWAR

ErrorMonster was originally based on a mod called RogueSpam, which worked to disable the text error messages in the center of the screen ("Not Enough Energy," for example). A rogue tends to spend a lot of time spamming a single button, waiting for the next energy tick. Each time the player clicks one of these buttons and doesn't have enough energy, a red error message displays in the center of the screen. This addon comes with a large number of filters to disable these basic combat spam messages, and doesn't require any configuration.

Warlocks

The two main challenges for Warlocks are their sheer number of abilities and their dependence on damage over time spells. Pet control can take a back seat when it comes to addons because the macro system provides much of the necessary flexibility. Most of the addons in this section, therefore, are designed either to condense abilities into a few buttons or to provide feedback on your various DoTs and other spells.

Necrosis LdC

Original Necrosis created by dudedigital, updated and maintained by Lomig

CURSE-GAMING	WOWINTERFACE	WORLDOFWAR

The ancestor of all the "circle" or "osis" addons, Necrosis provides compact access to nearly all of a Warlock's offerings and helps manage your soul shards, demons, stones, and DoTs. The central button activates Life Tap by default and displays a count of your soul shards (see Figure 8-26). The Healthstone button provides one-click trading of Healthstones with your target. Other buttons in the default layout include the other types of stones; demon, curse, and general spell menus; and a button to summon your steed.

In addition to its capability management, Necrosis has a few other goodies: a Spell Durations window that shows you how much time is left on your DoTs and what mobs they're applied to; cooldown progress bars for your various combat spells; and even options for having your character say random things when you summon demons, mount, or cast certain spells. It will also ask for help from party members when you begin the Ritual of Summoning.

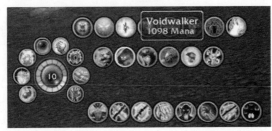

FIGURE 8-26: Necrosis with summoning message and buttons expanded.

InstaBolt

Addon created by Photonic

`CURSE-GAMING`   `WOWINTERFACE`   `WORLDOFWAR`

The InstaBolt addon may seem to be simple and single-minded, but the job it does is invaluable to Affliction of Destruction Locks. When the Nightfall or Backlash talents are triggered, this addon makes the notification more obvious. It has options to play a sound as well as to display a full-screen glow effect of a configurable color when the specified ability is ready.

ShardTracker/ShardAce

ShardTracker Classic

Addon created by Kithador, updated by Cragganmore, maintained by Indus

`CURSE-GAMING`   `WOWINTERFACE`

ShardAce

Addon created by Norque

`WOWINTERFACE`

ShardTracker and ShardAce (an Aced version of the former) share a good deal of functionality with Necrosis, except for Necrosis' Spell Durations. Instead of their own UIs, however, these addons' buttons encircle the minimap (see Figure 8-27). Some of the buttons are multipurpose; the shard count button, for instance, summons your mount on left-click, casts your highest armor spell on right-click, opens the configuration screen on Shift+left-click, and shows the demon menu when you hover.

FIGURE 8-27: Shard Tracker (left) and ShardAce (right).

Note

There may be some slight differences between ShardTracker and ShardAce; be sure to read their documentation. Both addons are designed to serve the same general purpose.

ShardTracker requests help from your party when summoning and provides audible and visual feedback to remind you when your Soulstone's cooldown is up. For other classes, it provides a Healthstone button when you have one in your inventory.

Grimoire Keeper

Addon created by Ayradyss

    CURSE-GAMING   WOWINTERFACE   WORLDOFWAR

Every Warlock past level 10 knows this pain: You go to your trainer, learn all your new skills, and then it's time for the grimoires. Unfortunately WoW provides no way for you to know which skills your pets already know without summoning them. That is, of course, unless you keep track of them yourself, which is exactly what Grimoire Keeper does. When you summon a demon, it goes through its spell book and makes note of what you've taught it so far. The next time you visit a grimoire vendor, it highlights in green any book you've already purchased and used, so you know exactly which ones you should buy. Figure 8-28 shows a page from a spell book.

FIGURE 8-28: Grimoire Keeper's window.

Hunters

Hunters are capable of doing large amounts of damage from a distance, as long as they can multi-task. Their pets have skills that can be used to assist during combat, but finding and training the pets can be a difficult business. Hunters are capable of laying a number of traps but they take time to arm, and have varying cooldowns. The following addons can make a hunter's life a bit easier.

Fizzwidget's Hunter Helper

Addon created by Gazmik Fizzwidget

Once you've learned how to tame pets with your hunter, it will be useful to know what skills you can learn from a given pet. Fizzwidget's Hunter Helper provides a simple way to get that information, by adding it to the tooltip when you mouse-over a tameable beast in the world. If you are looking for a specific skill, you can use the /huntershelper slash command with the name of the spell you'd like to find (for example, "Bite 6"). The addon will display a list of beasts that can teach the specified skill, sorted by the zone that is closest to your current location.

FIGURE 8-29: Hunter Helper's tooltip.

Note Check out Gazmik Fizzwidget's Superior Gadget & Doodad Emporium for a whole bunch of useful addons by the same author. The web address is http://fizzwidget.com.

Venantes

Addon created by Zirah

Venantes is the hunter edition of Necrosis/Serenity/etc. Many of the same options apply because these addons share a number of similar components. Having a single place to keep track of your aspects, traps, and other miscellaneous tasks helps you free up space on your action bar. You can customize the behavior of almost every button on the sphere (see Figure 8-30), giving you a nice place to tuck those buttons you don't use very often, but still need to have available.

FIGURE 8-30: Venantes sphere buttons.

Every class in World of Warcraft has a unique set of skills and abilities that makes playing that class a challenge. While each class can be played using the default user interface, this chapter has shown you a number of addons that can help you stay organized as you play.

Addon Compilations

Not everyone has the time or the desire to sort through the thousands of addons out there to find the few they want to use. In fact, maybe that's one of the reasons you got this book in the first place. The process of installing and configuring addons one by one isn't everyone's favorite activity either; and that's where compilations come in.

Addon compilations are pretty much exactly what they sound like: multiple addons that are packaged together. Someone else is doing the legwork of picking and choosing for you, although you still have to pick and choose among the compilations. There are basically three kinds:

- **Compilations of many individually authored addons:** The major-ity of compilations contain a variety of addons written by other people. These collections are a double-edged sword for you; on one hand you're getting a whole bunch of addons all at once without the trouble of handpicking them yourself, but on the other hand, the collection and the addons it contains are only as good as the person who put it together, and it's much easier to put together a collection of addons than it is to write one. Even so, these packs are a good way to sample many addons at once. An example of this type of pack is Mirage UI.

- **Team- or author-centered compilations:** Some compilations contain components that are wholly created by a single author or a team of people. In this case, all the addons in the package are designed to work together, generally affecting the interface as a whole. The benefit to these packs is consistency; everything is designed from the start as a whole, so there's no need for added glue to hold every-thing together and everything is generally less jumbled. An example of this type of compilation is CTMod.

- **Aesthetic compilations:** A large percentage of compilations aim to change the "look" of the interface completely. Instead of the compiler simply choosing his or her favorite addons, these packs aim to improve upon Blizzard's default "look and feel" (and let's face it, there's plenty to improve upon) by changing the layout of the screen, hiding and reorganizing redundant information, and using custom textures to design and unify the theme. These packs generally utilize multiple addons written by other authors to create a singular experience. An example is PhotekUI.

Many addon compilations combine aspects from several of these categories. This chapter covers a few of the more noteworthy compilations and interfaces. Be warned, though, that the learning curve can be high. When you install one new addon, there's a limited amount of new information to process: one or two new windows, a handful of slash commands, and some new functionality. A compilation is a whole different story. Cosmos, for example, contains over 70 addons, in addition to an addon manager, a self-patcher, and an in-game configuration system. Even the simplest compilations are more complicated than single addons; and the more pieces there are, the more likely it is that something will go wrong.

Note Some compilations include addons that may be out of date. When you install a new compilation, it's probably a good idea to see whether any of the addons are flagged as "Out of Date" and ensure that you check the "Load out of date addons" checkbox if necessary.

Replacing Game Fonts

Some addon compilations change the default fonts by including a `Fonts` directory that sits in the root WoW folder and contains one or more carefully named font files. Because the client looks for the files it needs in that folder first, before looking in the game's compressed archives, these font files are used instead of the built-in ones as long as they have the same name. You can experiment with substituting in your own TrueType fonts. The following are the names of the four built-in fonts that you need to use:

- `arialn.ttf`: Arial Narrow is used for input fields and chat boxes.
- `frizqt__.ttf`: Friz Quadrata is the general interface font, used everywhere.
- `morpheus.ttf`: Morpheus is used for handwritten messages and mail.
- `skurri.ttf`: Skurri is used for the large damage/healing numbers on unit frames.

Cosmos: Addon Control and Auto-Updates

Compilation created and maintained by the Cosmos UI Team

Cosmos was one of the first addon compilations on the scene and is still one of the most well known packages. It consists of some of the best addons currently available, all glued together with a system called Khaos, which provides a centralized means of configuration. Furthermore, Cosmos can keep itself up to date with a patcher and addon management program. Cosmos is an extremely large compilation if the default selection of addons is used.

Cosmos falls somewhere in between an author-centric compilation and an assortment of mods by many authors. It's a suite of addons, which all use a single configuration GUI that has one project lead. It's kind of an odd case in that most of the addons are Khaos driven and all written by the same team, but they also include addons that other people have written.

Cosmos may appeal to you if you don't want to wade through thousands of addons one by one and would rather jump right into deep water. It's a great way of testing out a ton of new features without worrying about whether any of them are going to conflict with each other. Also, while Khaos may be confusing at first, having so many settings in the same place is a convenience. On the whole, Cosmos can be somewhat overwhelming.

On the Web Cosmos is large, and there's a lot to learn about it — much more than can be covered in this book. If you need more information, the best place to start looking is the Cosmos FAQ at www .wowwiki.com/Cosmos_FAQ.

Downloading and Installing Cosmos

Download Cosmos from www.cosmosui.org, the official website (which is also a great place to find documentation and discussion regarding the project). You can download several different packages, but to start off you should get the patcher application for your operating system. Some manual distribution packages are also available that you can install just like any other addon, but they won't update themselves.

If you're using Windows, the ZIP file you download will contain a file called Cosmos.exe. On a Mac, it'll be called Cosmos.app. You can extract this file anywhere, although a good place to keep it is in the root folder of your WoW directory. If you use this program to run the game instead of the default WoW shortcuts, your Cosmos files will always be kept up to date. When you first run the Cosmos application, you are presented with the screen shown in Figure 9-1.

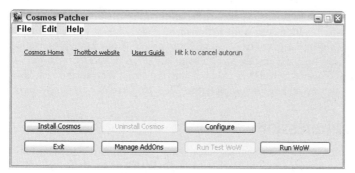

FIGURE 9-1: The main Cosmos window.

By default, Cosmos is configured to provide you with the latest full release of the compilation; however, other packages are available. Click the Configure button to select the distribution you want. For most users, the Complete distribution is the best choice, because it contains everything. There are additional packages for beginners or developers. Click the Install Cosmos button to start the installation. After you select your WoW folder and run through a few progress bars, the window shown in Figure 9-2 appears.

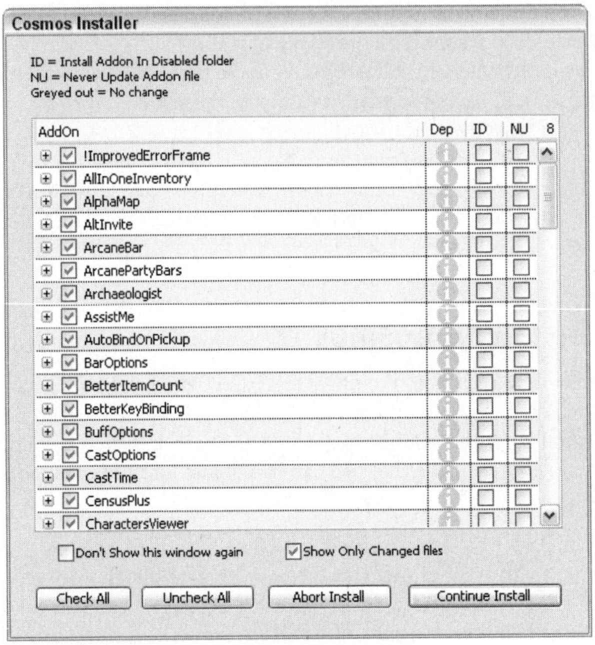

FIGURE 9-2: The Cosmos Installer window.

If you want the full Cosmos package, just click the Continue Install button. Otherwise, you can pick and choose which addons you want to download and enable. If you're new to Cosmos, leave everything alone for now and continue on with the install. A few more progress bars (as the Cosmos addons download and install) and an installation report and you're done. You'll notice that the Install Cosmos button has now become the Patch Cosmos button. Use this button whenever you want to check for new updates. Click Run WoW to start the game.

Cosmos First Impressions

When you first enter the game after installing Cosmos, you'll be presented with a small dialog box asking you to select a configuration (see Figure 9-3). At this point, there are only two configurations to choose from: Empty or Initial. The Empty configuration turns off as much as possible, while the Initial setting has a number of features turned on by default. You should probably stick with the Initial configuration. You should also select the checkbox shown in Figure 9-3; otherwise you'll be presented with this dialog box each time you enter the world. Doing so ties the selected configuration profile to your current character. Finally, click the Use button.

FIGURE 9-3: This small dialog box pops up when you enter the world after installing Cosmos.

Now that you're in-game, there are a lot of differences and a lot of new little windows. Any compilation takes some getting used to, and Cosmos is certainly no exception. There's a lot to adjust, move around, tweak, and learn. Some of the interface windows you're familiar with will look different now, such as the Key Bindings interface. The trade-off for getting so many addons at once is the overwhelming presence of new, unfamiliar things onscreen. There's no way to cover each of the addons included in Cosmos (the current version has 76 of them), so as far as individual features go, you're on your own. Many of the addons that come with Cosmos are discussed elsewhere in this book.

Using the Earth Feature Menu

The Earth Feature Menu can be opened via one of the new minimap buttons, specifically the one with the little blue C on it (not to be confused with the large yellow C button; that's for your new CensusPlus addon).

The Earth Feature Menu is basically the Cosmos main menu, where many of its major features are listed and accessible (see Figure 9-4). Also, a number of the larger Cosmos addons (such as SCT, AlphaMap, and MobInfo2) can have their own options panels opened from here. Even though the majority of Cosmos settings are centralized, these larger addons are still configured on their own.

FIGURE 9-4: The Earth Feature Menu.

If you look in the upper-left corner of the menu, you'll see the button for Khaos, which opens the configuration panel. You can also open Khaos from WoW's main menu (when you press Escape); there's a new button for it added to the top of the list.

Using Khaos

When you first open Khaos, you'll see a window with two frames: an index on the left and settings on the right. You can select and enable (or disable) various Cosmos addons from the index frame, all of which are grouped by category, and then configure their individual options on the right. There's enough here to configure to keep you busy for hours.

If you'd like to take things up a notch, change the User Skill setting from Beginner to Average (or higher) using the drop-down menu above the index frame. Immediately, a third frame will appear on the left side of the window; this is the profiles frame (see Figure 9-5) from which you can manage various profiles of Khaos settings (so each of your characters can have different settings, for example). Raising the User Skill level also changes the number of options that are displayed for each individual addon. Raise the skill level to Master to see every available option.

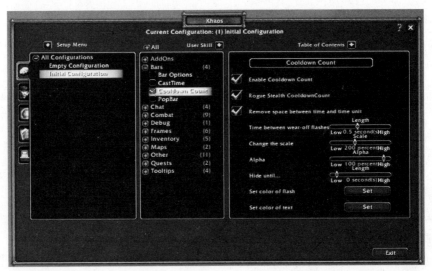

FIGURE 9-5: The Khaos configuration panel.

Note   A good piece of advice regarding Khaos is to pay attention to the mouse-over notes. When you hover your cursor over an addon or even a specific setting, more often than not there's a corresponding note that will appear in blue at the bottom of the window. These notes can help you decipher many of the more obscure settings.

Uninstalling Cosmos

There may come a time when you want to remove Cosmos from your system. Take the following steps to get your WoW installation back to default. Note that the intro cinematic will play the next time you start the game, and that you'll also have to agree to the World of Warcraft Terms of Use again. This is normal.

Caution This process will delete all your video settings, addons, and custom macros, so proceed with caution. If necessary, back up your settings first.

1. Make sure WoW is closed.

2. Browse to your root WoW directory.

3. Delete the `Interface` folder.

4. Delete the `WTF` folder.

5. Delete the Cosmos executable.

6. Delete any text files that have Cosmos in their name.

Note Because it's considerably larger and more complicated, Cosmos shouldn't be treated like any other compilation. Use caution, and, before jumping in headfirst, have its documentation available on hand.

Mirage UI: Tons of Features

Compilation created and maintained by LedMirage

| WORLDOFWAR | CURSE-GAMING | WOWINTERFACE |

The Mirage UI (formerly known as the Insomniax Recompilation), like Cosmos, is a huge collection of addons that's focused primarily on added functionality. Unlike Cosmos, there's no external executable portion of the package, so the completion is installed just like any other addon and must be updated manually. Many of the addons appearing in the Mirage UI have been tweaked to fit in better (the myriad of new minimap icons are already nicely arranged when you first enter the game). Also, useful tooltip notes have been added to many objects. Many of the CTMod addons (see the section on CTMod next) are included in this compilation as well.

At the time of this writing, the Mirage UI contains 108 addons, making it one of the largest popular compilations. Be prepared to spend some quality time configuring your interface and arranging bars and windows after installing this package, because you won't be able to play with the default settings right away. You should install Mirage UI only after clearing out your Interface and WTF folders first.

On the Web   The Mirage UI has its own forum at `http://ledmirage.net/forums/`.

CTMod: Targeted Interface Improvements

CTMod is a suite of addons that have all been created by the same team (for the most part) and are designed to work either side by side or individually. Also, unlike some of the compilations out there, CTMod focuses on adding new features to the game rather than changing the overall appearance or layout of the interface.

This compilation has been around for a long time, and is quite mature. One of the CTMod addons, CT_RaidAssist (CTRA), has become extremely popular and is required by many raiding guilds (the details of this mod are covered in Chapter 7). The core CTMod addons are also found at the heart of a number of other addon packages.

Getting CTMod

The CTMod website is the best place to download the package, and is also a good source of news and information. The address is `www.ctmod.net`.

On the CTMod download page you have the option to download the basic package, an advanced package, or a custom selection of addons. It's a good idea to start with one of the packages and then expand from there. To install the package, simple copy all of the directories from the downloaded ZIP file into your `Interface/AddOns` folder, just like you would with any other addon or compilation.

About the CTMod Addons

The basic CTMod package contains 4 addons while the advanced package contains all 13. Each one is described in Table 9-1.

Table 9-1   CTMod Addons

Addon	Description
CT_Core	Adds several small features and tweaks to the Blizzard UI, for example hp and mana regen per tick, level of quests, and more.
CT_BarMod	Adds 6 customizable hotkey bars and improves the Blizzard hotkey bars.

Table 9-1 *Continued*

Addon	Description
CT_BottomBar	You can break up the game's main menu bar apart to move or hide each piece individually.
CT_BuffMod	Allows a customizable buff display.
CT_ExpenseHistory	Tracks repair costs as well as several other expenses across all of your characters.
CT_MailMod	Adds several mailing options to your mail window and enables sending several items at once.
CT_MapMod	Enables you to add small text notes to the world map.
CT_PartyBuffs	Allows displaying of buffs on the party frames.
CT_RaidAssist	Advanced raiding tool for monitoring the raid's overall status.
CT_RABossMods	Adds the Boss Mods section to CT_RaidAssist.
CT_Timer	Adds a simple timer that can be used both as a stopwatch and as an alarm clock.
CT_UnitFrames	Adds customizable health and mana numbers for yourself, your target, your pet and party.
CT_Viewport	Allows you to shrink the game view, allowing you to fit the UI outside the game area.

CTMod has a central configuration panel that can be opened with the CT button on the mini-map. This panel (see Figure 9-6) can be used to configure all CTMod addons.

FIGURE 9-6: The CTMod configuration panel.

PhotekUI: Form and Function

Compilation created and maintained by photek

CURSE-GAMING

PhotekUI is a more recent UI that's built almost exclusively around the Ace2 library for speed and efficiency. Ace2 is a modular addon development library that aids authors in the creation of addons and also attempts to eliminate the redundancy of commonly used routines. PhotekUI combines both form and function: It includes a number of functional addons (41 in total) and combines them into a pre-designed interface layout (see Figure 9-7) that's vastly different from the default Blizzard look.

 On the Web For more information about Ace2, see www.wowace.com.

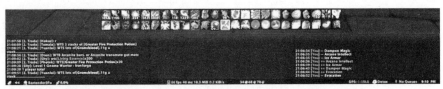

FIGURE 9-7: PhotekUI provides a complete replacement for the default UI.

Follow these instructions to install PhotekUI once you've downloaded it:

1. Remove the Interface and WTF folders from your WoW directory. If you're not worried about losing your settings, you can delete them. Otherwise, you should back them up on your desktop or somewhere else that's safe.

2. Open the file you downloaded and unzip the PhotekUI folder anywhere.

3. Open the PhotekUI folder and copy the WTF, Fonts, and Interface folders into your WoW directory.

4. Open the WTF folder, go into the Account folder, and rename the YOURACCOUNTNAME folder to the actual name of your account.

   Your account name must be written in all capitals.

5. Open the folder you just renamed, and then rename the YourServerName folder to the actual name of your server.

   For example: Jaedenar

6. Once again, open the folder you just renamed, and then rename the `YourCharacterName` folder to the actual name of your character.

For example: `Nine`

7. Once in-game, type `/sct menu` and load the `Photek` profile.

Note To uninstall PhotekUI, simply delete the WTF, Fonts, and Interface folders from your root World of Warcraft directory.

MazzleUI: Stunning Complexity

Compilation created and maintained by Mazzlefizz

`CURSE-GAMING` `WOWINTERFACE`

MazzleUI is a stunning collection of addons tied together by an in-game installer and configuration manager (see Figure 9-8). One of the philosophies behind MazzleUI is that it should be both as efficient and uncluttered as possible. Some of the things that make this compilation stand out are an insane attention to detail, the fact that it actually *works* very well, and the Mazzifier; an in-game wizard-style installer addon. Once configured, the final UI is beautiful (see Figure 9-9).

FIGURE 9-8: The Mazzifier, MazzleUI's in-game installation tool.

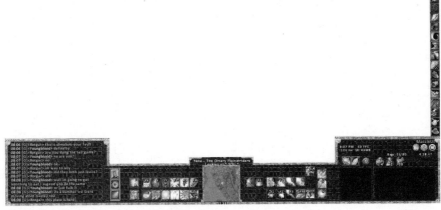

FIGURE 9-9: MazzleUI configured and running.

For downloads and documentation, visit MazzleUI's portal page at WoWInterface:

```
http://mazzlefizz.wowinterface.com/
```

Make sure to read and follow the detailed installation instructions that come with the download. They're clear and concise, and will have you up and running in no time!

Other Compilations

Because pretty much anyone can throw a bunch of addons together and zip them up, there are literally hundreds of other compilations out there, and you should try many of them out for yourself or even create your own. Generally, you should search the addon websites for the term "UI" to locate many of them. Compilations are built around certain classes, libraries, philosophies, and aesthetics.

When it comes to the distribution of user-created compilations, there seems to be slightly less consistency as compared to straight addons. Some compilations have executable installers, some don't. Some include a WTF folder that you need to modify while others only come with addon folders. A few have in-game configuration systems, and many have custom artwork.

Building Your Own UI

Do you like the "look" of some of the custom interfaces you've seen, but think you could do it better yourself? Maybe you don't want to take the time to learn someone else's setup. In any case, you might want to try creating your own UI from scratch. Take a look at the addons in Chapter 4 especially and check the addon sites to see what recent offerings are available. Start with a sketch or mock-up of your idea.

With the right combination of addons, your interface can look like pretty much anything you want. Designing a complete UI is a task that can take anywhere from a few minutes to a few days. It all depends on how much tweaking you want to do and how drastic you want your changes to be.

My Simple UI

These days I'm using a pretty simple custom UI (see Figure 9-10). I don't want anything flashy that will slow down the game. I want WoW to be a cinematic, visual experience, so I don't want my view cluttered up; the interface elements should be separated from the scenery as much as possible. This interface took about an hour to build from start to finish.

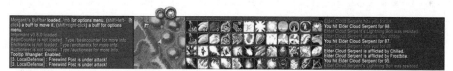

FIGURE 9-10: My custom interface.

Next is a list of the addons I used to create this interface, and a brief description of how I configured them to achieve the desired effect. They're listed in order of installation:

- **Bongos:** This allows precise control over the action bars and other parts of the main bar. I lined up action bars 1 through 4 into a block, placed them at the bottom of the screen and scaled them all to 75 percent. I aligned the XP bar above them and resized it to fit. I also hid the bag bar and main menu bar because I don't need them onscreen; I use hotkeys to open all the necessary windows.

- **simpleMinimap:** This repositions the minimap and allows it to be reshaped. I moved the minimap down next to the action bars, reshaped it into a square, and hid many of its frames, including the location text and zoom buttons, because it can be zoomed with the mouse wheel now. Then I scaled it to be the same height as everything else.

- **ChatMOD:** This allows you to tweak the chat boxes. I removed the chat buttons, enabled mouse scrolling, and repositioned the edit box to the top of the main chat frame. Then, using the built-in controls, I separated the combat log from the general chat window, changed the size of the text, colored the backgrounds, and dragged each frame into position. Finally, I resized them to fit precisely and locked them in place.

- **CT_Viewport:** This changes the area of the screen in which the world is rendered. Because there was now a solid bar of information at the bottom of the screen, I didn't want the world to be rendered behind it, cutting off the terrain and part of my character. I used CT_Viewport to set the bottom of the rendered area to the exact top of the strip.

- **Tooltip Wrangler:** This repositions and re-anchors the tooltip. The tooltip was appearing on top of the combat log, which looked cluttered and made it hard to read. I turned on the Tooltip Wrangler target frame, positioned it in the center of the screen, directly above the bottom strip, and set the anchor to bottom-center. Then I locked it in place.

- **MetaHud:** This replaces the player and target frames with centered curved bars. I didn't want my vision to be focused on the unit frames in the upper-left corner of the screen during fights, so I chose MetaHud for its centralized location, slick graphics, and overall classy presentation. I tweaked the layout (my info on the left, the target's info on the right) and adjusted some of the display options, hiding things I didn't need and changing the font.

- **MobHealth3:** This allows MetaHud to display enemy health numerically.

- **vBagnon:** This consolidates all bags into a single window, which is a feature I can't live without. I changed the layout of the inventory window so it would fit next to the auction house window without overlapping.

- **Morganti's Buffbars:** This modifies how and where buffs are displayed. I wanted my buffs to appear near the bottom of the screen, so I needed an addon that would let me move them around.

That's pretty much it. However, when you're completely rearranging everything like this its important to remember that there are other, invisible frames to take into account, such as the durability frame (movable with simpleMinimap), the dice roll frame (movable with Bongos), and the party frame (in this case, fine where it is by default). As you encounter different in-game situations (rolling for loot, going on a raid, or crafting, for example) you may find that something isn't quite right with your new layout, and further tweaking (or a new addon altogether) is required. Creating a complete UI is an ongoing, fluid process.

Backing Up and Sharing Your UI

Once you have everything the way you want it, make a copy of your Interface and WTF folders and save them in a safe place. This way, if you ever need to, you can get things back to the same state. If something in your active WTF folder gets corrupt and it needs to be reset, you'll end up going back to Blizzard's UI and the backup will come in handy.

If you want to share your interface with other people, you need to give them those two folders (Interface and WTF), but there are a few additional things to keep in mind:

- They should delete their Interface and WTF folders before copying yours into place.

- Your settings are only going to look right at your current screen resolution. If they're using a different resolution, the layout is going to need a lot of reworking.

- Before they can use your settings, they need to go into the new `WTF` folder and rename some directories. The folder directly within the `Account` folder needs to have their account name in capital letters. Inside that, the folder with your server's name needs to be changed to theirs. Finally, inside that, the folder with your character's name needs to be changed to theirs as well.

- If you're distributing a UI for general consumption by the public, trim the `WTF` folder down so it only contains folders for a single character, and rename your specific account, server, and character folders to something generic like `ACCOUNT`, `Server`, and `Character`. Provide typed instructions for setting everything up, and make sure to have your friends test it all out before you upload anything. Finally, you should always contact the authors of any addons you're going to include in a public UI, and ask them for permission to redistribute their work. If they say no, you must respect their wishes.

Summary

In this chapter you learned about the different sorts of addon compilations that are out there, and how to get started using a handful of them, namely Cosmos, Mirage, CTMod, Photek, and Mazzle. You also learned how to manually replace the in-game fonts without using an addon. Finally, you got a brief look into what creating your own UI might involve, and a good sense of which kinds of addons you need at the core.

In the next chapter, you're going to break away from looking at addons that already exist and begin thinking about creating your own!

Advanced Hacks: Creating Your Own Addons

part

Addon Anatomy

Now that you're familiar with a ton of different addons and hopefully have had a chance to play with several of them, it's time to get your hands even dirtier by creating an addon yourself.

This chapter walks you through the steps of building a simple yet functional addon from scratch. The next few chapters are going to be in the form of a tutorial. Don't worry if you've never written a computer program before; we'll go slowly and everything will be explained as it happens. The only thing you'll need is a familiarity with computers (you *do* play WoW after all) and some common sense. Hopefully, by the end of the project you'll have enough experience to take the next steps on your own.

Defining the Pieces of an Addon

Before jumping into the larger project, you will explore the various components that make up a typical addon, and then take a look at the source code of an extremely simple example.

Examining the Folder

By now you're familiar with the fact that each addon has its own folder. In fact, each addon *needs* to live in a separate folder, even if it depends on or communicates with other addons. Some addon projects (such as vBagnon or Auctioneer) are actually comprised of multiple addons, and thus come with multiple folders, one for each module.

The name of each folder is also important because while the WoW client is loading, it searches the folder for a table of contents (TOC) file with the exact same name as the folder itself (plus a `.toc` extension). The name of an addon's folder can be different from the name that the Addon List displays because the latter is defined in the TOC file. (In case you've forgotten since Chapter 1, the Addon List is the listing of currently installed addons that's accessible from the character-select screen.) For example, the ScrollingCombatText addon lives in a folder called `sct`.

Within the folder, an addon usually contains somewhere between two and ten files, with three being a typical number. Some addons come with many more files than this, but there are only a few different *types* of files from which addons are built. Many addons also come with documentation, in the form of text or HTML files.

The Table of Contents (TOC)

The table of contents (TOC) is a file in the root directory of an addon's folder. This file is absolutely necessary and each addon needs to have exactly one. Basically, the TOC contains metadata about the addon, including (but not limited to) its name, the version of the interface it's designed for, its dependencies, and the variables that the game should save between sessions. The TOC also informs the game which additional files need to be loaded for the addon to function. The name of the TOC file depends on the folder name. For example, the Atlas addon lives in a folder called `Atlas` and its TOC is called `Atlas.toc`.

The TOC file has two parts: the header and a list of files. The order of information in the TOC really isn't important, but it's easier to think about it as a two-part deal. Most TOCs are structured like this. The header is where all the metadata goes, and each line of the header is marked with two number symbols (##). For example, pretty much every TOC begins with the line:

```
## Interface: XXXXX
```

The Xs are replaced with a number known as the *interface number* or *TOC number*, which represents the version of the interface that the addon is designed to work with. For example, `11200` was the interface number for the 1.12 patch. Sub-patches such as 1.12.1 don't generally increment the interface number, but every once in a while they do.

Note As of this writing, the current patch level is 2.0.10, but the TOC number is still 20003. All major patches update the interface number, but only some of the sub-patches do. As an addon author, you need to stay on top of every new patch (major or minor) that's released, and update your addon's TOC number accordingly (after making sure everything works, of course).

Technically, metadata is unnecessary for simply loading an addon, although if you don't include the interface number, your addon will be marked as out-of-date in the Addon List and won't load unless out-of-date addons are enabled. Whenever a major patch is released, addon authors must rerelease their addons with an updated interface number (they also need to fix any issues the new patch might have introduced). There are many other TOC metadata codes in addition to the interface number, but they're unimportant for the time being.

As mentioned earlier, the TOC also needs to include a list of the addon's files. The TOC parser assumes that each line that doesn't begin with ## is the name of a file to look for. These additional files comprise the logic and layout of the addon, and are either Lua or XML files. Usually, both types of files are present, although some simple addons contain only one or the other.

Some addons list only their XML files in the TOC. The XML files, in turn, reference the Lua files. Using this method doesn't make a difference in the end, but it does determine the order in which files are loaded. Because listing all your files in the TOC is much more straightforward, that's the method this book will illustrate.

If you're interested in the other method, in which XML files reference Lua files, please see the Scripts section of:

```
http://wowwiki.com/XML_User_Interface
```

You may also want to check out an article that describes the order in which Lua files referenced in this way are loaded:

```
http://wowwiki.com/UI_Code_Load_Order
```

The Logic (Lua)

These files hold the core logic of the addon, which is written in the Lua programming language. Lua is similar to C in many ways, but it's interpreted rather than compiled, so the source code itself is distributed rather than a binary executable. In fact, Lua files (and XML files, too) can be modified and reloaded without exiting the client at all. This means that in many cases you can tweak an addon and test it without even restarting the game. However, if you change the TOC file at all, you must restart.

Note   For more information about the Lua programming language, visit its official website at www.lua.org. The site contains extensive technical documentation.

Typically, instead of running code right away, Lua scripts define several functions (also called subroutines). Functions are blocks of code that can be called at any time to perform specific tasks. Functions are usually called based on events happening in-game. User-interface elements such as buttons, sliders, and typed commands generate many of the events that are relied upon to call functions.

The Layout (XML)

The vast majority of addons have user-interface elements in the form of windows, dialog boxes, options panels, and onscreen text (one notable exception is WeaponQuickSwap because it adds no visible elements to the interface). The easiest way to define the appearance of these elements is to use eXtensible Markup Language (XML).

Note   You're not strictly required to use XML when defining onscreen elements. The WoW API includes several Lua functions for dynamically creating and manipulating interface objects. However, those functions fall outside the scope of this book.

Wikipedia describes XML simply as "a way of describing data." XML is actually a general-purpose markup language that has been customized by Blizzard for the specific purpose of describing World of Warcraft's hierarchical user-interface elements.

Addons typically define the appearance of each window with a separate XML file. Each element in the window is described and relevant events are tied to functions in your Lua file. You can even include snippets of Lua code right in the XML. For example, an XML file called MyAddon.xml could define a button called MyButton that's 60 units wide, 20 units tall, says "Click Me" on it, and calls the function MyButton_OnClick() when the user clicks it. This function would be implemented in a corresponding Lua file called MyAddon.lua.

Note There's a special XML file that any addon can include called `Bindings.xml`. This file is used to define all of an addon's key bindings. You don't have to list it in your TOC file because the client finds it automatically if it exists.

Custom Artwork (TGA or BLP)

Many addons make use of the artwork that's built into the game, but that isn't always sufficient. Some addons come with their own artwork for textures, icons, or maps, even though this greatly adds to their size because images take up a lot more space than text files. The images need to be either Targa (TGA) files or BLP files (a custom Blizzard texture format). While most graphics programs support TGA files natively, only a few tools are available for manipulating BLPs. However, many addons use them anyway because they offer a higher degree of compression and take up less space.

Creating a Simple "Hello, Azeroth!" Addon

Let's take a look at the source code for an extremely simple addon. All it does is pop up a dialog-box greeting when you first enter the game. Go ahead and implement this simple example to get the feel for manipulating an addon's files and seeing them run in-game. Follow these steps to build the addon:

1. Go to your `Interface/AddOns` directory.

2. Create a new folder called `HelloAzeroth` and open it.

3. Open Notepad (or TextEdit if you're on a Mac) and type these four lines:

```
## Interface: 20003
## Title: Hello, Azeroth!
## Notes: The simplest addon ever.
HelloAzeroth.lua
```

Note This book will be slightly out-of-date as soon as Blizzard releases a new patch that changes the TOC number. To find out the current TOC number, go to `http://wdn.wowinterface.com` and look for the most recent "Live Server" release. If the TOC number isn't `20003`, use the new one instead.

4. Save the file as `HelloAzeroth.toc` in the `HelloAzeroth` folder.

5. Create a new text document and type this line:

```
message("Hello, Azeroth!");
```

6. Save this file as `HelloAzeroth.lua` in the same folder.

7. Start WoW and go to the Addon List. Make sure that Hello, Azeroth! is listed. Mouse-over the entry to see its description (see Figure 10-1).

8. Enter the world. The greeting will appear (see Figure 10-2).

FIGURE 10-1: The HelloAzeroth addon in the Addon List.

FIGURE 10-2: A greeting is displayed when you enter the game.

Dissecting the Code

Congratulations, you've just created your first addon! Now let's dissect the four lines of the TOC file even though you might already have a pretty good idea of what they do:

```
## Interface: 20003
```

This tells the client that the addon is designed to work with a specific version of WoW (2.0.3 in this case, or any sub-patches after it that didn't change the TOC number). If there were any other value here, or if this line were missing, the addon would be marked as out-of-date in the Addon List, but would function fine otherwise.

```
## Title: Hello, Azeroth!
```

This defines how the addon's title is displayed in the Addon List. If you didn't include this line, the name of the addon's folder (in this case HelloAzeroth) would be used as the title.

```
## Notes: The simplest addon ever.
```

Similarly, this optional line defines the description that appears in the addon's tooltip.

```
HelloAzeroth.lua
```

This line doesn't begin with ##, which means it's the name of a file to be loaded. When you enter the world, the client looks for this file, finds it, opens it, and executes the single line:

```
message("Hello, Azeroth!");
```

This line is a *call* to the `message()` function, which is a built-in part of the WoW API. The `message()` function knows how to draw a simple dialog box onscreen. It uses the data that's passed to it between the parentheses for its message — in this case, a string of text. Text-data like this (called a *string*) is enclosed in quotes so the Lua interpreter knows to take it literally rather than try and interpret it as part of the programming language.

Also note that a semicolon ends the line. Semicolons aren't required at the end of lines in Lua, but because you'll be working with Blizzard's own code in some places, this book presents code in a similar style. Blizzard's lines end with semicolons; so will yours. You can think of the semi-colon as the programming equivalent of a period at the end of a sentence. In the future you'll encounter certain lines of Lua code that specifically *cannot* end with a semicolon. Pay careful attention to the examples, and you'll get the hang of it.

Introducing Variables

If you're already familiar with variables, skip this section. If you're not, here's a brief introduc-tion. You can think of a *variable* simply as a container for data. The addon you just created didn't use any variables, but it could easily be modified to use one. Consider this code:

```
local myMessage = "Hello, Azeroth!";
message(myMessage);
```

In the first line, a variable called myMessage is created, and a value is assigned to it. Variables in Lua are automatically created the first time they're referenced. Here, the assigned value is a string of text. Then in the second line, the variable is passed to the message() function. Variables are one of the most important concepts in programming. You'll be seeing much more of them in the chapters ahead.

Scope: Local Variables versus Global Variables

You might be wondering about the meaning of the local keyword in the preceding example. For the current purpose, it isn't really necessary because the example would work perfectly without it. However, including it presents an opportunity to talk about the difference between a *local variable* and a *global variable*, as well as the concept of *scope*.

The scope of a variable determines how widely it can be used. Any variable created without the keyword local automatically becomes a global variable. Global variables can be used anywhere, by any part of your addon, or even by other addons. This means you have to be careful when creating a global variable, because it's possible that one with the same name already exists. That would cause a conflict that could easily lead to errors, or even worse, a case in which parts of the interface stop working but no errors appear. This is the hardest kind of problem to debug.

By simply defining myMessage with the keyword local, you turn it into a local variable, effectively reducing its scope. It can now be used only by code inside the Lua file in which it appears. If a local variable is declared inside a function, it can be used only within that func-tion. Now, another addon that creates a global variable called myMessage won't cause a conflict. However, you wouldn't be able to reference it either, because your local myMessage variable takes precedence within its scope. In general, always define variables with the smallest practical scope.

Of course, many addons (most, in fact) need to make use of global variables. Those variables are always named carefully to minimize the risk of potential conflicts. Typically, this involves appending the addon's name to them. For example, the variable Atlas_GlobalVariable is unlikely to be used by any addon besides Atlas.

Starting the Larger Addon Project

Now that you've seen a very basic example, it's time to get started on the real deal. This process involves specifying an addon's features and behavior, and then implementing it all with Lua and XML. Instead of beginning with programming fundamentals, you'll use the addon's source code as a starting point. As you build the addon piece by piece, you should be able to follow along even if you've never programmed anything before. This and the next few chapters divide the development process into manageable chunks.

Designing the Addon

Before you write even one line of code, it's important to lay out exactly what you're going to construct. Even though most addons aren't built this way (it can be a lot of fun to jump right in with a rough idea and see what happens), planning ahead is a great habit to get into, and it makes the programming stage a lot easier when you get to it.

The question is: What's your addon actually going to do?

The Big Picture

By the time you complete the next few chapters, you'll have created an addon that displays your character's current coordinates in a little window onscreen. If you're not already familiar with WoW's coordinate system, check out the beginning of Chapter 3. Basically, coordinates give you a numerical representation of your location within an outdoor zone, enabling you to accurately talk to other players about where things are.

You might be asking, why make a coordinates addon when a bunch of them already exist? Well, there are a couple of reasons. First, this project focuses on the basic aspects of development common to all addons, including creating windows, handling events, displaying information, saving data, and implementing configuration options. A more complicated project would put the focus on the logic itself, something that would be more appropriate for an advanced programmer. The core logic of this addon is simple: Request a piece of information from the client and display it. *How* you display this information is the fun part, which brings me to the second reason: configuration.

There are thousands of ways to display even the simplest piece of data. What most coordinates addons lack is the capability to tweak where their data is displayed. This is the strength of this addon: It can be moved anywhere onscreen.

Furthermore, building a number of display options enables you to explore what's going on under the hood. Various topics can be covered, such as how to create a slash-command system, make a frame moveable, create sliders, and save the user's settings between sessions. This kind of flexibility in an addon is useful; if someone wants to tweak his or her interface to perfection, each element's appearance needs to be fluid.

What's this addon's name? One-word names are perfect for addons because they're easy to remember. "Whereabouts" is simple and accurately describes the addon's purpose.

Specifying the Addon's Features

Now that you have a broad view, it's time to hammer out some concrete specifications. How does the addon behave and what kinds of features should it have? Take a look at the following list of behaviors and options. Notice that programming terms are avoided here; this list is about *what* the addon does, not *how* it's going to be implemented.

- The frame is small and is located in the center of the screen, from where the user can easily move it to a location of his choice.

- The coordinates are displayed in yellow as numbers between 0 and 100, and are separated by a comma.

- The background of the frame is dark and slightly transparent.

- When the coordinates are both zero, the frame displays three dashes.

- The frame is draggable and can be locked in place with a slash-command or a checkbox on the options panel. The frame is clamped, meaning that it can't be dragged off-screen.

- The options panel can be opened by right-clicking on the frame.

- When the mouse is hovering over the frame, a tooltip pops up telling the user what mouse actions are available. The tooltip can be disabled if desired.

- A display of your current coordinates is added to the World Map frame. This feature can also be turned off.

- The options panel is also a clamped, draggable window. All settings update the display of the Whereabouts frame in real time.

- Every setting is available as a slash-command option with `/whereabouts` or `/wa`. Either command by itself prints out a complete list of slash-commands.

Whereabouts' slash-command options are outlined in Table 10-1.

Table 10-1   Whereabouts Slash-Command Options

Option	Description
options	Toggles the options panel
show	Shows the coordinates window
lock	Locks the coordinates window in place
tooltip	Enables the tooltip display
worldmap	Enables coordinates on the World Map
alpha <number>	Sets the transparency of the window

Choosing a Text Editor

Because you'll be doing a lot of typing over the next few chapters, it's important to use a text editor that you're comfortable with. The built-in offerings (Notepad on Windows and TextEdit on Mac) are missing some incredibly useful features when it comes to writing code:

- Because you're dealing with multiple files at once, you'll benefit from an editor that has a tabbed interface, enabling you to rapidly switch between files.

- Syntax highlighting can make your life a lot easier. Lua-specific keywords and formatting are automatically color-coded.

- If you encounter error messages from the client (typos happen), they're always marked with the line that generated the error. Line numbering helps you retrace your steps to the block of code that's causing a problem.

Here are a few free source code editors to consider:

- **Notepad++** (Windows):

  ```
  http://notepad-plus.sourceforge.net
  ```

- **Crimson Editor** (Windows):

  ```
  http://crimsoneditor.com
  ```

- **jEdit** (Windows, Mac, Linux):

  ```
  http://jedit.org
  ```

- **SciTE** (Windows, Linux):

  ```
  http://scintilla.org/SciTE.html
  ```

In addition, Jim Whitehead, the coauthor of this book, maintains a modified release of SciTE called SciTE-WoWInterface. It has the WoW API built in for reference, which means the editor can make suggestions about WoW-specific programming terms while you're coding, reducing the chance of typos and errors. You can find it at:

```
http://wowinterface.com/downloads/info4989-SciTE-
WOWInterface.html
```

Laying the Groundwork for Whereabouts

Now that you're set up with your editor and you know the details of the addon you're writing, it's time for the fun part: making it!

Creating the Folder and Source Files

The first thing Wherabouts needs is a folder to call home. Create a new folder in your `Interface/AddOns` directory called `Whereabouts`. Next, you need to create the source code files for the various parts of the addon: the main window, the options panel, and the World Map addition. You also need to create the TOC file as well as a file in which to store all of the text strings (so they can easily be translated). Create these seven empty text files in the `Whereabouts` folder:

- `Whereabouts.toc`: Contains metadata and a file list
- `Whereabouts.xml`: Defines the layout of the window
- `Whereabouts.lua`: Contains the majority of the logic
- `Whereabouts_Options.xml`: Defines options panel
- `Whereabouts_Options.lua`: Controls options panel
- `Whereabouts_WorldMap.xml`: Adds World Map coords
- `enUS.lua`: Consolidates all text strings into one place

These are all the files you'll need for this project.

Starting on the TOC

Now you'll populate the TOC file you just created with metadata. Afterward, the WoW client will recognize it, put an entry for Whereabouts in the Addon List, and load the addon when you enter the world. This step isn't too different from what you just did in the HelloAzeroth example. Once again, the interface number should be brought up to date if necessary.

Open `Whereabouts.toc` and add these lines:

```
## Interface: 20003
## Title: Whereabouts
## Notes: Displays your coordinates in a movable window.
enUS.lua
Whereabouts.lua
Whereabouts.xml
Whereabouts_Options.lua
Whereabouts_Options.xml
Whereabouts_WorldMap.xml
```

The major difference between this and the TOC you created in the HelloAzeroth example is that now you're listing more than one file in the TOC. Each filename goes on its own line.

Go ahead and start the game. Open the Addon List; Whereabouts should be listed there. Unfortunately, it doesn't do anything yet. That'll change in the next chapter.

What's Next?

In this chapter, you learned how addons are structured and the kinds of files they're made of. You also completed a small example to get the hang of manipulating files and testing them out in-game. You were introduced to several programming fundamentals, including functions, variables, strings, and variable scope. Finally, you saw the planning that goes into a larger-sized addon and created the groundwork necessary to begin coding it. In the process, you set yourself up with an appropriate source code editor.

In the next chapter, you develop the visual elements of the Whereabouts addon, including its window, border, and text, by defining its primary XML file, and learn a lot about the World of Warcraft Widget API during the process.

XML, Frames, and Event Handlers

I n this chapter, you write the first half of a basic fully functional version of the Whereabouts addon. In the following chapters you'll expand it with additional features, slash-command options, and a visual control panel.

Now that the addon's relatively simple TOC file is finished, it's time to dive into XML (eXtensible Markup Language). XML provides the most common way of defining the onscreen elements that comprise addons. You already know a little bit about XML, how it defines hierarchical data, and that it is versatile and can be customized for specific purposes, such as a shopping list, the materials necessary to build a house, or the various UI elements in a World of Warcraft addon.

Blizzard uses XML to define virtually every aspect of the game's visual interface, as you'll see in this chapter.

Introducing XML

As previously mentioned, Blizzard has customized XML to fit its purposes. A specific XML customization is called a *schema*. A schema contains specifications for all the different kinds of objects that can be defined, how these objects relate to each other, and what their settings can be.

Note Blizzard's schema for the WoW interface is stored in a file called UI.xsd in the Interface/FrameXML folder. This file (as well as the entire folder) is compressed in the game's MPQ archives. You need to use Blizzard's Interface Kit to extract the game's interface files before you can open and view them normally.

It's not necessary to know the entire schema to start creating an XML file for your addon. In fact, if you look at the UI.xsd file right now, you probably won't be able to make much sense of it unless you're already familiar with XML. In case you don't have much experience, this chapter covers XML's basic syntax.

The Basic Syntax of XML

If you've ever written a website in HTML, then you've had a taste of markup language, and the following examples should look somewhat familiar.

XML consists of *tags*, *attributes*, and *content*. You can think of a tag as a pair of bookends; one goes at the beginning of content and one goes at the end. In between can be more tags, content, or nothing at all. For example, consider the following:

```
<House>
```

That's the first half. The second half would be:

```
</House>
```

That's the generalized form of opening and closing tags. Anything between the two would be considered part of the House object. For example:

```
<House>
    <Room>
    </Room>
</House>
```

Now the house contains a Room. If this Room object doesn't contain anything itself, there's a shorthand way of writing it that combines the opening and closing tags into one line:

```
<House>
    <Room/>
</House>
```

The hierarchy of these tags describes their relationship to each other.

Attributes and Content

Attributes describe objects that have been created with tags. Typically, the possible values of an attribute are finite, although this isn't always the case. For example, consider the following:

```
<House color="white">
    <Room type="kitchen"/>
</House>
```

In this example, `color` and `type` are attributes, and `"white"` and `"kitchen"` are their values. Each attribute needs a value. Attributes aren't objects themselves; they simply give more information about objects that have already been created. In your addons, you'll commonly use an attribute to give each element a name, among other things.

Content is used in more free-form situations, like this:

```
<House color="white">
    <Room type="kitchen"/>
    <Address>
        269 South St.
    </Address>
</House>
```

In this case, you could say that the Address element contains content. This content has all kinds of possible values, like "Apartment 12b," "1165 Industrial Way," or "The dilapidated shack at the end of the windy dirt road." While it's true that this information *could* be specified by an attribute, it wouldn't be practical. In general: Short, finite values are implemented as attributes, while large blocks of information are implemented as content. An even more important distinction between attributes and content is made in the case of WoW XML files.

When you are working with WoW addons, any content is automatically assumed to be Lua code. This enables you to insert blocks of logic directly into your XML files, if you choose to do so. In fact, you could insert all of your Lua code into XML files and omit having separate Lua files altogether. In practice, though, that's rarely done. Usually, you'll want to place only small chunks of Lua in your XML files, and keep the larger functions separate.

Differences Between XML and HTML

If you've ever written HTML, you probably noticed some similarities between XML and HTML. However, with HTML you might be used to getting away with some sloppiness such as unpaired `<p>` and `<br>` tags, as well as overlapping sets of tags like the following:

```
This text is <b>bold, <i>bold, and italic,</b> and just italic.</i>
```

This sort of thing isn't allowed in XML; a strict hierarchy must be followed, which is why indenting your XML code carefully is always a good idea. Also, unlike HTML, XML is case-sensitive. "Frame" and "frame" are not the same thing. Finally, XML files must be complete; you can get away with omitting the `<html>` and `<body>` tags in an HTML file, but your XML files must include absolutely everything.

XML in Terms of WoW

The Blizzard schema details exactly what kinds of objects you can create, and what kind of attributes they can have. On the largest scale, every WoW XML file needs to have one overarching object called Ui. Everything else goes inside this element. Directly within it you'll commonly find one or more Frame objects. A Frame is akin to the house used in earlier examples; it represents a window onscreen. While a house contains individual rooms, furniture, and appliances, a frame contains buttons, images, text, and sometimes more frames.

Note Because you're working in an XML file throughout this chapter, there are many instances in which you should be adding certain lines of code to your file. In general, new code that you should add appears in bold. If some text is bold and some isn't, that means the regular text should already exist and you only need to insert the bold text.

Specifying the Outer Shell

Open the `Whereabouts.xml` file in your editor. As you know, each WoW XML file must have the same outermost element. Everything else in your file goes inside that element. Technically, the only thing you need for your addon to function is:

```
<Ui>
</Ui>
```

However, it's customary to include a bit more. Specifically:

```
<Ui xmlns="http://www.blizzard.com/wow/ui/" ↵
xmlns:xsi="http://www.w3.org/2001/XMLSchema-instance" ↵
xsi:schemaLocation="http://www.blizzard.com/wow/ui/ ↵
..\FrameXML\UI.xsd">
```

What a start! Don't worry; this is about as complicated as it gets, and it's not important that you understand everything in these lines perfectly. These few lines associate your XML document with the schema defined by Blizzard in the `UI.xsd` file, as well as the W3C's specification of XML itself. The World Wide Web Consortium (W3C) is an organization that drafts specifications for languages such as XML and HTML, and helps maintain web standards. W3C can be found online at `www.w3.org`.

More About Schemas

You can think of the XML schema as the rules for building your metaphorical house. Every XML document must abide by the most basic of rules: It must be well formed with tags that are closed properly and it must declare attributes in the correct manner. In addition, it must follow an additional set of rules set forth by the schema. An XML schema clearly defines the kinds of elements you can create, which elements can have which attributes, and which values are valid for each attribute. Consider the following excerpt taken directly from Blizzard's WoW XML schema:

```
<xs:element name="AbsDimension">
    <xs:complexType>
        <xs:attribute name="x" type="xs:int" use="required"/>
        <xs:attribute name="y" type="xs:int" use="required"/>
    </xs:complexType>
</xs:element>
```

This code defines an element called `AbsDimension` that takes two attributes named `x` and `y`. Both attributes are required and must be integer values. By providing this specification, you can validate an XML file for correctness. This is done outside of the game with a third-party tool such as XMLSpy (available at `www.altova.com`). I won't go into the specifics of doing this, but check out the XMLSpy documentation if you're interested. Note that XMLSpy is commercial software, although a trial version is available.

More About Schemas *Continued*

Validating your XML document isn't vitally important at this stage, so feel free to move on without worrying about it. This information is included specifically for those of you who are interested in what's going on behind the scenes. As you work more and more with XML, you'll become more comfortable with the schema. Eventually, you might want to explore some of the editors that are available that make writing XML code easier. Stick with your current source code editor for now, though.

Creating the Main Frame

The tangible WoW user interface is based on the concept of frames. Pretty much everything onscreen is a frame. Your backpack, the auction window, your character sheet — all of these are frames. Many of the objects in these windows — such as buttons, sliders, and textures — are *descendants* of frames, which means they have all the functionality of frames plus some additional specialized behavior. In XML, you use the Frame element to define a frame.

The Whereabouts addon is no different; it needs a Frame in which to display its data. Before you specify the Frame object, though, review the overall project. You're going to display the player's *x* and *y* coordinates in a small window. The two values are going to be separated by a comma. The window itself needs a simple border and a background. Unlike most coordinates addons, which display your coordinates as integers between 0 and 100, this addon is going to increase the precision to two decimal places, so you'll need a little extra width for the extra digits. Figure 11-1 is a simple sketch of what you're trying to accomplish.

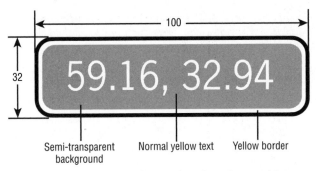

FIGURE 11-1: Specification of the basic Whereabouts addon.

In addition, the addon includes the following behaviors and options:

- The frame is draggable and can be locked in place with a slash-command or a checkbox on the options panel. The frame is clamped, meaning that it can't be dragged off-screen.
- A display of your current coordinates is added to the World Map frame. This feature can also be turned off.

- All settings update the display of the main Whereabouts frame in real time.

- Every setting is available as a slash-command option with /whereabouts or /wa. Either command by itself prints out a complete list of slash-commands.

It's always good to have in mind exactly what you're moving toward. The next thing to define in your XML file is Whereabouts' primary Frame object, which goes directly after the Ui opening tag. You have to name the frame so you can reference it from elsewhere in your code. Add this code to your file:

```
<Ui>
    <Frame name="Whereabouts_Frame">
    </Frame>
</Ui>
```

Note   The attributes for Ui have been omitted from this block of code to save some space. In general, when new code is introduced, only the objects immediately surrounding it will be included, and their attributes will usually be removed. That way, you can figure out where the new code should go but you don't need to wade through everything you've already written.

Setting the Rest of the Frame's Attributes

In addition to a name, Frame objects often need to have several other attributes set. In this case, use the following:

```
<Frame name="Whereabouts_Frame" toplevel="true" ↵
frameStrata="HIGH" enableMouse="true" movable="true" ↵
parent="UIParent" clampedToScreen="true">
```

What do all these attributes mean? Let's take a look at each of them:

- toplevel: Defines whether a frame will rise above other frames when the user clicks it. When true, if your frame is partially obscured by another frame and then clicked, it rises to the top, obscuring the frame that was covering it.

- frameStrata: Specifies the screen *layer* on which your Frame should exist. HIGH is a fine layer for your frame, although I encourage you to change this value and observe the results. The screen is separated into eight stacked layers, which are called (from top to bottom):

  - TOOLTIP

  - FULLSCREEN_DIALOG

  - FULLSCREEN

  - DIALOG

  - HIGH

  - MEDIUM

  - LOW

  - BACKGROUND

- enableMouse: Allows the frame to receive mouse events.

- movable: Allows the object to be moved. This attribute alone does not enable you to drag the frame around; you still need to specify much of that behavior, as you'll see later in the chapter.

- parent: The WoW UI is a hierarchical system involving *parents* and *children*. UIParent is the object at the top of the hierarchy. When a parent frame is modified, all of its children (and their children, and so on) are modified in exactly the same way. However, if you modify a child frame, its parent is unaffected. Soon you'll parent an object to something other than UIParent.

- clampedToScreen: Specifies whether your frame can be dragged off-screen. If enabled, the frame simply stops when one side of it reaches the edge.

This isn't a comprehensive list of Frame attributes, but it's all you need for now.

Setting the Frame's Size

To set the frame's size, you include the Size object within the two Frame tags, like so:

```
<Frame>
    <Size>
    </Size>
</Frame>
```

Size doesn't have any attributes; instead it has two possible elements that can go inside it:

- AbsDimension: Sets the size of an object in absolute units.

- RelDimension: Sets the size of an object as a percentage of its parent's size.

For Whereabouts, use the AbsDimension element, like this:

```
<Size>
    <AbsDimension x="100" y="32"/>
</Size>
```

Because AbsDimension doesn't contain anything else, you can use its shorthand form. This line indicates that the Whereabouts window should be 100 units wide and 32 units tall. Note that these are "units" and not "pixels." The WoW user-interface system isn't measured in pixels; its screen coordinates are resolution-independent. The interface is always 768 units high, no matter the actual resolution. The width then varies based on the current aspect ratio. Thus, a 4:3 screen is 1024 × 768, a 5:4 screen is 960 × 768, and a 16:10 screen is 1228.8 × 768. The virtual root frame UIParent, which all non-parented frames are children of, is given this normalized size.

Also, note that the screen coordinate system's origin (0, 0) is in the upper-left corner.

For more information, see http://wowwiki.com/UI_Coordinates.

Note If you use `RelDimension`, you should know that its `x` and `y` attributes need to be decimal values between 0 and 1. For example, 0.32 specifies 32 percent.

Anchoring the Frame

Anchors define where objects appear onscreen. Essentially, you need to pick a side or corner of one object and hook it onto the side or corner of another. Alternatively you can pick two points on the frame, and then omit the `Size` element entirely; your frame will grow and shrink in accordance with whatever it's anchored to. All this behavior is defined in the `Anchors` element. This element always contains one or more `Anchor` objects. Add the following code to your `Whereabouts.xml` file:

```
<Frame>
    <Anchors>
        <Anchor point="CENTER"/>
    </Anchors>
</Frame>
```

Because `Whereabouts_Frame` is parented to `UIParent`, your frame will appear in the exact center of the screen when it's first loaded. Eventually you'll make the frame draggable so it can be positioned anywhere onscreen. The nice thing about user-positioned windows is that the WoW client automatically remembers their position between game sessions, so they'll stay put once they've been moved somewhere.

The possible values for `point` are:

- CENTER
- TOPLEFT
- TOP
- TOPRIGHT
- RIGHT
- BOTTOMRIGHT
- BOTTOM
- BOTTOMLEFT
- LEFT

The CENTER value represents the overall center of an object. The TOP, RIGHT, BOTTOM, and LEFT values represent the exact center of their respective sides, while the rest of the values represent corners.

In addition to point, you can use two other attributes when specifying an Anchor:

- relativePoint: Defines the point *on the parent* to which the current object will be anchored. If you only specify point, then the same value will be used for this. You only have to specify relativePoint when it needs to be different from point. For example, these two lines are equivalent:

```
<Anchor point="RIGHT" relativePoint="RIGHT"/>
<Anchor point="RIGHT"/>
```

- relativeTo: Enables you to anchor your frame to something other than its parent. For example:

```
<Anchor point="TOPLEFT" relativeTo="PlayerFrame"/>
```

You can use both of these attributes at the same time, if you need to.

The final thing to know about Anchor elements is that they can also contain Offset, which in turn contains either AbsDimension or RelDimension, just like Size. For example, to center your frame horizontally, but have it only 20 units from the top of the screen vertically, you could theoretically use the following code:

```
<Frame>
    <Anchors>
        <Anchor point="TOP">
            <Offset>
                <AbsDimension x="0" y="-20"/>
            </Offset>
        </Anchor>
    </Anchors>
</Frame>
```

Using Textures to Define the Frame's Appearance

The Backdrop element enables you to define the appearance of your window's background and border. This element also goes directly within the Frame object, and has two important attributes: edgeFile and bgFile. These attributes point to textures for the border and background respectively. To start with, your Backdrop code should look like this:

```
<Frame>
    <Backdrop edgeFile="Interface\Tooltips\UI-Tooltip-Border" ↵
bgFile="Interface\Tooltips\UI-Tooltip-Background">
    </Backdrop>
</Frame>
```

About Texture Paths

Wherever textures are concerned, you have the choice of either using the game's built-in textures or your own. In the case of Whereabouts, you'll use built-in textures, resulting in a smaller, distributable package. If you ever decide to use your own artwork, be aware that the texture's path is determined in relation to the root World of Warcraft directory.

For example, if you had a file called `Whereabouts-Background.tga` located in the `Whereabouts` folder, its texture path would look like this:

```
"Interface\AddOns\Whereabouts\Whereabouts-Background"
```

Notice how there's no file extension in the path. That isn't a mistake; the file extension is always omitted, no matter what kind of file it is. It's also important to remember that WoW supports only TGA and BLP2 textures.

For your `edgeFile`, use the default tooltip border because it's thin and simple. The tooltip's background also suffices for the `bgFile`; it's a solid color and can be modified. Both of these files are already located in the game's MPQ archives, so they don't need to be distributed with the addon.

 Note If you're interested in making your own borders and backgrounds, it can be a little tricky. Check out `http://wowwiki.com/EdgeFiles` for more information about their structure.

The next step in creating the `Backdrop` is setting the *inset values*, which determine how close the background texture gets to the border texture. If you don't include these values, the background will appear slightly outside of the border, resulting in a really sloppy look. To define the insets, use `BackgroundInsets` and `AbsInset` as follows:

```
<Backdrop>
    <BackgroundInsets>
        <AbsInset left="4" right="4" top="4" bottom="4"/>
    </BackgroundInsets>
</Backdrop>
```

This keeps the background 4 pixels away from the edge of the frame on every side, leaving just enough room for the border, but not enough room to create a gap.

`EdgeSize` determines what size to stretch the various chunks of the `edgeFile` texture. A value of 16 is perfect here. In general, each `edgeFile` has an ideal `EdgeSize` setting. Other values will look scaled and awkward. Add the following code:

```
<Backdrop>
    <EdgeSize>
        <AbsValue val="16"/>
    </EdgeSize>
</Backdrop>
```

The last two elements you're going to use in Backdrop are Color (which affects the color of the background texture) and BorderColor (which affects the color of the border). These elements tint the textures based on the colors you specify. They can also set each texture's transparency. Use the r, g, b, and a attributes for the red, green, blue, and alpha channels respectively. The following values provide a semitransparent black background and slightly transparent yellow border:

```
<Backdrop>
    <Color r="0" g="0" b="0" a="0.4"/>
    <BorderColor r="1" g="0.8" b="0" a="0.8"/>
</Backdrop>
```

Experiment with your own values. Note that an alpha setting of 0 will make the texture completely transparent (invisible).

The completed Backdrop definition looks like this:

```
<Backdrop edgeFile="Interface\Tooltips\UI-Tooltip-Border" ↵
bgFile="Interface\ChatFrame\ChatFrameBackground">
    <BackgroundInsets>
        <AbsInset left="4" right="4" top="4" bottom="4"/>
    </BackgroundInsets>
    <EdgeSize>
        <AbsValue val="16"/>
    </EdgeSize>
    <Color r="0" g="0" b="0" a="0.4"/>
    <BorderColor r="1" g="0.8" b="0" a="0.8"/>
</Backdrop>
```

Using MyWarcraftStudio to Explore Built-In Artwork

Reusing the game's internal textures is a great way to design your addon because it cuts down on size. Why make people download new textures when they already have great ones sitting around? On the other hand, it can be difficult to figure out which built-in textures to use.

Several third-party applications are available that enable you to view the game's internal files. Check out MyWarcraftStudio, which lets you browse through the game's textures and even export them if you want to. The program is available directly from its creator's website, http://cnitblog.com/linghuye.

The page is mostly in Chinese, but if you search for "MyWarcraftStudio" you should be able to find the download link. Fortunately, the program's interface is in English.

Because these kinds of third-party programs don't modify your in-game experience in the slightest, they're not going to get you in trouble with Blizzard. In fact, you can't even run MyWarcraftStudio and World of Warcraft at the same time.

Once you have the application open, you need to point it to one of WoW's MPQ archives in the Data folder (which is within your WoW installation).

Displaying a Line of Text

So far, you've created a frame, set its size and location, and defined its general appearance. In terms of XML, there are two things left to do: Create an object to display a line of text in your window, and set up event handlers so that the text is updated and the frame can be moved around. Let's start with the text object, which must exist on a *layer*.

Splitting a Frame into Layers

Objects like text and textures exist on various layers within a frame. Just to confuse you, these layers are different from the overall interface layers mentioned earlier. These internal layers determine what overlaps what, but on a different scale: This time it's about the various images, buttons, and text strings within a frame. Before you get into the content of the layers themselves, take a look at how they're defined. Your frame needs only one line of text, so you need to create only one layer in which to put it. Add the following code to your project:

```
<Frame>
    <Layers>
        <Layer level="OVERLAY">
        </Layer>
    </Layers>
</Frame>
```

As you can see, the layer you just created is given a specific value in its `level` attribute. The values for `level` are (from highest to lowest):

- HIGHLIGHT
- OVERLAY
- ARTWORK
- BORDER
- BACKGROUND

Note   Anything in the HIGHLIGHT layer is automatically shown when the cursor is on top of the frame and automatically hidden when it leaves, so put things on this layer only when that sort of behavior is appropriate.

Displaying Text with the FontString Object

To display text you use the `FontString` object, which goes inside the `Layer` tags you just created. The `name` attribute gives the `FontString` a name, so you can reference and update it later from another block of code. `FontString` elements can have a lot of settings, but you rarely need to set any of them yourself. Instead, you'll borrow the text's appearance from a built-in *template*.

A template is an object definition that's marked with the `virtual="true"` attribute. That prevents it from showing up onscreen, but allows other objects to *inherit* from it, essentially copying all of its predefined settings. For this project, you'll inherit from a template called `GameFontNormal` that's built into the game's default user interface files:

```
<Layer>
    <FontString name="$parent_Text" inherits="GameFontNormal">
        <Anchors>
            <Anchor point="CENTER"/>
        </Anchors>
    </FontString>
</Layer>
```

This template generates medium-sized yellow text in the default in-game font. An `Anchor` object is used inside the `FontString` object to center the text in the middle of the window. Because of the XML file's inherent hierarchy, this `FontString` object automatically becomes a child of `Whereabouts_Frame`; it doesn't need to be explicitly parented. Also, notice how `$parent` is used in the object's name. This special code is automatically replaced by the name of the parent, resulting in the `FontString` having the name `Whereabouts_Frame_Text`.

Because it will change constantly, you can't set the actual text to be printed right now. Instead, you'll create a script to automatically update it with the player's current coordinates as often as possible.

This brings you to the last part of the XML file: widget event handlers.

Setting Up Your Widget Event Handlers

The WoW interface is event-driven, meaning that whenever you do something like click a button, slide a slider, or move your mouse over a window, an event is fired. There are actually two different kinds of events in World of Warcraft:

- **Game events:** Fired in response to the actions of your character. For example:

    - MAIL_SEND_SUCCESS

    - PET_ATTACK_START

    - ZONE_CHANGED

- **Widget events:** Fired in response to interaction with UI objects. For example:

    - OnLoad

    - OnUpdate

    - OnMouseWheel

Right now you're only going to be dealing with widget events. "Widget" refers to the broad category of visual objects that the interface provides, such as buttons, sliders, and text strings.

The main window (`Whereabouts_Frame`) needs to respond to a number of different events of this sort, and for that you'll use the `Scripts` object. It goes right inside the `Frame` tags, like this:

```
<Frame>
    <Scripts>
    </Scripts>
</Frame>
```

For each widget event to which the frame needs to respond, you create a new object inside `Scripts`. A good starting point is the `OnLoad` event. The addon will use `OnLoad` to register its slash-commands (`/whereabouts` and `/wa`) as well as perform a few other one-shot administrative tasks. For now, the handler calls a single function, which will be implemented later when we move on to the Lua side of this project.

Continue by adding the following code:

```
<Scripts>
    <OnLoad>
        Whereabouts_OnLoad(self);
    </OnLoad>
</Scripts>
```

This is the first time you're using content in an XML file. As mentioned earlier, content like this is always interpreted as Lua code. So in this case, you're telling the client to call the global Lua function `Whereabouts_OnLoad()` when your main window fires the `OnLoad` event. `OnLoad` fires when your frame is first loaded, right as your character enters the world. Of course, you haven't written the `Whereabouts_OnLoad()` function yet, but you will in the next chapter.

While you're at it, add a handler for the `OnUpdate` event as well. It fires right before your computer redraws the screen (roughly 60 times a second), so it should be used sparingly. If you put too many calculations in this event handler, you'll see a performance hit. However, the player's coordinates sometimes change so fast that you need to use an `OnUpdate` handler to update them fast enough. Also, requesting the player's coordinates from the game hardly requires any computation. There also aren't any relevant game events that are fired when the player's coordinates change, so using the `OnUpdate` widget event is the only solution. Create the handler and its associated function-call as follows:

```
<Scripts>
    <OnUpdate>
        Whereabouts_OnUpdate(self, elapsed);
    </OnUpdate>
</Scripts>
```

Using Widget Events to Enable Frame Dragging

There are three more widget events to handle, all of which work together to allow the window to be dragged around the screen. Because there isn't much code for these handlers, they'll house their Lua code directly in the XML file instead of calling more functions from `Whereabouts.lua`. Take a look at the code now:

```
<Scripts>
    <OnMouseDown>
        if ( button == "LeftButton" ) then
            self:StartMoving();
            self.isMoving = true;
        end
    </OnMouseDown>
    <OnMouseUp>
        if ( self.isMoving ) then
            self:StopMovingOrSizing();
            self.isMoving = false;
        end
    </OnMouseUp>
    <OnHide>
        if ( self.isMoving ) then
            self:StopMovingOrSizing();
            self.isMoving = false;
        end
    </OnHide>
</Scripts>
```

Spend some time with this block of code and see how much of it you can make sense of on your own. Several new concepts are at work here so don't sweat it too much. I'll cover each one of them individually in the next few sections.

Dissecting the Dragging Code

The events themselves are pretty clear. OnMouseDown and OnMouseUp fire in response to the two actions that make up a single mouse click and OnHide fires when the window is hidden altogether. The functions StartMoving() and StopMovingOrSizing() are also clear, although their usage with the keyword self might be a little confusing.

The concepts with which you may not be familiar are conditional statements, event handler arguments, widget functions, and referencing a table entry. The following sections tackle those new concepts.

Conditional Statements

A conditional statement is the most straightforward way for a computer to make a decision. The if statement is the most common implementation of a conditional statement. In its simplest form, an if statement in Lua always involves three keywords: if, then, and end. Everything that's written between if and then is *evaluated*, meaning that it's reduced to a simple value of either true or false. Parentheses help to clarify what's being evaluated and make the code more human-readable. Here's an example straight from the code:

```
if ( self.isMoving ) then
```

The `self.isMoving` variable's value is evaluated (more about `self` and the period in a second). If it's equal to `true`, the code between `then` and `end` is executed; otherwise the code is skipped. Numerical values always evaluate as `true` if they're not equal to zero. If a variable is uninitialized, it has the value `nil`, which evaluates as `false`.

You can also *compare* things to each other, as in the line:

```
if ( button == "LeftButton" ) then
```

In this case, the variable `button` (more on this in a second, too) is compared to `"LeftButton"` — a string of text. If the value of `button` is equal to `"LeftButton"` exactly, the statement evaluates as `true` and the code that follows is executed. If the value happens to be `"RightButton"` or anything else, the code that follows is skipped.

Note Why use two equals signs instead of one? In Lua, one equals sign (=) is an assignment operator. It assigns the value of whatever's on the right side to whatever's on the left side. Two equals signs (==) perform a check to see if the two objects in question are equal to each other, and then return `true` or `false` depending on the outcome of the comparison.

Event Handler Arguments

Widget events come with something called *arguments*. Arguments are variables that come preloaded with information that's pertinent to the event that was just fired.

In the `OnMouseDown` handler that you just wrote, for example, two variables are referenced: `self` and `button`. These are the two arguments that this event receives when it's fired. The `self` variable references the object that generated the event, and the `button` variable contains information about which mouse button was clicked. Because you only want the window to be draggable when the left mouse button is used, you need to check the value of the `button` variable with a conditional statement before calling the `StartMoving()` function. The last line of code you examined in the previous section makes this check.

Table 11-1 contains a list of all known widget event handlers and their associated arguments. While this information won't be very useful to you right now, it will hopefully come in handy later as a quick reference.

Table 11-1   Widget Events and Their Arguments

Name	Arguments
default	self
OnAttributeChanged	self, name, value
OnChar	self, text
OnCharComposition	self, text
OnClick	self, button, down

Table 11-1 *Continued*

Name	Arguments
OnColorSelect	self, r, g, b
OnCursorChanged	self, x, y, w, h
OnDoubleClick	self, button
OnDragStart	self, button
OnEnter	self, motion
OnEvent	self, event, ...[a]
OnHorizontalScroll	self, offset
OnHyperlinkClick	self, link, text, button
OnHyperlinkEnter	self, link, text
OnHyperlinkLeave	self, link, text
OnInputLanguageChanged	self, language
OnKeyDown	self, key
OnKeyUp	self, key
OnLeave	self, motion
OnMouseDown	self, button
OnMouseUp	self, button
OnMouseWheel	self, delta
OnMovieShowSubtitle	self, text
OnScrollRangeChanged	self, xrange, yrange
OnSizeChanged	self, w, h
OnTooltipAddMoney	self, cost
OnUpdate	self, elapsed
OnValueChanged	self, value
OnVerticalScroll	self, offset
PostClick	self, button, down
PreClick	self, button, down

[a]OnEvent is passed an arbitrary number of arguments that are stored in a special variable. For more information see the Lua language documentation.

Source: post by Iriel on the official Blizzard forums

Widget Functions

When you name an XML element, a global Lua variable is created with that name, enabling you to reference the object from Lua code anywhere. Each XML element has various functions that can be called in the form:

```
ElementName:DoSomething();
```

`DoSomething()` is referred to as a widget function. `StartMoving()` and `StopMovingOrSizing()`, both of which you used in the previous block of code, are widget functions that can be used with `Frame` objects and their descendants.

Because `self` points to the object that generated the widget event, you can call that object's widget functions without typing its full name, instead using the following:

```
self:StartMoving();
```

This lets you create more general code that you can easily reuse.

You might be wondering why you use this syntax (with a colon) instead of passing the element's name (or `self`) as an argument to the function. The difference is that your XML elements actually *contain* their own widget events. This means that if it needed to, a frame and a button could contain slightly different `StartMoving()` functions. You never need to worry about the difference because you call them in exactly the same way. This book doesn't go into the subject in-depth, but it's worth noting that this is one of the benefits of object-oriented programming. Anyhow, functions contained within another object like this are sometimes referred to as *methods*.

Note For a daunting list of all widget functions, see `http://wowwiki.com/Widget_API`.

Referencing a Table Entry

As you've just seen, there are structures in Lua that can store other variables and functions (which are secretly the same thing) within them. These structures are called *tables*. The variable that's created when you name an XML element is actually a table that can contain any number of additional variables and methods. Consider the following line of code:

```
self.isMoving = true;
```

This references a variable called `isMoving` within the `Whereabouts_Frame` table and sets its value to `true`. If the variable doesn't exist, it will be created. If you're still a little uneasy about tables, don't worry; they're going to be discussed in much greater detail later on in Chapter 13.

Finishing Up with XML

That's it for the XML portion of the Whereabouts addon, for the time being! If you're itching to test it out, you need to make two little changes to prevent getting errors when you enter the game. Because two of the functions you call from your event handlers haven't been written yet, you need to comment out two lines of code.

In Lua, anything following two dashes (--) on a line is considered a comment. Comments are ignored completely by the game's parser. So, you need to change two of the function calls in your widget event handlers to look like this:

```
--Whereabouts_OnLoad(self);
--Whereabouts_OnUpdate(self, elapsed);
```

Then fire up World of Warcraft, enable the addon, and enter the world. You should see a small rectangular window with a yellow border in the center of the screen. Click and drag to move it around. When you're done, uncomment the two lines you just modified and save the file. For reference, Listing 11-1 is the complete Whereabouts.xml file.

Listing 11-1   Whereabouts.xml

```
<Ui xmlns="http://www.blizzard.com/wow/ui/" ↵
xmlns:xsi="http://www.w3.org/2001/XMLSchema-instance" ↵
xsi:schemaLocation="http://www.blizzard.com/wow/ui/ ↵
..\FrameXML\UI.xsd">
    <Frame name="Whereabouts_Frame" toplevel="true"
frameStrata="HIGH" ↵
enableMouse="true" movable="true" parent="UIParent"
clampedToScreen="true">
        <Size>
            <AbsDimension x="100" y="32"/>
        </Size>
        <Anchors>
            <Anchor point="CENTER"/>

        </Anchors>
        <Backdrop edgeFile="Interface\Tooltips\UI-Tooltip-Border" ↵
bgFile="Interface\Tooltips\UI-Tooltip-Background">
            <BackgroundInsets>
                <AbsInset left="4" right="4" top="4" bottom="4"/>
            </BackgroundInsets>
            <EdgeSize>
                <AbsValue val="16"/>
            </EdgeSize>
            <Color r="0" g="0" b="0" a="0.4"/>
            <BorderColor r="1" g="0.8" b="0" a="0.8"/>
        </Backdrop>
        <Layers>
            <Layer level="OVERLAY">
                <FontString name="$parent_Text" ↵
inherits="GameFontNormal">
                    <Anchors>
                        <Anchor point="CENTER"/>
                    </Anchors>
                </FontString>
            </Layer>
        </Layers>
```

continued

Listing 11-1 *Continued*

```
<Scripts>
    <OnLoad>
        Whereabouts_OnLoad(self);
    </OnLoad>
    <OnUpdate>
        Whereabouts_OnUpdate(self, elapsed);
    </OnUpdate>
    <OnMouseDown>
        if ( button == "LeftButton" ) then
            self:StartMoving();
            self.isMoving = true;
        end
    </OnMouseDown>
    <OnMouseUp>
        if ( self.isMoving  ) then
            self:StopMovingOrSizing();
            self.isMoving = false;
        end
    </OnMouseUp>
    <OnHide>
        if ( self.isMoving ) then
            self:StopMovingOrSizing();
            self.isMoving = false;
        end
    </OnHide>
</Scripts>
</Frame>
</Ui>
```

Summary

This chapter provided a crash course in XML. You learned about its syntax and structure, how Blizzard makes use of it, what a schema is, and how to create your own objects and frames. You began working on the Whereabouts addon by creating a simple window, defining its size and position onscreen, and decorating it with built-in textures. You also learned about two kinds of events (game events and widget events) and created event handlers for several widget events. You even wrote some Lua that allows the window to be dragged around. Finally, you got a tiny taste of conditional statements, tables, widget functions, and comments!

In the next chapter you plunge into Lua and implement the core logic that runs the Whereabouts addon.

The Lua Side

With the Whereabouts addon's XML code taken care of, you're ready to go in and write its Lua script. You had a little taste of Lua when you dealt with the widget event handlers that allowed the window to be dragged around in Chapter 11. Now you'll take care of the rest of the Lua. Over the course of this chapter you'll develop five different Lua functions:

- `Whereabouts_OnLoad()`: Registers your slash commands. This is called when your frame is first loaded.

- `Whereabouts_SlashCommand()`: Called whenever the user types one of the slash commands you registered. It will eventually parse them, but for now, it's just going to call a toggle function.

- `Whereabouts_Toggle()`: Performs the actual toggling of the main window's visibility, hiding it if it's shown and showing it if it's hidden.

- `Whereabouts_OnUpdate()`: Calculates, formats, and updates the player's coordinates onscreen. This is the heart of the addon, and is called once every time the screen is redrawn.

- `round()`: Lua's built-in math library doesn't have a rounding function, so you need to create (or find) your own. It is called when formatting the coordinates. It's `local`, so its name doesn't need to have "Whereabouts_" preceding it.

The Nuts and Bolts of Functions

Before you begin working on the actual code for Whereabouts, let's take a more in-depth look at what functions are, as well as how they're declared and used. Consider this line of code:

```
function AddTwoNumbers(n1, n2) end
```

This is a function *declaration*. Alternatively, you could write:

```
AddTwoNumbers = function(n1, n2) end
```

Either way is correct, but the second example helps illustrate the fact that a function is just a special kind of value that can be held by a variable. In practice, the syntax of the first example is more commonly used.

A function describes a specific process that you can use anywhere else in your code, or in response to events. These two examples both declare functions that are perfectly legitimate, but don't do anything. Essentially, they end before anything happens. You'll take a look at the contents of functions in a minute. First you need to know a little something about arguments.

Passing Data with Arguments

Both of the preceding declarations indicate that the function should receive two arguments (n1 and n2) when called. *Arguments* are values that need to be passed to the function whenever it's used. If the function (which presumably adds two numbers together) were called without any arguments, how would it know what to add together? The answer is: it wouldn't. That's why you pass arguments to functions.

A call to this function might look something like this:

```
AddTwoNumbers(1035, 57);
```

This function call would be pretty useless on its own, though, because nothing is being done with the result of the whole operation. Some functions (such as this one) need to return a value when they're done. The logical thing for this function to return is the result of the addition. Some more useful calls to it might look like:

```
local result = AddTwoNumbers(12, 95);
message(AddTwoNumbers(834, 221));
```

The first line of code assigns the result of the function to a variable, while the second line prints the result in a dialog box. You can pass variables to functions (as arguments) if they hold the appropriate kind of data. In fact, that's what you'll do more often than not:

```
local price1 = 49;
local price2 = 120;
local total = AddTwoNumbers(price1, price2);
```

The Content of a Function

In between the name of a function (including its arguments) and the end keyword, you use Lua code to define what your function actually does. Here is a complete, working declaration for the AddTwoNumbers() function:

```
function AddTwoNumbers(n1, n2)
   local output = n1 + n2;
   return output;
end
```

This function is so simple you'd never realistically use it; you'd just do the addition manually. But it's an example that's easy to follow along with. When the function is called, a new local variable called `output` is declared and its value is initialized to the sum of the two arguments. Then the value of `output` is returned. There are a couple of important concepts at work here: variable scope and return values.

Variable Scope

First of all, the `local` keyword is used before the `output` variable is declared to limit its *scope*. Scope refers to how widely a variable can be used. A local variable can be used only within the function in which it's declared. A local variable declared within an `if` statement can be used only inside that `if` statement.

Why limit a variable's scope? Defining a variable as `local` prevents it from conflicting with global variables that share the same name, perhaps created by other addons or by the game itself. Any variable (including a function) created without the `local` keyword is considered a global variable, and global variables can be referenced anywhere. It's a good idea to use local variables whenever you can.

Return Values

I added an extra line to the preceding function just so I'd have an excuse to talk about local variables. The function's core code could easily be simplified to just one line:

```
return n1 + n2;
```

The `return` keyword here specifies the value returned by the function. A `return` statement like this immediately concludes the execution of a function, even if more lines of code follow it. The returned value is what a function call evaluates to. You can use conditional statements to return different values based on the circumstances, as in the following example:

```
function IsLessThanOne(n)
    if ( n < 1 ) then
        return true;
    end
    return false;
end
```

Registering Slash Commands

The `Whereabouts_OnLoad()` function is called by the Whereabouts window's `OnLoad` widget event handler. This event fires once when the window is first loaded into memory, and provides a perfect opportunity for you to register any slash commands that Whereabouts needs to use. The handler function is used for several other initialization tasks as well, but those don't need to be covered yet.

Registering a slash command involves adding it to the list of commands that the client recognizes, and then hooking it up with a slash-command handler, a separate function that's called whenever the user enters one of your registered commands.

Declaring the OnLoad Function

Open the `Whereabouts.lua` file in your editor and begin by entering the following two lines:

```
function Whereabouts_OnLoad(self)
end
```

This is a completely valid function that doesn't do anything yet.

Unfortunately, registering slash commands is a slightly non-intuitive process. It's not exactly complicated, but it is a little strange, especially for a beginning programmer.

The first thing to do is initialize two precisely named global variables. As mentioned earlier, a variable is considered *global* if you don't use the `local` keyword when you declare it. Global variables can be used anywhere; in any of your functions, and in other addons' functions as well. Be careful with them; it's easy to cause a conflict if a global variable doesn't have a unique name. Functions are actually stored in variables, which is why all of your functions have `Whereabouts_` at the beginning of their names — to make sure they're unique no matter what other addons the user has loaded.

Anyhow, these variables need to be global. Add the following two lines to the body of the function declaration, between the function's name and the `end` keyword (I suggest you indent them for clarity):

```
SLASH_WHEREABOUTS1 = "/whereabouts";
SLASH_WHEREABOUTS2 = "/wa";
```

Remember, the names of these variables are important. Even if you were only registering one slash command, the first variable would still need to have that `1` at the end of it. The WoW client's internal logic dictates the naming convention.

Next, add the following line of code to the function, below the two variable definitions:

```
SlashCmdList["WHEREABOUTS"] = Whereabouts_SlashCommand;
```

When a player types a slash command into the WoW client, it checks `SlashCmdList` (a pre-existing global variable whose value is a keyed table) to figure out what to do next. This table keeps track of all of the game's slash commands, and the associated functions that have been registered to handle each one.

In the preceding line of code, the key `"WHEREABOUTS"` is created in the table, and then associated with the value of a variable called `Whereabouts_SlashCommand`. This is going to be the variable that holds your slash command handler function.

This is a lot to take in for three little lines of code. Don't worry too much if you didn't understand all of that. The two main things to understand are as follows:

■ The key used with `SlashCmdList` needs to be exactly the same as the part of the global variable's name that follows the underscore and precedes the number:

SLASH_**WHEREABOUTS**1

■ The function you insert into the table is called whenever the user types one of your registered slash commands. This is the slash command *handler*.

The completed function looks like this:

```
function Whereabouts_OnLoad(self)
    SLASH_WHEREABOUTS1 = "/whereabouts";
    SLASH_WHEREABOUTS2 = "/wa";
    SlashCmdList["WHEREABOUTS"] = Whereabouts_SlashCommand;
end
```

Don't worry about the argument (self) now; you'll use it later on.

Creating the Slash Command Handler

In the next chapter, you'll expand the slash command handler into a parser and add a bunch of slash-command options. For now, just declare it and make it simply toggle the window on and off, no matter what the user types in after the initial command.

Below the previous function declaration, create a new one:

```
function Whereabouts_SlashCommand(msg)
    Whereabouts_Toggle();
end
```

This function has a mysterious argument as well: msg. When called, the game passes your slash-command handler anything the user typed in after the slash command. You'll use this information when you implement slash-command options.

For now, all you need to do is implement the Whereabouts_Toggle() function.

Toggling the Whereabouts Window

A window's *toggle* function has two simple rules:

- If the window is currently shown, hide it.
- If the window is currently hidden, show it.

Fortunately, that's pretty much exactly what the Lua code looks like:

```
function Whereabouts_Toggle()
    if ( Whereabouts_Frame:IsShown() ) then
        Whereabouts_Frame:Hide();
    else
        Whereabouts_Frame:Show();
    end
end
```

The functions IsShown(), Hide(), and Show() are all widget functions that you can use with Frame objects. The functions themselves are pretty self-explanatory. The IsShown() function returns either true or nil, depending on whether the frame is shown. Fortunately, a value of nil evaluates as false in a logical expression.

The other interesting thing at work here is the `else` statement. You already learned about how code in an `if` block is executed only when the tested expression evaluates to `true`. Code in an `else` block (which always needs to immediately follow an `if` block) is executed only if the expression is `false`. In the next chapter, you'll learn about the `elseif` statement.

You're almost ready to test the code you've written so far, but first you need to declare the `Whereabouts_OnUpdate()` function. Right now, this function is going to be called by the `OnUpdate` handler before every screen refresh; if it's not declared, an error will be generated. For now, simply declare the function with nothing inside it:

```
function Whereabouts_OnUpdate(self, elapsed)
end
```

Once again, don't worry about the arguments; they'll be used later. Now save your work and load the game. The Whereabouts window is still empty, but you can type `/whereabouts` or `/wa` to toggle it.

Updating the Coordinates

You'll finish this script off with the core of the addon's functionality: a function that updates the displayed coordinates. As already mentioned, the `OnUpdate` event handler fires once before each screen refresh, calling the function `Whereabouts_OnUpdate()` many times per second. This function needs to do three things each time it's called:

1. Get the player's current coordinates.

2. Format them properly for display.

3. Update the object that prints them onscreen.

You get the player's coordinates by inserting the following line into the empty `Whereabouts_OnUpdate()` function:

```
local x, y = GetPlayerMapPosition("player");
```

This function actually returns two values, which is why you need two variables to store the results. The variables are defined with the `local` keyword because you only need them for the duration of this function. The `GetPlayerMapPosition()` function is part of the general World of Warcraft API. The reason you pass the string `"player"` to this function is because it can also be used to get the coordinates of party or raid members, so it requires an argument that specifies the unit that you're interested in.

The WoWWiki website has the most complete documentation of the World of Warcraft API currently available. See `http://wowwiki.com/World_of_Warcraft_API`.

The coordinate values returned by this function are floating-point values between 0 and 1. If the player is in an instance or another area in which coordinates aren't available, both returned values will be 0. Here's an example of the unmodified values:

```
0.36775401234627, 0.57326972484589
```

Unfortunately, numbers with 14 decimal places aren't very useful for charting your character's location, so you need to modify them into something more readable. Many players are used to coordinates being represented as integers between 0 and 100. The same coordinates in this format would look like:

```
37, 57
```

Much better! However, providing two decimal places makes Whereabouts a little bit more accurate and also more responsive as the player moves around:

```
36.78, 57.33
```

How do you transform the original values into this form? You can multiply them by one hundred, round them to two decimal places, and then force their output to exactly two decimal places (otherwise numbers such as `27.40` with trailing zeros will appear as `27.4`, which would be inconsistent). Because there are so many different ways to round numbers, Lua doesn't assume a specific method, and leaves it for the programmer to implement. The following section outlines one possible method.

Rounding Numbers

You're not the first person who's needed to round numbers with Lua, so you can look online for an existing algorithm and save some time. Fortunately, some enterprising Lua programmers at the lua-users website have tackled this particular problem; see `http://lua-users.org/wiki/SimpleRound`.

Add this function declaration directly above the `Whereabouts_OnUpdate()` function in your `Whereabouts.lua` file:

```
local function round(num, idp)
    local mult = 10 ^ (idp or 0);
    return math.floor(num * mult + 0.5) / mult;
end
```

You have to add it before the function in which it's used because it's a local function and must be declared prior to the first time it's referenced; otherwise the game assumes that your references to `round()` refer to a global function, and errors will be thrown.

To use it, simply pass it the number you want rounded and the number of decimal places you want it rounded to as arguments. In case you're wondering about the function's code, `math.floor()` returns the closest integer that's less than the floating-point value it's passed.

Note The math library is built into Lua, and provides many useful routines, including abs (returns the absolute value), sqrt (returns the square root), and random (returns a random number).

Returning to the OnUpdate Function

Before you process the returned decimal values, remember how some areas of the game don't report coordinates, and instead return both values as zero? Let's check for this, and then display dashes if the player is in an area in which coordinates are unavailable.

Back in `Whereabouts_OnUpdate()`, declare a local variable to store the final text output. This should follow the last line you wrote:

```
local text;
```

It doesn't need to be initialized because you'll give it a value shortly. Next, check to see if the values you got from `GetPlayerMapPosition()` are both zero, and if so, set `text` equal to three dashes:

```
if ( x == 0 and y == 0 ) then
    text = "---";
```

The keyword and signifies that *both* `x == 0` and `y == 0` must evaluate to `true` for the entire statement to be interpreted as `true`. If either part of the expression isn't `true`, the whole statement is `false`. Although it's theoretically possible to be standing on the very, very corner of a zone, where both coordinates would be legitimately equal to zero, it's practically unachievable.

Next, you use an `else` statement to prepare the coordinates for display when they *are* available (when one of them doesn't equal zero). You need to format the string so that both values are always displayed with two decimal places (trailing zeros and all) and are separated by a comma. For that, you can use the built-in `string.format()` function:

```
else
    x = round(x * 100, 2);
    y = round(y * 100, 2);
    text = string.format("%.2f, %.2f", x, y);
end
```

The string provided as the first argument to `string.format()` is scanned for *identifiers*, each of which represents a placeholder in the final output. The identifiers are used to determine how the output should be formatted. In this case, the identifier `"%.2f"` means "format this variable as a number with two decimal places." The other characters in the string (the comma and space separating the two identifiers) are interpreted literally. The remaining arguments to `string.format()` are put in the placeholders, according to the specification of the identifiers.

Note   For a list of other identifiers that can be used with `string.format()` and documentation on the string library, see `http://lua-users.org/wiki/StringLibraryTutorial`.

The last step is to update the text string displayed by your `FontString` object using a widget function called `SetText()`:

```
Whereabouts_Frame_Text:SetText(text)
```

That's it!

Here's the completed `Whereabouts_OnUpdate()` function for reference:

```
function Whereabouts_OnUpdate(self, elapsed)
   local x, y = GetPlayerMapPosition("player");
   local text;
   if ( x == 0 and y == 0 ) then
      text = " — -";
   else
      x = round(x * 100, 2);
      y = round(y * 100, 2);
      text = string.format("%.2f, %.2f", x, y);
   end
   Whereabouts_Frame_Text:SetText(text);
end
```

Testing Your Code

Save everything, launch WoW, enter the world, and you should have a fully functional coordinates display that updates as your character moves around. Try going into an instance, and you should see the coordinates replaced with three dashes (see Figure 12-1) indicating that they're not available.

FIGURE 12-1: The Whereabouts addon displaying coordinates (left) and its unavailable message (right).

Congratulations, you're finished with your first functional addon! For reference, Listing 12-1 is the entire `Whereabouts.lua` file.

Listing 12-1   Whereabouts.lua

```
function Whereabouts_OnLoad(self)
   SLASH_WHEREABOUTS1 = "/whereabouts";
   SLASH_WHEREABOUTS2 = "/wa";
   SlashCmdList["WHEREABOUTS"] = Whereabouts_SlashCommand;
end

function Whereabouts_SlashCommand(msg)
   Whereabouts_Toggle();
end

function Whereabouts_Toggle()
   if ( Whereabouts_Frame:IsShown() ) then
      Whereabouts_Frame:Hide();
```

continued

Listing 12-1 *Continued*

```
      else
          Whereabouts_Frame:Show();
      end
end

local function round(num, idp)
      local mult = 10 ^ (idp or 0)
      return math.floor(num * mult + 0.5) / mult
end

function Whereabouts_OnUpdate(self, elapsed)
      local x, y = GetPlayerMapPosition("player")
      local text
      if ( x == 0 and y == 0 ) then
          text = " - -"
      else
          x = round(x * 100, 2)
          y = round(y * 100, 2)
          text = string.format("%.2f, %.2f", x, y)
      end
      Whereabouts_Frame_Text:SetText(text)
end
```

A Good Milestone

In this chapter you completed the basic version of the Whereabouts addon. It's still lacking some nice features, but it's fully functional nonetheless. You also learned how functions are declared, called, and implemented in Lua. You registered your addon's slash commands, created the framework for a slash-command handler, and declared a toggle function. Finally, you wrote the core code that constantly updates the coordinates, which included a general-purpose function for rounding numbers to an arbitrary length.

If you've worked through this project from the beginning, this is a great stopping point. So far, you've absorbed a ridiculous amount of new material! The code is only going to get more complicated from here on out. In the next chapter you expand this addon with some slash-command options; then in the following chapter you add a visual control panel.

Expanding the Whereabouts Addon

In this chapter you expand on the basic version of the Whereabouts addon that you completed in the previous chapter by adding several additional features:

- Tooltip information, which includes the name of the addon, its function, its locked status, and what various clicks on it do.
- A display of the player's coordinates on the World Map.
- A slash-command system that can be used to set all of the following options as well as toggle the options panel. It also includes documentation of the available commands.
  - Show/hide the coordinates window (*default is shown*).
  - Lock/unlock the window (*default is unlocked*).
  - Enable/disable the tooltip (*default is enabled*).
  - Enable/disable the World Map display (*default is enabled*).
  - Set the level of transparency (*default is opaque*).
- Full localization, so that the addon's text strings can be easily translated into different languages.

It's important to familiarize yourself with these features because you'll be using them in the next chapter when you build the addon's control panel. The panel allows the user to control each of these options with UI elements instead of slash-commands.

Saving the User's Settings

Because you're adding several settings to the addon, the user's decisions need to be preserved between sessions. The game should even remember if the Whereabouts window is shown or not. As mentioned already, the client saves the locations of windows automatically, but everything else you want to save must be explicitly specified in your code. Fortunately, Blizzard has made it really easy to specify which variables need to be saved between sessions, on a per-account or per-character basis.

To begin, you'll create the variables that will keep track of the state of all Whereabouts' settings. These same variables will be saved from session to session. Also, because of a programming construct in Lua called a *table*, you can create one master variable that holds all the others. You only need to tell the client to save the master variable and all the others will go along for the ride.

Introducing Tables

The concept of a table isn't unique to Lua; you might have heard the term thrown around elsewhere. A table is simply an object that's capable of containing a combination of zero or more other variables and tables (yes, you can have an empty table). Tables are often used to organize similar information, such as lists. They're also handy when it comes to simplifying your code. You'll use tables all the time.

Tables hold other variables in much the same way that variables hold data. For example, to keep track of the names of a character's items, you could use a table called myItems that contains a variable for each equipment slot. One of these variables would be myWeapon. There are several different ways to define or access tables and the variables they contain. The following three lines of code all do exactly the same thing; they create a table with one variable that holds the name of a weapon:

```
myItems.myWeapon = "The Sword of a Thousand Lies";
myItems["myWeapon"] = "The Sword of a Thousand Lies";
myItems = { myWeapon = "The Sword of a Thousand Lies" };
```

The syntax used in the third line is applicable only when you're creating a table and populating it; the other two techniques can also be used to reference data that's already in a table. For example, the following two lines are equivalent:

```
message(myItems.myWeapon);
message(myItems["myWeapon"]);
```

To make full use of tables, it's important to understand how they're implemented. Tables in Lua are *associative arrays* — that is, they're collections of paired elements. Each element pair consists of a *key* and a *value*. Without a key, there would be no way to access a specific piece of data in a table. Without a value, an element is considered to be uninitialized, and will be equal to the special value of nil if and when it's referenced. In the earlier example, the text string "myWeapon" is the key, and the text string "The Sword of a Thousand Lies" is its associated value. In addition to being strings, keys can be integer values as well. For example, consider this:

```
myFriends[5] = "Razark";
```

Notice that the integer is not surrounded by quotes. When an integer is used as a key, you cannot use the dot-syntax presented previously to reference it; you can only use the square-bracket syntax. However, the following operations are completely legitimate, and either one of them (combined with the previous line) would create a dialog box that says "Razark" in it:

```
--example one
local x = 5;
message(myFriends[x]);
```

```
--example two
local y = 4;
message(myFriends[y + 1]);
```

This goes to show how all kinds of tricks are at your disposal when creating or referencing tables and their elements. There are a few other things you should know about tables. First, you can initialize a table with more than one entry by separating each with a comma. You can also initialize tables without specifying keys; each value will be assigned an integer key starting with 1 and going up incrementally. For example, the following line of code combines both of these concepts:

```
myFriends = { "Razark", "Rotgar", "Youngblood", "Nyne" };
```

After making this table, you could execute the following line:

```
message(myFriends[2]);
```

The result would be a dialog box that says "Rotgar."

Finally, in some rare cases you need to create an empty table. The method is simple:

```
emptyTable = {};
```

Hopefully this brief crash course has given you enough information to follow along as tables are created and manipulated throughout the rest of this tutorial. As with all programming fundamentals, the more you put a concept to use, the more you'll understand it.

Note For more introductory information about using tables in Lua, check out this page: http://lua-users.org/wiki/TablesTutorial.

Creating a Table of Variables for Whereabouts to Save

Open the Whereabouts.lua file and add the following lines to the very top:

```
Whereabouts_Options = {
    show = true,
    lock = false,
    tooltip = true,
    worldmap = true,
    alpha = 1
};
```

The master Whereabouts_Options variable is a table, just like the ones discussed in the previous section. Remember that when you initialize a table like this, the individual elements must be separated with commas. Why does each variable in the table already have a value assigned to it? Well, the first time this addon is loaded by the user, there won't be any saved variables to load from disk, so these initial values will be used as defaults. Each time thereafter, these default values will be loaded when the file is first parsed, and then be overwritten when the client loads the saved variables from the hard drive.

Let's explore this process a little bit more. When an addon is first loaded, all of its Lua code is executed immediately. During that process, the Whereabouts_Options table is created and populated with the entries shown; each entry is initialized to the value listed. After all the addon's files are loaded and executed in this manner, the game loads any saved variables (if they exist), possibly overwriting some of the variables and tables that have just been created. If the user has loaded the addon before, his or her custom settings will overwrite the defaults listed here.

You instruct the game to save this structure in the addon's TOC file.

Specifying Saved Variables in the TOC

Open Whereabouts.toc and add the following line just below the Notes entry:

```
## SavedVariablesPerCharacter: Whereabouts_Options
```

You can save multiple variables this way, separating each one with a comma. If a table is specified, the entire table will be saved. As you may have noticed, this command informs the client to save the variables on a per-character basis. If you want them saved on a per-account basis instead, use the SavedVariables command. Variables saved per-account are stored in the following file:

```
WTF\Account\<Account>\SavedVariables\<Addon>.lua
```

Whereas variables saved per-character can be found in:

```
WTF\Account\<Account>\<Server>\<Character>\SavedVariables\<Addon>.lua
```

Per-character saving makes more sense for the Whereabouts addon, and many other addons for that matter, because each character tends to require a different interface arrangement. Even if they don't, it's no sweat for a player to configure an addon once for each character they have. It's annoying for a user to have to constantly switch a setting back and forth whenever they switch characters. More complex addons generally implement *profiles*, allowing players to easily copy their settings from one character to another. Whereabouts doesn't need this kind of feature though, because it has only a few settings.

The implementation of profiles is a complex undertaking, and is outside the scope of this book. However, there are many, many addons out there that have some kind of profile system built-in. Because all addons are effectively open source, you can freely dig around inside them to see how their profile systems are implemented.

Building a Slash-Command Parser

Parsing a string of text involves breaking it down into individual words and then checking to see if any of those words are recognized. This sounds like a difficult task, but it's not really as hard as you might think. When a slash-command is entered, the client takes care of parsing out the base command from the rest of the typed message, so you only need to deal with the latter part, which is passed to the slash-command handler as an argument.

For example, a user types the following:

```
/whereabouts alpha 0.5
```

The `/whereabouts` chunk is examined first. Because you previously registered this slash-command, the game knows to call the appropriate parser function in the Whereabouts addon's Lua file. Then it snips out the initial slash-command from the rest of the message and passes only the string "`alpha 0.5`" on to the parser.

The next step is to separate each word in that string into a separate variable, but first you need to have a preliminary understanding of loops.

Examining a Loop

One of the most fundamental concepts in programming is a *loop*. Loops are used when you want to do the same thing over and over an arbitrary number of times. Loops are often used when you want to *iterate* over a number of objects — to execute the same code once for every entry in a table, for example. This section explains a structure called a `for` loop.

Here's an example table:

```
theNumbers = { 4, 8, 15, 16, 23, 42 };
```

What if you want to increment each of the entries by one?

You could use the following code:

```
theNumbers[1] = theNumbers[1] + 1;
theNumbers[2] = theNumbers[2] + 1;
theNumbers[3] = theNumbers[3] + 1;
theNumbers[4] = theNumbers[4] + 1;
theNumbers[5] = theNumbers[5] + 1;
theNumbers[6] = theNumbers[6] + 1;
```

However, that's probably the least elegant solution possible. In addition, it's not versatile at all: If you add one more entry to the table of numbers, you'd also have to add another line of code. Fortunately, there's a much better way, as shown in the following example:

```
for i = 1, getn(theNumbers) do
   theNumbers[i] = theNumbers[i] + 1;
end
```

See how much more concise that is?

Let's examine how it works. First, right after the `for` keyword there are two expressions separated by a comma. They're followed by the `do` keyword. The first expression (`i = 1`) creates a local variable called `i` and sets it equal to 1. This variable (`i`) is called the *control variable*. The second expression (`getn(theNumbers)`) specifies a value for `i` that will cause the loop to stop. The built-in function `getn()` returns the number of elements in the table passed to it, which in this case is six. You can optionally specify a third expression that is used to increment the control variable each time the loop runs. This is called the *step*. If omitted, the step is assumed to be 1. Just for reference, the following line is equivalent to the one in the preceding example, although the declaration of the step is explicit:

```
for index = 1, getn(theNumbers), 1 do
```

The contents of the loop is then executed the appropriate number of times. Each time, the control variable is incremented by 1, so that each element in the table is modified once, in order, and then the loop stops. How is this any different than the original six-line solution to the problem? The benefit here is that this same three-line block of code can be used with a table of any size! You could add a seventh value to your table, for example, and the code would work the same.

As you can see, loops enable you to write code that's both more concise and more versatile. Because of this fact, you should use them often.

Separating a Message into Individual Words

In `Whereabouts.lua`, start by removing the one existing line from `Whereabouts_SlashCommand()` because you don't need it anymore. Replace it with the following block of code:

```
msg = string.lower(msg);
local args = {};
for word in string.gmatch(msg, "[^%s]+") do
    table.insert(args, word);
end
```

A lot of things are going on in these five little lines!

The first line utilizes the built-in `string.lower()` function to convert any uppercase characters in the incoming message into lowercase ones. This makes it easier to match known words because it allows the user to input slash-command options in either upper or lowercase (or a mix of the two). You only need to check them against lowercase strings.

Next, the `args` variable is initialized as an empty table. This is done for two reasons. First, because we want the variable to be `local`, and second, because the `table.insert()` function used in the fourth line requires `args` to be predefined as a table.

Following this is a `for` loop. However, it's a little different from the one you saw in the previous example. That was a *numeric* `for` loop; this is a *generic* `for` loop. Instead of incrementing a numeric control variable after each loop, this construct uses a special kind of function called an *iterator*. The `string.gmatch()` function is one such iterator. It searches a string (specified in its first argument) for a pattern (specified in its second argument). Because it's an iterator, it returns the next available result each time it's called. When there are no more results, the loop concludes.

Combined with the pattern you're passing to it (`"[^%s]+"`), the entire call to `string.gmatch()` can be literally translated as "find anything in the `msg` string that's not a space, then return everything until you reach a space or the end of the string." Because it's being used in a generic `for` loop, each returned value is placed into the local variable `word`. The loop continues until `string.gmatch()` doesn't have any more words to return.

The content of the loop is only one line. Using the built-in `table.insert()` function, the most recently returned `word` is placed into the `args` table for later reference. Entries in the `args` table are arranged in the order in which they were inserted, which means the first one (if there is one) is the slash-command option and any additional ones are arguments to it. The first entry inserted in this way is given the key 1, followed by 2, 3, 4, and so on.

The first edition of the book *Programming in Lua* by Roberto Ierusalimschy is available free of charge online and is a great resource for picking up the finer points of the language. Numeric `for` loops are discussed in section 4.3.4, generic ones in 4.3.5, and patterns are covered in section 20.2. The address is `http://lua.org/pil/`.

Looking for a Command Match

Now that each word in the command has been separated into its own table entry, you can check to see if the user has entered a valid command. First you check to see if there actually were any words entered in addition to the slash-command. If so, see if the first one matches any of the slash-command options you care about. In addition to the five settings outlined earlier, one additional command (`options`) will toggle the options panel.

Add the following lines to `Whereabouts_SlashCommand()`, right below the block of code you just finished:

```
if ( args[1] ) then
    if ( args[1] == "options" ) then
        Whereabouts_Options_Toggle();
    elseif ( args[1] == "show" ) then
        Whereabouts_Toggle();
    elseif ( args[1] == "lock" ) then
        Whereabouts_Options.lock = not Whereabouts_Options.lock;
    elseif ( args[1] == "tooltip" ) then
        Whereabouts_Options.tooltip = not ↵
Whereabouts_Options.tooltip;
    elseif ( args[1] == "worldmap" ) then
        Whereabouts_WorldMap_Toggle();
```

The notation `args[1]` refers to the first entry in the `args` table. If no words were placed into it by the previous loop, then a reference to it returns `nil`, a special value indicating the absence of data. A value of `nil` evaluates to `false` in an `if` statement. This check needs to be made first because comparing `nil` to a string (as you would do in the subsequent `if` and `elseif` statements) would generate an error message.

You begin checking one-by-one to see if the command is recognizable, first with an `if` statement, then with `elseif` statements. The `elseif` keyword can follow an `if` statement (or another `elseif` statement) and is evaluated only if all the previous statements in the chain are `false`. Because `args[1]` can match only one of the values you're checking it against, why bother checking every single one of them if a match has already been found?

You can see that most of the time, when a match is found, a simple toggle function is called (two of which don't exist yet). However, for `"lock"` and `"tooltip"` there's no frame to toggle, only a variable, so you use the not keyword to toggle the variable's value. When preceding a statement, not causes it to return the opposite of what it would otherwise evaluate to. So, in the seventh line of the preceding code, if Whereabouts_Options.lock is equal to false, it will be assigned the value true by the not statement to the right of the equals sign. Any Boolean value is simply reversed when paired with the not keyword.

Handling a Command That Requires an Argument

Unlike the rest of the settings, which are Boolean, the Whereabouts_Options.alpha setting is numerical. To be more specific, it requires a floating-point number between 0 and 1, with 0 representing complete transparency and 1 representing complete opacity. The user needs to enter a number following /whereabouts alpha. Fortunately, because of how things have already been set up, that number (if it exists) will reside in args[2].

Make sure you align the following block of code with the rest of the elseif statements so that the long chain of them is continued:

```
elseif ( args[1] == "alpha" ) then
   local alpha = tonumber(args[2])
   if ( alpha and alpha >= 0 and alpha <= 1 ) then
      Whereabouts_Options.alpha = alpha;
      Whereabouts_Frame:SetAlpha(alpha);
   else
      Whereabouts_Message(WHEREABOUTS_OPTIONS_ALPHAWRONG);
   end
```

To a computer, there's a fundamental difference between the character 5 followed by the character 4 in a string of text, and the numerical value 54. That's where the tonumber() function comes in. It takes a string as an argument, and if that string looks like a number, its numerical value is returned.

Once it's been determined that the user entered the "alpha" command, an elaborate check is made on its argument. The check involves three questions, in order:

1. Is it a number? The tonumber() function returns nil if the string isn't a recognizable number, which will cause the entire statement to be false.

2. Is the number greater than or equal to zero?

3. Is the number less than or equal to one?

If the value passes all three conditions, then the setting is stored in memory and the widget function SetAlpha() is called to set the transparency of the window.

If it fails any of the three checks, you can print a message telling the user which values are appropriate. The Whereabouts_Message() function hasn't been written yet, but when it is, it will display any message passed to it in the main chat window. You might also be wondering about the bizarre global variable WHEREABOUTS_OPTIONS_ALPHAWRONG, which is a good segue into the topic of *localization*.

The Basics of Localization

Millions of people play World of Warcraft and a whole lot of them don't speak English. They still might want to use the addons you create though, and that's why you should spend the time to make sure they're easily localizable; it's not even very much work.

The basic concept is this: Instead of hard-coding text strings into your scripts, like this:

```
myFontString:SetText("I do not speak French");
```

Create a separate Lua file called enUS.lua (or something similar), set it up in your TOC to load before your addon's other files, and populate it with global variables containing any strings your addon needs, such as the following:

```
MYADDON_NOFRENCH = "I do not speak French";
```

Then, in your addon's code, simply reference the variable instead of writing out the string:

```
myFontString:SetText(MYADDON_NOFRENCH);
```

When a French-speaking player comes along and decides to localize your addon, she only needs to copy your localization file, rename it to something like frFR.lua, and replace all of your strings with French ones:

```
MYADDON_NOFRENCH = "Je ne parle pas français";
```

Then she surrounds all the variables with a big if statement that looks like:

```
if ( GetLocale() == "frFR" ) then
    MYADDON_NOFRENCH = "Je ne parle pas français";
end
```

Finally, she adds the French file to the addon's TOC right after the English one. When the addon is loaded, a player in the United States will see the English strings. However in France, the if statement will evaluate to true and the global variables will be overwritten with the alternate French versions. Now everyone can use your addon, and your code doesn't have to change one bit!

Here's a list of the various WoW region codes:

- DeDE: German
- enGB: English (Great Britain)
- enUS: English (United States)
- esES: Spanish
- frFR: French
- koKR: Korean
- zhCN: Simplified Chinese (China)
- zhTW: Traditional Chinese (Taiwan)

It's generally a good idea to leave one language's global variables (probably yours) outside of an `if` statement. List that language first in the TOC file (before any other languages). This ensures that all necessary variables are initialized to something. Then if any of them are left out of the various translations, they'll just show up in the default language.

Adding Strings to Your Localization File

You created a localization file called `enUS.lua` in Chapter 10. Open it now, and add the following line:

```
WHEREABOUTS_OPTIONS_ALPHAWRONG = "Alpha must be between 0 and 1";
```

Now switch back to `Whereabouts.lua` to finish up the slash-command handler.

At the end of the long list of `elseif` statements comes your final `else` statement. The situation in which this code is executed comes about when the user types something after the slash-command that's not a recognizable option. In that case, you print a message informing him that his command doesn't exist and that he can type `/wa` for help:

```
else
    Whereabouts_Message(WHEREABOUTS_NOCOMMAND);
end
```

Then add the necessary string to `enUS.lua` as well:

```
WHEREABOUTS_NOCOMMAND = "That's not an option, type \"/wa\" ↵
for help";
```

> **Note** This text string might look like it has some typos in it, but that's not the case. The double-quote character signifies the beginning and end of a string in Lua, so you need a special way to insert it into the string itself. Do this by prefixing the quotation mark with a backslash.

Printing a List of Commands

Now that you've taken care of the case in which `args[1]` exists (the user typed *something* following the slash-command), it's time to deal with the alternative. If `args[1]` doesn't exist, that means the user typed `/wa` or `/whereabouts` without anything else. If this is the case, you can print out some help in the form of a list of valid slash-commands:

```
else
    Whereabouts_Message(WHEREABOUTS_USAGE);
    Whereabouts_Message("options - "..WHEREABOUTS_OPTIONS);
    Whereabouts_Message("show - "..WHEREABOUTS_OPTIONS_SHOW);
    Whereabouts_Message("lock - "..WHEREABOUTS_OPTIONS_LOCK);
    Whereabouts_Message("tooltip - "..WHEREABOUTS_OPTIONS_TOOLTIP);
    Whereabouts_Message("worldmap - "..WHEREABOUTS_OPTIONS ↵
_WORLDMAP);
    Whereabouts_Message("alpha <#> - "..WHEREABOUTS_OPTIONS_ALPHA);
end
```

Notice anything strange? How about those two periods in most of the lines? Two periods next to each other is called the *concatenation* operator. It's a fancy name, but what it does is simply join together the two strings on either side of it.

Don't forget to update enUS.lua too, with the following lines:

```
WHEREABOUTS_USAGE = "Usage: /whereabouts <option> or /wa ↵
<option>";
WHEREABOUTS_OPTIONS = "Toggle the options panel";
WHEREABOUTS_OPTIONS_SHOW = "Show the coordinates window";
WHEREABOUTS_OPTIONS_LOCK = "Lock the coordinates window in place";
WHEREABOUTS_OPTIONS_TOOLTIP = "Enable the tooltip display";
WHEREABOUTS_OPTIONS_WORLDMAP= "Enable coordinates on the World ↵
Map";
WHEREABOUTS_OPTIONS_ALPHA = "Set the transparency of the window";
```

Finally, cap the whole function off with one last end. Listing 13-1 shows your Whereabouts_SlashCommand() function as it is now.

Listing 13-1   Whereabouts_SlashCommand()

```
function Whereabouts_SlashCommand(msg)
   msg = string.lower(msg);
   local args = {};
   for word in string.gmatch(msg, "[^%s]+") do
      table.insert(args, word);
   end
   if ( args[1] ) then
      if ( args[1] == "options" ) then
         Whereabouts_Options_Toggle();
      elseif ( args[1] == "show" ) then
         Whereabouts_Toggle();
      elseif ( args[1] == "lock" ) then
         Whereabouts_Options.lock = not ↵
Whereabouts_Options.lock;
      elseif ( args[1] == "tooltip" ) then
         Whereabouts_Options.tooltip = not ↵
Whereabouts_Options.tooltip;
      elseif ( args[1] == "worldmap" ) then
         Whereabouts_WorldMap_Toggle();
      elseif ( args[1] == "alpha" ) then
         local alpha = tonumber(args[2])
         if ( alpha) and alpha >= 0 and alpha <= 1 ) then
            Whereabouts_Options.alpha = alpha;
            Whereabouts_Frame:SetAlpha(alpha);
         else
```

continued

Listing 13-1 *Continued*

```
Whereabouts_Message(WHEREABOUTS_OPTIONS_ALPHAWRONG);
          end
      else
          Whereabouts_Message(WHEREABOUTS_NOCOMMAND);
      end
   else
      Whereabouts_Message(WHEREABOUTS_USAGE);
      Whereabouts_Message("options - "..WHEREABOUTS_OPTIONS);
      Whereabouts_Message("show - "..WHEREABOUTS_OPTIONS_SHOW);
      Whereabouts_Message("lock - "..WHEREABOUTS_OPTIONS_LOCK);
              Whereabouts_Message("tooltip - ↵
"..WHEREABOUTS_OPTIONS_TOOLTIP);
              Whereabouts_Message("worldmap - ↵
"..WHEREABOUTS_OPTIONS_WORLDMAP);
              Whereabouts_Message("alpha <number> - ↵
"..WHEREABOUTS_OPTIONS_ALPHA);
   end
end
```

Writing Messages to the Chat Window

Your slash-command parser made ample use of the `Whereabouts_Message()` function, so let's get its declaration out of the way. Add the following to `Whereabouts.lua`:

```
function Whereabouts_Message(msg)
    DEFAULT_CHAT_FRAME:AddMessage("[Whereabouts] "..msg);
end
```

`DEFAULT_CHAT_FRAME` is a global variable that points to exactly what its name implies — the default chat frame. The main purpose of this function is to concatenate a little tag onto the beginning of all Whereabouts' messages so the user knows exactly where they came from.

Note   Messages printed to the chat window using this method are white by default. Additional arguments to the function allow you to change the color of the text; see WoWWiki for more information.

At this point, you can load up the game (and Whereabouts) without getting any errors. Type `/wa` to see the slash-command list and localization file in action (see Figure 13-1). Unfortunately, if you try to use the `options` or `worldmap` commands, you get an error because you haven't created those UI elements yet. `lock` and `tooltip` also don't do anything yet, but `show` and `alpha` work great.

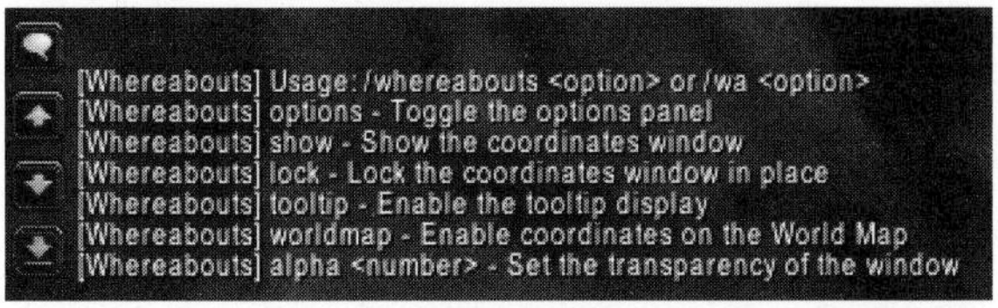

[Whereabouts] Usage: /whereabouts <option> or /wa <option>
[Whereabouts] options - Toggle the options panel
[Whereabouts] show - Show the coordinates window
[Whereabouts] lock - Lock the coordinates window in place
[Whereabouts] tooltip - Enable the tooltip display
[Whereabouts] worldmap - Enable coordinates on the World Map
[Whereabouts] alpha <number> - Set the transparency of the window

FIGURE 13-1: The Whereabouts slash-command handler spits out some help.

Locking the Whereabouts Frame in Place

The locking feature in Whereabouts is probably the simplest one to implement. Because the dragging operation is initiated in a specific place, all you need to do is check the status of Whereabouts_Options.lock. If it's true, you can block the dragging operation from taking place. Open Whereabouts.xml and go down to the line:

```
if ( button == "LeftButton" ) then
```

You're already making a check to see if the drag should happen, so all you have to do is throw in another check using the and keyword, like this:

```
if ( button == "LeftButton" and not ↵
Whereabouts_Options.lock ) then
```

You only want to drag when Whereabouts_Options.lock is equal to false, so you have to use the not keyword in front of it to reverse the Boolean result of the statement. That's it; the locking option is now enabled.

Adding Information to the Tooltip

Instead of each UI element having its own tooltip object, there's one main tooltip object (called GameTooltip) that's constantly being modified. In this section, you add two widget event handlers to your frame — one for the mouse hovering over the Whereabouts window, and one for when it leaves. In the former situation, you take control of the tooltip, add text to it, change the color of some of the text, and update it for display. In the latter, you simply hide the tooltip.

To start, add two new widget event handlers to Whereabouts.xml:

```
<OnEnter>
    Whereabouts_OnEnter(self);
</OnEnter>
<OnLeave>
    GameTooltip:Hide();
</OnLeave>
```

Setting up and displaying the tooltip takes some work, and it'll be easier to shuttle the process off into a separate function. Only one line of code is needed for the OnLeave handler, so you might as well put it in the XML file. You've already encountered the widget function Hide() and its use here is no different; the tooltip will be hidden when the mouse leaves the Whereabouts window.

Switch to Whereabouts.lua and create a new function declaration:

```
function Whereabouts_OnEnter(self)
   if ( Whereabouts_Options.tooltip ) then
      GameTooltip_SetDefaultAnchor(GameTooltip, self);
      GameTooltip:SetText(WHEREABOUTS_TOOLTIP_TITLE);
      GameTooltip:AddLine(WHEREABOUTS_TOOLTIP_SUBTITLE);
      if ( Whereabouts_Options.lock ) then
         GameTooltip:AddLine(WHEREABOUTS_TOOLTIP_LOCKED);
      else
         GameTooltip:AddLine(WHEREABOUTS_TOOLTIP_LEFTCLICK);
      end
      GameTooltip:AddLine(WHEREABOUTS_TOOLTIP_RIGHTCLICK);
      GameTooltipTextLeft1:SetTextColor(1, 1, 1);
      GameTooltipTextLeft2:SetTextColor(1, 1, 1);
      GameTooltip:Show();
   end
end
```

Let's go through this step-by-step. First, you check the status of Whereabouts_Options.tooltip; if it's false you can skip the whole process entirely.

Next, GameTooltip_SetDefaultAnchor() is a pre-existing function that sets up the tooltip in the lower-right corner of the screen. Many of the default UI elements use this configuration. The alternative is to use GameTooltip:SetOwner(), which enables you to set an anchor point manually. You don't need to bother with that right now, though.

The SetText() method populates the first (large) line of the tooltip, and then subsequent calls to AddLine() insert smaller lines of text below it. The tooltip's lines are actually separated into left-aligned and right-aligned entries (check out the formatting on an item's tooltip to see exactly what I mean), so when you reference individual lines, it's important to use the correct names. All text is aligned left by default, so when re-coloring lines with the SetTextColor() method, you need to reference the left-aligned objects. This method takes three arguments (red, green, and blue) as floating point values between 0 and 1.

Note   You might be wondering about the strangely named tooltip objects referenced in the previous block of code. Basically, each line of the tooltip exists as two discrete objects: one for the left-aligned text and one for the right. For more information about how these objects are named, refer to http://wowwiki.com/UIOBJECT_GameTooltip.

As you can see, you're performing a little logic in the middle of the function to display a different message based on whether the window is locked or not. Finally, after adding lines to the tooltip, a call to the Show() function is required to resize it properly.

Of course, you need to update enUS.lua with some new strings as follows:

```
WHEREABOUTS_TOOLTIP_TITLE = "Whereabouts";
WHEREABOUTS_TOOLTIP_SUBTITLE = "Zone Coordinates";
WHEREABOUTS_TOOLTIP_LOCKED = "This window is locked in place.";
WHEREABOUTS_TOOLTIP_LEFTCLICK = "Left-click and drag to
move this window.";
WHEREABOUTS_TOOLTIP_RIGHTCLICK = "Right-click to toggle
the options panel.";
```

Now you can enter the game again to test the locking and tooltip features (see Figure 13-2). Turn them on and off with /wa lock and /wa tooltip.

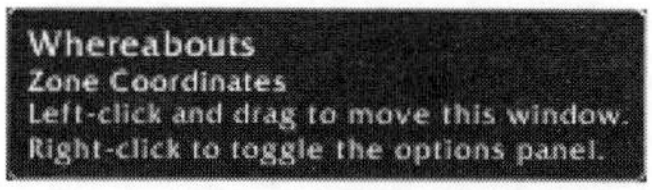

FIGURE **13-2: The freshly minted Whereabouts tooltip.**

Adding Coordinates to the World Map

The last major feature left to implement (besides the options panel) is the display of coordinates on the World Map. Because of the way parenting works, you can create a new frame that's parented to the existing World Map frame. That means your addition will essentially become part of the World Map, hiding and showing along with its parent automatically. All you have to do is format, anchor, and update it.

In Chapter 10 you created a file called Whereabouts_WorldMap.xml. When an addon starts getting more complicated, it's a good idea to separate different features into individual files. The general rule is that each Frame object gets its own XML file, and each XML file gets its own Lua file. However, this feature is simple enough that it doesn't even need a Lua file of its own. When you work on the options panel in the next chapter, it will have its own Lua and XML files.

The Whereabouts_WorldMap.xml file needs to have the same outermost Ui element; simply copy and paste from Whereabouts.xml. Your Frame definition changes a bit, though. The name needs to be unique, and the parent should be set to WorldMapFrame:

```
<Ui xmlns="http://www.blizzard.com/wow/ui/" xmlns:xsi="http:
//www.w3.org/2001/XMLSchema-instance" xsi:schemaLocation=
"http://www.blizzard.com/wow/ui/ ..\FrameXML\UI.xsd">
    <Frame name="Whereabouts_WorldMap_Frame"
parent="WorldMapFrame">
    </Frame>
</Ui>
```

All you need is a single `FontString` element to display the coordinates, so you don't have to worry about the size and positioning of the overall `Frame` object, just the `FontString`. You can jump right in with the `Layers` element and everything it contains. Remember, all of this goes inside the `Frame` object's opening and closing tags:

```
<Layers>
    <Layer level="OVERLAY">
        <FontString name="$Parent_Text" ↵
inherits="GameFontHighlightSmall">
            <Anchors>
                <Anchor point="BOTTOM" ↵
relativeTo="WorldMapPositioningGuide">
                    <Offset>
                        <AbsDimension x="0" y="11"/>
                    </Offset>
                </Anchor>
            </Anchors>
        </FontString>
    </Layer>
</Layers>
```

Notice how your `FontString` is positioned relative to the `WorldMapPositioningGuide` object. Because the World Map is dynamically scaled to the size of the player's screen, positioning an object relative to `WorldMapFrame` results in inconsistent results with different screen resolutions. Using `WorldMapPositioningGuide` instead solves this problem.

Also, `GameFontHighlightSmall` is a font template for small white text.

On the Web Although the page itself is about a specific API call, a decent list of font templates is available at `http://wowwiki.com/API_Button_SetTextFontObject`.

Your `Frame` object also needs an `OnUpdate` handler to update the text, just like the main Whereabouts window. Why use `OnUpdate` instead of `OnShow` when the player can't be seen or controlled while the World Map is open? Well, it's conceivable that they're still moving if they have auto-run turned on, if they're following someone, or if they're on a mount or vehicle. The display should reflect that their coordinates are changing.

You'll also need a handler for `OnHide` because of how the World Map operates. The coordinates you're using from `GetPlayerMapPosition()` are actually designed to place the marker for your character on the World Map, so as you change maps the coordinates change as well. Unfortunately, when you close the World Map this function continues outputting coordinates for the last map you were looking at, which isn't necessarily the zone the character is in. Thus, when the frame is hidden, you need to call `SetMapToCurrentZone()` so the normal Whereabouts window keeps displaying the correct numbers.

The widget event handler definitions should look like this:

```
<Scripts>
   <OnUpdate>
      Whereabouts_OnUpdate(self, elapsed);
   </OnUpdate>
   <OnHide>
      SetMapToCurrentZone();
   </OnHide>
</Scripts>
```

But wait; why are you using the same `Whereabouts_OnUpdate()` function that the main Whereabouts window uses? Well, it seems unnecessary to duplicate the code, and with a minor modification outlined in the next section, you can make it work for both UI objects.

`Whereabouts_WorldMap.xml` is now complete, so you can save and close it.

Using getglobal() and GetName() Together

Open `Whereabouts.lua` and find `Whereabouts_OnUpdate()`, specifically the line:

```
Whereabouts_Frame_Text:SetText(text);
```

To modify this function to affect `Whereabouts_WorldMap_Frame_Text`, you could just add this line below it:

```
Whereabouts_WorldMap_Frame_Text:SetText(text);
```

But that's not a very elegant solution.

A better solution lies in the use of the variable `self`. If you remember, `self` is always equal to the object calling the function, which in one case is `Whereabouts_Frame` and in the other case is `Whereabouts_WorldMap_Frame`. If you could just append `_Text` onto the end of whichever object called the function, you'd be all set. Fortunately, you can, thanks to:

- `getglobal()`: Passes a string; returns an object that has the same name, if it exists.
- `GetName()`: Widget function; returns the name of the object as a string.

Combine the two of them to get your solution:

```
getglobal(self:GetName().."_Text"):SetText(text);
```

As you can see, naming XML objects consistently and using the `$parent` keyword can have hidden benefits down the road. In this case, it enabled you to write elegant, versatile code.

Toggling the World Map Coordinates

The last thing you have to do about the World Map coordinates is to create the toggle function. Because this display is optional, you need to have a way to turn it on and off. You've already created a call to the `Whereabouts_WorldMap_Toggle()` function from the slash-command handler, so all you need to do now is implement the function. Create the following function declaration in Whereabouts.lua:

```
function Whereabouts_WorldMap_Toggle()
   if ( Whereabouts_WorldMap_Frame:IsShown() ) then
      Whereabouts_WorldMap_Frame:Hide();
      Whereabouts_Options.worldmap = false;
   else
      Whereabouts_WorldMap_Frame:Show();
      Whereabouts_Options.worldmap = true;
   end
end
```

As you can see, this is very similar to the previous toggle function you wrote, except that this time the state of the frame is stored in a variable that's preserved between sessions. In fact, you need to go back to the old Whereabouts_Toggle() function and update it to do the same thing:

```
function Whereabouts_Toggle()
   if ( Whereabouts_Frame:IsShown() ) then
      Whereabouts_Frame:Hide();
      Whereabouts_Options.show = false;
   else
      Whereabouts_Frame:Show();
      Whereabouts_Options.show = true;
   end
end
```

Now's a good time to fire up the game and check out the new World Map display. If you don't see anything, remember to toggle it on with /wa worldmap.

Creating a Traditional Event Handler

Remember the description of the difference between traditional in-game events and widget events? So far you haven't had to interact with traditional events at all, but that's about to change.

You may have noticed that even though your settings variables are being stored and retrieved between sessions, the appearance of the Whereabouts frame and the status of the World Map display don't persist when you log out and log back in. Why?

The reason is this: Although you have values stored in variables, they have nothing to do with the actual state of the frames yet. When the player logs in, the frames simply take their default state, which is visible with full opacity. When you tweak the settings using the slash-command options, the frames are updated. The problem is that they're not yet being updated when the user enters the world.

Unfortunately, saved variables aren't available immediately when the game loads. There's a specific moment during the loading process when they become available; and that moment is marked by a game event.

In addition, you might have noticed that the coordinates in the Whereabouts window don't change when your character moves from one zone to another. You'll use a different event to refresh the coordinates whenever a new zone is entered.

Registering Events

Individual events must be registered to `Frame` objects, and whenever a registered one is fired, that frame's `OnEvent` widget handler is called with the name of the event as an argument. The traditional place to register events is in a frame's `OnLoad` handler. The events you need to look for are as follows:

- `VARIABLES_LOADED`: When this event fires, you know for sure that your saved variables have been loaded and are available.

- `ZONE_CHANGED_NEW_AREA`: This event fires whenever you enter a new zone.

Open `Whereabouts.lua` and go to the `Whereabouts_OnLoad()` function. Right before the end of the function, add these two lines:

```
self:RegisterEvent("VARIABLES_LOADED");
self:RegisterEvent("ZONE_CHANGED_NEW_AREA");
```

Then in `Whereabouts.xml`, add the following widget event handler:

```
<Scripts>
   <OnEvent>
      Whereabouts_OnEvent(self, event, ...);
   </OnEvent>
</Scripts>
```

Now the `Whereabouts_OnEvent()` function will be called whenever either of the two events fires.

Creating an Event Handler

Creating the event handler itself is trivial. You need to check the `event` variable to see which event was actually fired, and then act accordingly. Create the following function in `Whereabouts.lua`:

```
function Whereabouts_OnEvent(self, event, ...)
   if ( event == "VARIABLES_LOADED" ) then
      Whereabouts_InitDisplay();
   elseif ( event == "ZONE_CHANGED_NEW_AREA" ) then
      SetMapToCurrentZone();
   end
end
```

The `Whereabouts_InitDisplay()` function is where the addon looks at its saved variables and updates the various frames as necessary. You'll implement it in the next section.

The `SetMapToCurrentZone()` function is a built-in function that does exactly what you need — it changes the current map displayed by the World Map to the one for the zone your character is in. This effectively updates the current coordinates as well. When you move from one zone to the next, the coordinates will instantly change over.

Initializing Whereabouts

Of all your saved values, only the following need to be initialized:

- `Whereabouts_Options.show`: The Whereabouts window is visible by default. If this variable is false, the window should be hidden.

- `Whereabouts_Options.worldmap`: Likewise, World Map coordinates are visible by default, and should be hidden if this variable is false.

- `Whereabouts_Options.alpha`: The transparency of the window is 1 by default. You can simply set the transparency to the value of this variable.

Both `lock` and `tooltip` are passive; they don't affect the state of something else, and their value directly determines the behavior of their respective features, so you don't need to worry about them here. Create the initialization function in `Whereabouts.lua`:

```
function Whereabouts_InitDisplay()
   if ( not Whereabouts_Options.show ) then
      Whereabouts_Frame:Hide();
   end
   if ( not Whereabouts_Options.worldmap ) then
      Whereabouts_WorldMap_Frame:Hide();
   end
   Whereabouts_Frame:SetAlpha(Whereabouts_Options.alpha);
end
```

And that brings us to the end of the chapter; all of the addon's features are completed and working properly. All of them except the options panel, of course.

Whereabouts Is Almost Finished

In this chapter you implemented the bulk of Whereabouts' extra features, including saved settings, a slash-command parser, a World Map display, and a localization system, all of which flesh out the addon considerably. You also learned about the somewhat daunting concepts of tables and loops, and how to use them.

In the next chapter, you finish Whereabouts by creating its options panel. That task involves a combination of both XML and Lua code. Fortunately, you'll be going into it with some experience in both of these languages!

The Whereabouts Options Panel

This chapter focuses solely on building an options panel for the Whereabouts addon. If your addon has more than one or two basic settings, seriously consider creating a control panel for it. World of Warcraft is a visual, point-and-click game in which users (for the most part) expect to control settings with widgets, not necessarily typed commands. A well-conceived options interface will instantly make your addon more accessible and user-friendly.

The Whereabouts options panel needs to provide control over the five main options in the addon:

- show — Checkbox: Is the window displayed?
- lock — Checkbox: Is the window locked in place?
- tooltip — Checkbox: Is the tooltip enabled?
- worldmap — Checkbox: Are coordinates shown on the World Map?
- alpha — Slider: How transparent is the window?

In addition, the options window has to be created (a Frame object). It needs a title and some info (two FontString objects), labels for all of the controls (fortunately, text labels are built into most widget templates), and a means to close it when the user is finished (a Button object).

In Chapter 13, you determined the two ways in which the user would access the options panel — using the slash command /wa options or right-clicking the window — and programmed the first one. Now you'll implement the second.

Right-Clicking to Open the Options Panel

Before starting on the options panel itself, you'll first take care of the second method of accessing it: right-clicking on the main Whereabouts frame. Because you've already set up this frame to be draggable using a widget event handler, this should be somewhat familiar territory.

Open `Whereabouts.xml` and scroll down to the handlers, specifically the `OnMouseDown` handler. You want to add a button-checking `elseif` statement right below the `if` statement that's already there. Add the following two lines before the `end` keyword:

```
elseif ( button == "RightButton" ) then
   Whereabouts_Options_Toggle();
```

You also have to implement the toggle function itself. The toggle function doesn't need to update a variable because the state of the options panel doesn't have to be preserved between game sessions. Open `Whereabouts_Options.lua`, and add the following code:

```
function Whereabouts_Options_Toggle()
   if ( Whereabouts_Options_Frame:IsShown() ) then
      Whereabouts_Options_Frame:Hide();
   else
      Whereabouts_Options_Frame:Show();
   end
end
```

Creating the Frame's XML Code

The XML definition of the Whereabouts options frame is similar to the definition of the Whereabouts window itself, at least at first. In fact, you can copy and paste the appropriate code from `Whereabouts.xml` and then tweak it, but make sure you catch all the changes provided for the options frame. Open the `Whereabouts_Options.xml` file and start it off with the following code:

```
<Ui xmlns="http://www.blizzard.com/wow/ui/" xmlns:xsi="http:↵
//www.w3.org/2001/XMLSchema-instance" xsi:schemaLocation↵
="http://www.blizzard.com/wow/ui/
..\FrameXML\UI.xsd">
   <Frame name="Whereabouts_Options_Frame" hidden="true" ↵
toplevel="true" frameStrata="HIGH" enableMouse="true" movable↵
="true" parent="UIParent" clampedToScreen="true">
      <Size>
         <AbsDimension x="340" y="260" />
      </Size>
      <Anchors>
         <Anchor point="CENTER" />
      </Anchors>
      <Backdrop edgeFile="Interface\Tooltips\UI-Tooltip-Border" ↵
bgFile="Interface\Tooltips\UI-Tooltip-Background">
         <BackgroundInsets>
            <AbsInset left="4" right="4" top="4" bottom="4" />
         </BackgroundInsets>
```

```
        <EdgeSize>
           <AbsValue val="16" />
        </EdgeSize>
        <Color r="0" g="0" b="0" a="0.8" />
        <BorderColor r="1" g="1" b="1" a="1" />
     </Backdrop>
   </Frame>
</Ui>
```

The `Ui` definition always remains the same. Then the name of the `Frame` is set. All of its attributes can remain the same except for one addition: Specifying `hidden="true"` changes the default state of the window so that when the UI is first loaded this window won't be visible.

Then the absolute dimensions are modified because the options frame is much larger than the coordinates window. You can use the same `Backdrop` textures, the same inset values, and the same `EdgeSize` setting. The colors are tweaked a bit so the background is darker (less transparent) and the border is opaque white.

Giving the Frame a Title

Next you add a title to the frame, and a line of text that lets the user know he can drag it around. These lines of text are defined in much the same way that you defined the coordinates display `FontString` on the main window. However, this time they're static so you don't need to worry about any updates or events. As always, they need to go inside a `Layer` object. Here's the code:

```
<Layers>
   <Layer level="OVERLAY">
      <FontString inherits="GameFontHighlightLarge"↵
text="WHEREABOUTS_OPTIONS_TITLE">
         <Anchors>
            <Anchor point="TOPLEFT">
               <Offset>
                  <AbsDimension x="20" y="-20"/>
               </Offset>
            </Anchor>
         </Anchors>
      </FontString>
      <FontString inherits="GameFontDisableSmall"↵
text="WHEREABOUTS_OPTIONS_LEFTCLICK">
         <Anchors>
            <Anchor point="TOPLEFT">
               <Offset>
                  <AbsDimension x="20" y="-36"/>
               </Offset>
            </Anchor>
         </Anchors>
      </FontString>
   </Layer>
</Layers>
```

Because you don't need to reference these FontString objects from anywhere else, you don't need to name them. The templates they inherit from (GameFontHighlightLarge and GameFontDisableSmall) produce large white text and small gray text respectively (see Figure 14-1).

Whereabouts Options
Left-click and drag to move this window.

FIGURE **14-1: The options frame gets a title.**

Also, take notice of the text attribute, which can be used as a one-time deal instead of the SetText() method you used earlier — you can still use SetText() later to overwrite the string if you need to. While you could put strings of text directly into the text attributes' values, the game first checks to see if they're equal to a global variable — and in this case, they are (since they'll be defined in the localization file).

> **Note** When using offsets to position an element onscreen (as you did in the preceding code), you always measure from the anchor point. Positive *x* values always denote going to the right and positive *y* values always denote upward movement.

Make sure you add two new entries to your enUS.lua file:

```
WHEREABOUTS_OPTIONS_TITLE = "Whereabouts Options";
WHEREABOUTS_OPTIONS_LEFTCLICK = "Left-click and drag to move this ↵
window.";
```

Creating the First Checkbox

Checkboxes, which are defined by the CheckButton object, are descendents of frames, which means they need to be defined inside the Frames element in your XML. Add the following code inside the Frame element, right below the end of the Layers definition:

```
<Frames>
    <CheckButton name="$Parent_ShowBox" ↵
inherits="OptionsCheckButtonTemplate">
        <Anchors>
            <Anchor point="TOPLEFT">
                <Offset>
```

```
                    <AbsDimension x="20" y="-60"/>
                </Offset>
            </Anchor>
        </Anchors>
        <Scripts>
            <OnLoad>
                OptionsCheckButton_SetText(WHEREABOUTS_OPTIONS_SHOW);
            </OnLoad>
            <OnClick>
                Whereabouts_Toggle();
            </OnClick>
        </Scripts>
    </CheckButton>
</Frames>
```

The good news is that most of the work is already done for you! Because you can make use of the built-in checkbox template called `OptionsCheckButtonTemplate`, you don't have to define the object's size, textures, colors, or behavior. It's important to name the object though, because its state (checked or unchecked) needs to be initialized when the options panel is first shown. As always, you also need to anchor and position the object; in this case, keep a 20-unit margin on the left and move the box 24 units down from the top of the `FontString` object above it (for a total of 60 units down from the top of the window).

The `CheckButton` object is descended from the `Frame` object, so it can contain its own widget event handlers, of which you need two: `OnLoad` and `OnClick`. You can't use the `text` attribute with a checkbox like you did with the `FontString` objects, so you need to use a built-in UI function in the `OnLoad` handler instead. Fortunately, you can reuse the same localization string that you used in the slash-command handler. Finally, when the box is clicked, `OnClick` fires and the Whereabouts window is toggled.

The danger posed by a checkbox is the possibility of it getting out of sync with the setting it controls; for example, if the box was checked when the frame was hidden or unchecked when the frame was shown, clicking it would toggle both states, keeping it out of sync permanently. That's why you need to initialize the checkbox, as well as be vigilant about any other ways your settings could possibly change. You'll revisit your slash-command handler at the end of the chapter to protect against these synchronization problems.

Creating the Rest of the Checkboxes

There are three more Boolean options that need checkboxes. It's simple — just rinse and repeat:

```
<CheckButton name="$Parent_LockBox" ↵
inherits="OptionsCheckButtonTemplate">
    <Anchors>
        <Anchor point="TOPLEFT">
            <Offset>
                <AbsDimension x="20" y="-90"/>
```

```xml
            </Offset>
          </Anchor>
        </Anchors>
        <Scripts>
          <OnLoad>
            OptionsCheckButton_SetText(WHEREABOUTS_OPTIONS_LOCK);
          </OnLoad>
          <OnClick>
            Whereabouts_Options.lock = not Whereabouts_Options.lock;
          </OnClick>
        </Scripts>
      </CheckButton>
      <CheckButton name="$Parent_TooltipBox" ↵
inherits="OptionsCheckButtonTemplate">
        <Anchors>
          <Anchor point="TOPLEFT">
            <Offset>
              <AbsDimension x="20" y="-120"/>
            </Offset>
          </Anchor>
        </Anchors>
        <Scripts>
          <OnLoad>
            OptionsCheckButton_SetText(WHEREABOUTS_OPTIONS_TOOLTIP);
          </OnLoad>
          <OnClick>
            Whereabouts_Options.tooltip = not ↵
Whereabouts_Options.tooltip;
          </OnClick>
        </Scripts>
      </CheckButton>
      <CheckButton name="$Parent_WorldMapBox" ↵
inherits="OptionsCheckButtonTemplate">
        <Anchors>
          <Anchor point="TOPLEFT">
            <Offset>
              <AbsDimension x="20" y="-150"/>
            </Offset>
          </Anchor>
        </Anchors>
        <Scripts>
          <OnLoad>
            OptionsCheckButton_SetText(WHEREABOUTS_OPTIONS_WORLDMAP);
          </OnLoad>
          <OnClick>
            Whereabouts_WorldMap_Toggle();
          </OnClick>
        </Scripts>
      </CheckButton>
```

Notice that each box is positioned 30 units down from the previous one (see Figure 14-2). Also, note how the actions taken in the OnClick handlers are precisely the same as the ones taken in the slash command handler you created in Chapter 13; either you toggle a variable, or you toggle a frame *and* a variable by calling one of your custom toggle functions.

If you test out the addon at this point, be aware that the sync problem hasn't been taken care of yet, so the checkboxes might display the wrong states.

FIGURE **14-2: The options panel is starting to look like an options panel.**

Adding a Slider to Control the Alpha Setting

The alpha (transparency) setting isn't Boolean, so a checkbox won't suffice. Instead, you'll use a *slider* — a widget that's designed to allow the user to select from a range of values.

Sliders are best suited to settings that have theoretically infinite values between a maximum and a minimum. They're also useful when only discrete steps between the min and max values are valid (like integers between 0 and 10). Even more limited, yet linearly related values such as high, medium, and low can be represented with a slider.

Sliders aren't any good for multiple choices in which there isn't a linear relationship among the elements (like apples, kiwis, or guavas, for example). It's best to use radio buttons or drop-down menus in those situations. These two types of widgets aren't covered in this book, although the WoW API does provide the means to create them.

Implementing the Slider object doesn't present any huge surprises, but it is slightly more complicated than the simple checkboxes. Add this code right below the last CheckButton tag, but still inside the Frames element:

```
<Slider name="$Parent_AlphaSlider"
inherits="OptionsSliderTemplate">
    <Anchors>
        <Anchor point="TOPLEFT">
            <Offset>
                <AbsDimension x="30" y="-210" />
```

```
                </Offset>
            </Anchor>
        </Anchors>
        <Scripts>
            <OnLoad>
                Whereabouts_SetupSlider(
                    self, WHEREABOUTS_OPTIONS_ALPHALABEL, 0, 1, 0);
            </OnLoad>
            <OnValueChanged>
                Whereabouts_Options.alpha = this:GetValue();
                Whereabouts_Frame:SetAlpha(Whereabouts_Options.alpha);
            </OnValueChanged>
        </Scripts>
    </Slider>
```

Much like the checkboxes, you inherit from a special template that provides the basic settings for the slider's size, behavior, and appearance. In terms of layout, the slider object gets a little bit more of a margin (the best appearance is achieved through trial and error; just tweak away) and is moved down until it isn't crowding the checkboxes.

Unlike checkboxes, sliders have quite a few values that need to be initialized, including their label, minimum and maximum values, and a setting called *step* that determines whether any value between the min and max is selectable or if there's a specific interval between values to which the slider should adhere. Because so much needs to be done, you'll create a function (discussed in the next section) that is passed all the necessary pieces of information as arguments. This turns what would normally be five lines of code per slider into only one. If you ever need to add another slider to this addon, you can use the same setup function.

The `OnValueChanged` handler, which is unique to sliders and status bars, is fired whenever the slider's value is changed (huge surprise there). When the event fires, you grab the slider's value, store it in your settings variable, and then update the transparency of the Whereabouts window. That gives you real-time feedback as the slider is moved around. The code is a little bit different than the slash-command handler's because the value here is coming from an interactive widget instead of a typed number.

A new localization string was also referenced in this block of code. Why not use the same string that you used in the slash-command help, as you did for all the checkboxes? Well, slider labels only have enough room for a couple of words, so you need a much shorter string here. Append this line to `enUS.lua`:

```
WHEREABOUTS_OPTIONS_ALPHALABEL = "Alpha";
```

Setting up a Slider

The earlier call to `Whereabouts_SetupSlider()` was passed five values: a reference to the slider object, a string, and three numbers. The string is the label and the numbers are the label, minimum value, maximum value, and step. Switch to the `Whereabouts_Options.lua` file and create the declaration for this function:

```
function Whereabouts_SetupSlider(self, text, myMin, myMax, step)
    getglobal(self:GetName().."Text"):SetText(text);
    getglobal(self:GetName().."Low"):SetText(myMin);
    getglobal(self:GetName().."High"):SetText(myMax);
    self:SetMinMaxValues(myMin, myMax);
    self:SetValueStep(step);
end
```

You use the `getglobal()` and `GetName()` trick discussed previously to set each label. When an object inherits from `OptionsSliderTemplate`, it gains all the objects that are defined in the template, some of which are `FontString` objects. These objects are named using the `$parent` keyword. Your slider is called:

```
Whereabouts_Options_Frame_AlphaSlider
```

So objects in the template named `$parentText`, `$parentLow`, and `$parentHigh` become known to your instance of the slider as:

```
Whereabouts_Options_Frame_AlphaSliderText
Whereabouts_Options_Frame_AlphaSliderLow
Whereabouts_Options_Frame_AlphaSliderHigh
```

That's why you can reference them dynamically using the `self` variable you passed to the function.

Anyway, `Text` is the overall label, `Low` is the minimum label, and `High` is the maximum label. The user doesn't need these labels, but it's helpful to display them. The labels are just informational, and setting them doesn't affect the inner workings of the slider at all. Your call to `SetMinMaxValues()` is what actually calibrates the slider, and the subsequent call to `SetValueStep()` takes care of the step quantity. You passed in a value of 0 for `step`, which means the interval is infinitely small. In reality, the possible values are limited by the width of the slider (it's only so many discreet units wide onscreen). As an experiment, set the `step` value to 0.1 and see what happens.

Your options panel is nearing completion (see Figure 14-3).

FIGURE **14-3:** The slider appears on the options panel.

Creating the Done Button

The last widget on the options panel is a simple Done button. Many operating system control panels and some of the control panels in WoW enable you to tweak settings without actually changing anything; and then you commit all the changes at once. Simple control panels like yours don't need that added layer of protection. There aren't any damaging controls in terms of lost time, lost data, or security; so every setting can go into effect immediately. That means you don't need a Cancel button. The only thing the Done button does is close the window.

The Button widget is about as simple as they come. Unlike the checkboxes, it doesn't even have two states to keep track of — just press it to make something happen. Insert the following code into Whereabouts_Options.xml right after the end of the Slider object:

```
<Button name="$Parent_DoneButton" ↵
inherits="OptionsButtonTemplate"↵
text="WHEREABOUTS_OPTIONS_DONE">
   <Anchors>
      <Anchor point="BOTTOMRIGHT">
         <Offset>
            <AbsDimension x="-20" y="20"/>
         </Offset>
      </Anchor>
   </Anchors>
   <Scripts>
      <OnClick>
         Whereabouts_Options_Frame:Hide();
      </OnClick>
   </Scripts>
</Button>
```

As you can see, Button objects support the text attribute (unlike checkboxes), making things even simpler. The offset of this widget isn't consistent with the others because this time the anchor point is the bottom right, standard for dialog-box button positioning. Finally, the OnClick handler doesn't even need to call a custom function; it just hides the options frame.

Back in enUS.lua, add the new string for the Done button's label:

```
WHEREABOUTS_OPTIONS_DONE = "Done";
```

And with that, your options panel is visually complete (see Figure 14-4). There are just a few odds and ends left to clean up, in terms of logic.

FIGURE 14-4: The Whereabouts options panel with all elements and controls in place.

Cleaning up Some Odds and Ends

The options panel should be draggable onscreen. Fortunately, you already have some experience in this area since you made the main Whereabouts frame draggable. Remember that the Scripts element goes outside Frames (where you've been doing most of your work recently) and directly within the overall Frame element:

```
<Scripts>
    <OnMouseDown>
        if ( button == "LeftButton" ) then
            self:StartMoving();
            self.isMoving = true;
        end
    </OnMouseDown>
    <OnMouseUp>
        if ( self.isMoving ) then
            self:StopMovingOrSizing();
            self.isMoving = false;
        end
    </OnMouseUp>
    <OnHide>
        if ( self.isMoving ) then
            self:StopMovingOrSizing();
            self.isMoving = false;
        end
    </OnHide>
</Scripts>
```

Initializing the Options Panel's Controls

Remember the syncing issues mentioned earlier in the chapter? Now you'll fix them. The problem arises from this: The default state for a checkbox is unchecked, but what if any of the settings that have been saved from the last session are `true`? When the control panel is first opened, the controls need to be *initialized* so they're synchronized with the current settings; otherwise they'll display the opposite value. You take care of this by adding an `OnShow` handler to the options frame.

Why not use `OnLoad` instead? If the variables haven't been loaded yet, you might get errors or the controls might initialize to the default values instead of the loaded ones. What about the `VARIABLES_LOADED` event, which the Whereabouts frame uses to initialize? Well, that would initialize the controls when the addon first loads, but what if one of the values changes before the control panel is actually opened? This would happen if the user toggled a setting with a slash command, for instance. Then things would be out of sync. Better to initialize whenever the options panel is displayed:

```
<OnShow>
    Whereabouts_Options_Init();
</OnShow>
```

Then create the initialization function in `Whereabouts_Options.lua`:

```
function Whereabouts_Options_Init()
    Whereabouts_Options_Frame_ShowBox:SetChecked(↵
        Whereabouts_Options.show);
    Whereabouts_Options_Frame_LockBox:SetChecked(↵
        Whereabouts_Options.lock);
    Whereabouts_Options_Frame_TooltipBox:SetChecked(↵
        Whereabouts_Options.tooltip);
    Whereabouts_Options_Frame_WorldMapBox:SetChecked(↵
        Whereabouts_Options.worldmap);
    Whereabouts_Options_Frame_AlphaSlider:SetValue(↵
        Whereabouts_Options.alpha);
end
```

You just go through each control one by one and set it to the value of its corresponding saved variable. Because the options panel is never visible by default, when the player enters the world there's no danger of this function executing before the variables have been loaded (and generating an error). You might have noticed that this function is named with `Init` at the end instead of with the name of the handler as usual, and there's good reason for this — you need to call the function from one other place.

Updating the Panel When a Slash Command Is Executed

If you think about it, there's a slightly obscure situation in which the controls could still get out of sync, even with your new `OnShow` initialization routine in place: If the options panel is open while the user changes a setting with a slash command. This is one of the dangers of having two ways to control settings, especially when one of them provides constant visual feedback. Although this is an unlikely situation, it's worth preventing.

Fortunately, there's a simple way to solve the problem. All you have to do is reinitialize the control panel (if it's open) after the user executes a slash command. Open `Whereabouts.lua` and navigate to the slash-command handler. Find the lines:

```
else
    Whereabouts_Message(WHEREABOUTS_NOCOMMAND);
end
```

Right after that is where you want to insert the new logic:

```
if ( Whereabouts_Options_Frame:IsShown() ) then
    Whereabouts_Options_Init();
end
```

Calling the initialization function isn't expensive (computationally), so there's no need to prove that a setting was actually changed. Placing it here is convenient as well, because the structure of the surrounding conditional statements is unaffected. The check is made whenever `args[1]` exists — that is, whenever the user types *something* after the slash command. It's important that the check be made after the rest of the code in the block, after a setting might have been altered.

Now, if the options panel is open when a slash command is executed, it's immediately reinitialized, bringing all the controls in sync.

Whereabouts Is Complete!

Congratulations! The addon is now complete. I encourage you to tweak the Whereabouts code you've written and just experiment. You learn the most when exploring on your own. Make a change, reload the UI (just type `/script ReloadUI()` in the chat window), and see what happens. Add features, add controls, and have fun!

Here are some suggestions for features you might want to try (be warned, some of them might be pretty difficult, depending on your programming familiarity):

- Add an option to change the color of the coordinates. Use a button on the options panel to open a color picker when clicked. Hint: investigate the `ColorSelect` and `ColorPickerFrame` objects. Then develop a way for the user to change the color with a slash command.

- Add radio buttons to the options panel to allow the user to change the font in which the coordinates are displayed. Hint: place a few fonts into the addon's directory, then use the `SetFont()` widget function to reference them.

- Create your own custom frame texture for the background of the window. While you're at it, create one for the options panel, too.

- Write a program to display which cardinal direction the character is traveling based on how the coordinates change over time.

Summary

In this chapter, you implemented the layout and functionality of an options panel for the Whereabouts addon, completing the project. You learned about a number of different widgets (checkboxes, sliders, and buttons), including how to define, label, initialize, and use them. You learned how to hook them up to the rest of the Whereabouts addon so they actually do something (besides just look pretty).

In the next chapter, you tackle a slightly more advanced addon development project: adapting the target-of-target frame into a standalone focus addon. Focus is a feature that was added to the game shortly before The Burning Crusade was released. It enables you to monitor another unit in addition to your current target. This provides a huge benefit to anyone, especially crowd-controllers like Mages and Warlocks. Unlike Whereabouts, which you built from scratch, the next project gives you a taste of what it's like to hack a piece of existing code to suit your own needs.

Hacking an Advanced Addon

You've been on a whirlwind tour of the addons that are available for World of Warcraft, and you've also learned how to create a simple configurable addon from scratch. In this chapter, you build a more advanced addon and become more familiar with Blizzard's customization system.

With the release of The Burning Crusade expansion, Blizzard has introduced a new unit called *focus*. Think of the focus unit as a second target that you can change at any time while retaining your original target. The focus unit is perfect for things such as crowd control (with Polymorph, Seduce, and so on) because it enables you to monitor the status of the mob you're controlling while still targeting the mob that's under attack.

Unfortunately, Blizzard doesn't provide a way to monitor the focus unit in the default user interface. It's handy for macros, but makes it somewhat difficult to use as a monitoring tool when you have no visual display. In this chapter you fill the gap by creating a unit frame to display your focus unit.

Understanding the Focus Unit

You may be wondering just what exactly a unit is, and how the focus unit factors into the game. Simply put, a *unit* is a character within World of Warcraft that has some relationship to your character. You may be more familiar with the more common units such as `player`, `pet`, `party1`, and `target` — your character, your pet (if you have one), your first party member, and your target respectively. These units (or UnitIDs) always refer to a specific slot in the game, regardless of what is actually in that slot. If you target yourself, both the `player` and the `target` units will point to the same character. Table 15-1 describes all currently possible UnitIDs.

Table 15-1   Valid UnitIDs

Unit	Description
player	Your character.
pet	Your combat pet, if summoned.
party1 - party4	Your party members in the order listed in the default interface. You are not considered your own party member, so your full party is player, party1, party2, party3, party4.
raid1 - raid40	Your raid members. These numbers don't correspond to the slots within the raid tab or have any order to them.
target	Your current target, if you have one.
focus	Your current focus.
mouseover	The character you are currently mousing-over in the game world, or the character belonging to the unit frame you are mousing-over (if you mouse-over the default player frame, the mouse-over is equivalent to player).
npc	The non-player-character you are currently interacting with.
partypet1 - partypet4	Your party member's pets, if summoned.
raidpet1 - raidpet40	Your raid member's pets, if summoned.
<unit>target	The given unit's current target (can be repeated indefinitely, although your performance may suffer if you overdo it).

The default user interface contains a few examples of the `<unit>target` usage, with both the target-of-target frame (Figure 15-1), and the target frames that are enabled in single raid pull-out frames (Figure 15-2).

FIGURE 15-1: Target-of-target frame.

FIGURE 15-2: Raid target frame.

In the first example, the game is simply looking at the `targettarget` unit, while in the second example the game uses `raidXtarget`.

You'll learn more about advanced macros in the next chapter, but it's important to understand how to use the focus unit if you're making an addon to display it. There are two basic slash commands that can be used to control your current focus: `/focus` and `/clearfocus`.

Brackets (`[]`) are commonly used in computing literature to show that an argument is optional, so `/focus [<unit> or <name>]` means that the `/focus` command can take either no arguments, or a UnitID, or a name. If you don't supply any argument, typing `/focus` sets your focus to be your current target, or clears your focus if you have nothing targeted. You could also use `/focus Thrall` to focus on the character Thrall, as long as you can currently see him. If you have a pet, you could use `/focus pettarget` to watch your pets target at all times.

The `/clearfocus` command simply clears your current focus unit, regardless of whether you have it set. You could always target nothing and type `/focus`, but having this as an option makes sense.

Developing an Idea

Before you begin creating an addon, it's a good idea to understand what you hope to accomplish. You've seen that playing with the focus unit can be somewhat handy, but it would be more useful if you could see the hit points and mana of your focus. All classes would benefit by being able to click a unit frame to target their focus if necessary, and being able to see the focus's buffs and debuffs could be helpful in many encounters.

As you'll find out, half of the reason Blizzard didn't add a focus frame is because it's difficult to find a place to put it! Non-pet users could put it below their player frame, but pet users already have screen issues to deal with. Your best bet is to make the frame draggable so the user can place it wherever he'd like, but the frame shouldn't be so big that it's difficult to place anywhere. That leaves the following requirements:

- Compact frame that displays the focus unit
- Shows health, mana, energy, rage, and so on
- Displays the character's name
- Shows buffs and debuffs
- Frame should be movable, and lockable

Lucky for you, there is already a frame in game that fits most of these requirements, and can be easily adapted to meet the other two needs: the target-of-target frame. The main advantage of using a Blizzard frame for inspiration is that the code and the artwork are already created for you, which makes your job one of adaptation, rather than creation.

Examining Blizzard's Files

Blizzard's default interface is written the same way addons are written, using XML to define the graphical elements, and Lua code to define the behavior of those elements. Normally all the interface code is packed up in Blizzard's game archives, but there is an easy way to extract and view this code. Blizzard provides a small program (for Windows and Mac) called the Interface AddOn Kit (see Figure 15-3) that automatically extracts all of these files into the Blizzard Interface Data (enUS) folder in your WoW directory (the enUS may be different depending on the area of the world in which you play the game). It can also extract the artwork for the interface, if you are interested in examining that. The addon kit comes with a solid tutorial for building addons; it contains two projects, located in the Blizzard Interface Tutorial directory.

FIGURE 15-3: The Interface AddOn Kit extracts core interface files and includes a tutorial.

You will find two directories under the Blizzard Interface Data (enUS) directory: one called AddOns and the other called FrameXML. The AddOns directory contains several Blizzard created addons that are official and part of the games. These addons are typically parts of the game that aren't accessed all the time, so they remain unloaded until needed (such as the Talent UI or the Auction House UI). The FrameXML directory contains all of the code that runs the rest of the default interface.

Note The Interface AddOn Kit is available for free from Blizzard's official support website. You can download it at `http:// blizzard.com/support/wow/?id=aww01671p`.

Viewing the Target-of-Target Frame

Once you've extracted the interface files, open the `TargetFrame.xml` file in the FrameXML directory. The file format should look familiar after your work on Whereabouts, so look for the frame named `TargetofTargetFrame` (you can use your text editor's search functionality to find it easily). Most of the code you write will come from this section of the file.

Tip If you don't know the name of a frame you can use the following script (or place it in a macro) to print the current frame to your chat window:

```
/script DEFAULT_CHAT_FRAME:AddMessage(GetMouseFocus():GetName())
```

Simply hover your mouse over a frame, and type that into your editbox, and you should get the name printed to your main chat window. If you receive an error, you either made a typo or you're not hovering over a frame with a name. This method isn't foolproof, but it's a nice and easy way to get a name in a pinch.

Creating an Addon Skeleton

Almost all addons begin as the same skeleton of files, so create those now:

1. Go to your Interface/Addons directory

2. Create a new folder called FocusFrame and open it.

3. Using your favorite text editor, create a new file in this directory called `FocusFrame.toc` and add the contents in Listing 15-1.

Listing 15-1 FocusFrame.toc

```
## Interface: 20003
## Title: FocusFrame
## Notes: Creates a movable focus frame
## SavedVariablesPerCharacter: FocusFrameOptions
FocusFrame.lua
FocusFrame.xml
```

4. Create a new empty file named `FocusFrame.lua`.

5. Next, create a new file named `FocusFrame.xml` and add the contents in Listing 15-2 to the file. This is the standard namespace declaration we used in Whereabouts that is used for validation.

Listing 15-2   Basic UI Tag for FocusFrame.xml

```
<Ui xmlns="http://www.blizzard.com/wow/ui/" ↵
xmlns:xsi="http://www.w3.org/2001/XMLSchema-instance" ↵
xsi:schemaLocation="http://www.blizzard.com/wow/ui/
..\FrameXML\UI.xsd">
</Ui>
```

Note The Interface number will change from version to version of the game (each time the UI files have a major update, specifically). Typically, you can just click Load Out-Of-Date Addons on the addon selection screen to load the addon, anyway, but it's good to ensure that you keep your addons up-to-date.

Remember, the `.toc` file is just a table of contents file that provides the game with details about the name of your addon, a short description, and a list of the files that need to be loaded. The `## SavedVariablesPerCharacter` lets the game know that you need your addon to save variables, and these should be kept per character, in the variable `FocusFrameOptions`, which you will define and use later in this chapter.

Buttons and Templates

Because you plan to make your unit frame clickable (for targeting purposes), it needs to be a button. Add the following within the `<Ui>` tag in `FocusFrame.xml`:

```
<Button name="FocusFrame" toplevel="true" movable="true" ↵
inherits="SecureUnitButtonTemplate" parent="UIParent" ↵
hidden="true">
</Button>
```

Most of this should seem familiar, except `inherits="SecureUnitButtonTemplate"`. You've used `inherits` before, but it was never really discussed. The XML system Blizzard created enables you to define a virtual frame that can be used by other frames as a basic template. A basic virtual frame might look like this:

```
<Button name="MyVirtualTemplate" virtual="true">
  <Size>
    <AbsDimension x="15" y="16"/>
  </Size>
</Button>
```

This code simply defines a new virtual frame called `MyVirtualTemplate` that can later be used in an `inherits` attribute, creating a 16 × 16 button. You'll see more complex examples of virtual frames later in this chapter, when you create the buff and debuff icons for your unit frame.

In this case, you are inheriting from `SecureUnitButtonTemplate`, which requires a bit of explanation. Any button that needs to cast a spell or target a unit (along with a few other protected actions) does so through the use of a number of secure templates. These secure frames are then limited in the following ways:

- You can only change the attributes of a secure frame (height, width, scale, and so forth) when the player is not engaged in combat.

- You must define what your secure frame does before entering combat, and these actions cannot be altered until you leave combat.

- Secure frames can only be hidden or shown in combat by defining visibility conditions before the player enters combat.

In exchange for these limitations, secure buttons do a ton of different things when they are clicked, such as changing the action bar pages, targeting, casting spells, and using items. You'll deal with these limitations later in the chapter (you want to be able to target your focus after all).

Note   `www.wowwiki.com/Secure_Frames_Overview` details the requirements of using secure frames and what is possible using that system.

If necessary, you can inherit from multiple templates when creating a new frame. Simply add each template with a comma to the `inherits` attribute like this:

```
<Button name="MyFrame" ↵
inherits="SecureUnitButtonTemplate,MyVirtualTemplate">
</Button>
```

Each frame needs to be given a size and be placed somewhere on the screen. Add the following code inside your `<Button>` definition in `FocusFrame.xml`:

```
<Size>
    <AbsDimension x="93" y="45"/>
</Size>
<Anchors>
    <Anchor point="CENTER"/>
</Anchors>
```

The first section simply defines the size of the frame, taking the numbers from `TargetofTargetFrame`. Because you're using Blizzard's artwork you can cheat and use its numbers, too. You also define the default position of the frame to be in the center of its parent, `UIParent`, which is the entire screen.

Layering Graphical Elements

Building graphics in World of Warcraft is a bit like making a pizza; you need to follow a recipe for everything to come together. Sure, you can make a pizza with the sauce on top, but it'd be awfully messy to eat! In your case, you need to layer the portrait, the health bar, and the mana bar below the frame artwork itself, to ensure that everything looks right all the time. You'll use layers to build the frame from the back to the front. Add the following inside the <Button> definition in FocusFrame.xml so you have a place to put them:

```
<Layers>
</Layers>
```

Adding a Subtle Background

It's a good idea to include a background behind your frame so the text remains legible in the middle of a hectic fight. Open the FocusFrame.xml file and add the following code in the <Layers> section you just defined:

```
<Layer level="BACKGROUND">
  <Texture name="FocusFrameBackground">
    <Size>
      <AbsDimension x="46" y="15"/>
    </Size>
    <Anchors>
      <Anchor point="BOTTOMLEFT">
        <Offset>
          <AbsDimension x="42" y="13"/>
        </Offset>
      </Anchor>
    </Anchors>
    <Color r="0" g="0" b="0" a="0.5"/>
  </Texture>
</Layer>
```

Again you get to cheat and use Blizzard's numbers, but this section defines a black background with 50 percent alpha (meaning that it's partially transparent).

Creating a Portrait Texture

The TargetofTarget frame shows the portrait of the unit, so you get to use that as well. You need to put a placeholder texture somewhere on the frame that can be used later to load that artwork, so add the following in the <Layers> section of FocusFrame.xml:

```
<Layer level="BORDER">
  <Texture name="FocusFramePortrait">
    <Size>
      <AbsDimension x="35" y="35"/>
    </Size>
    <Anchors>
      <Anchor point="TOPLEFT">
        <Offset>
```

```
            <AbsDimension x="6" y="-6"/>
         </Offset>
      </Anchor>
   </Anchors>
</Texture>
</Layer>
```

Here, you create a 35 × 35 square that will display the portrait (don't worry, the image itself is a circle). The texture is anchored to the top-left of the frame, offset slightly down and to the right.

Note All offsets are specified in game pixels, with positive x values moving a frame to the right, and positive y values moving a frame down.

Placing the Border Artwork

When you're baking a traditional pizza, the toppings typically go on top of the cheese. That way you can see what's on the slice before you eat it, and it makes sense from that standpoint. Placing the border artwork for your frame is a bit more difficult and requires some trickery to make it work.

When using the `<Layers>` section, you can give each part of artwork a different layer to ensure that everything is layered properly. Unfortunately status bars aren't textures, so they can't be placed in a layer, and any widgets (such as buttons and status bars) will display on top of the artwork defined in `<Layers>`. You want your status bars to be behind your frame's border artwork, so you have to wrap the artwork in a frame, and use a small trick to ensure that it displays properly. Open `FocusFrame.xml` and add the following section to your `<Button>` definition:

```
<Frames>
</Frames>
```

This code simply tells the game that you have some frames that will be children of the main frame. You will use this `<Frames>` section to place the artwork. Add the following within the `<Frames>` section:

```
<Frame name="FocusFrameTextureFrame" setAllPoints="true">
   <Layers>
      <Layer level="BORDER">
         <Texture name="FocusFrameTexture" ↵
file="Interface\TargetingFrame\UI-TargetofTargetFrame">
            <TexCoords left="0.015625" right="0.7265625" top="0" ↵
bottom="0.703125"/>
         </Texture>
      </Layer>
   </Layers>
</Frame>
```

The `setAllPoints="true"` tells this frame to attach itself to every part of its parent, so that they are the same size and they always move together. You then define a BORDER layer that contains a texture (as a child to the new subframe). The texture file is set to be the artwork from the target-of-target frame, using the same TexCoords numbers used in `TargetFrame.xml`. There are only a few more elements to go (health bar, mana bar, name, and text to signify when the unit is dead), so you can place the other decorations in this frame (the name and the dead text). Add the following to the new BORDER layer:

```
<FontString name="FocusFrameName" inherits="GameFontNormalSmall" ↵
justifyH="LEFT">
    <Size>
        <AbsDimension x="100" y="10"/>
    </Size>
    <Anchors>
        <Anchor point="BOTTOMLEFT">
            <Offset>
                <AbsDimension x="42" y="2"/>
            </Offset>
        </Anchor>
    </Anchors>
</FontString>
<FontString name="FocusFrameDeadText" ↵
inherits="GameFontNormalSmall" text="DEAD">
    <Anchors>
        <Anchor point="CENTER">
            <Offset>
                <AbsDimension x="15" y="1"/>
            </Offset>
        </Anchor>
    </Anchors>
</FontString>
```

Note You can find detailed information about textures and TexCoords tranformations at www.wowwiki.com/SetTexCoord_Transformations.

These definitions are relatively standard: Two font strings are created, given sizes, and placed. Because the font strings are defined after the border artwork, they will be displayed on top of those graphics.

You add one small bit of magic to make sure this frame is set on the right level (so the status bars are below it). You could either wrap it in another frame, which would push this one level higher, or you can use a function called `RaiseFrameLevel()`. This function can be used to move a frame to the highest level on its strata. Add the following section inside your `<Frame name="FocusFrameTextureFrame">` definition (after the `</Layers>` in that section):

```
<Scripts>
    <OnLoad>
        RaiseFrameLevel(self);
    </OnLoad>
</Scripts>
```

This script will be executed once, making sure your artwork is all layered properly.

Creating Health and Mana Bars

You've used basic buttons and textures already, but several widgets are available for crafting new frames. In this project you want to display a status bar, and the game provides a StatusBar widget to make that easier. Add the following code right after the end of your FocusFrameTextureFrame definition in FocusFrame.xml:

```
<StatusBar name="FocusFrameHealthBar" inherits="TextStatusBar">
   <Size>
      <AbsDimension x="46" y="7"/>
   </Size>
   <Anchors>
      <Anchor point="TOPRIGHT">
         <Offset>
            <AbsDimension x="-2" y="-15"/>
         </Offset>
      </Anchor>
   </Anchors>
   <BarTexture file="Interface\TargetingFrame\UI-StatusBar"/>
   <BarColor r="0" g="1.0" b="0"/>
</StatusBar>
```

The first thing you may notice is the use of StatusBar as the root tag rather than the Button or Frame type you've used previously. This simply tells the game that the object that follows is a status bar, and it enables you to specify things such as status bar texture and color in the XML definition. You could always change the bar texture to something else, but for now it's the default status bar texture, colored green.

You can use almost the same code to define the mana bar, with a blue color (you'll handle changing this later if the focus is a warrior or rogue). Add the following definition after the health bar:

```
<StatusBar name="FocusFrameManaBar" inherits="TextStatusBar">
   <Size>
      <AbsDimension x="46" y="7"/>
   </Size>
   <Anchors>
      <Anchor point="TOPRIGHT">
         <Offset>
            <AbsDimension x="-2" y="-23"/>
         </Offset>
      </Anchor>
   </Anchors>
   <BarTexture file="Interface\TargetingFrame\UI-StatusBar"/>
   <BarColor r="0" g="0" b="1.0"/>
</StatusBar>
```

You've now defined all your graphical elements except the buff and debuff icons, which you create in the next section. As you can see, layering graphical elements sometimes takes a bit of thought and planning to make sure things look right. If you're not graphically inclined, it can be helpful to use Blizzard's definitions and artwork to make your job easier.

Creating Virtual Frames

As you saw earlier, virtual frames are an easy way to make templates to cut down on duplicated code. The preceding example defined a 16 × 16 button, but you can include scripts, textures, and any other XML elements in your templates. The default party frames are all generated using templates, one master virtual frame that defines the graphical elements and the behavior of the frame, and four simple frames that just inherit the virtual frame. You can use this same technique for your buff and debuff icons.

Defining the Template

You want to define a basic size for your frame and create a layer with a single texture, so open your FocusFrame.xml, and at the top of the file, right inside your <Ui> tag, add the following definition:

```
<Frame name="FocusFrameBuffTemplate" virtual="true" hidden="true">
    <Size>
        <AbsDimension x="12" y="12"/>
    </Size>
    <Layers>
        <Layer level="ARTWORK">
            <Texture name="$parentIcon" setAllPoints="true"/>
        </Layer>
    </Layers>
</Frame>
```

Here you're creating a new template called FocusFrameBuffTemplate, setting it to hidden by default, giving it a default size, and creating a simple texture called $parentIcon that is the same size as the actual frame. You may remember from Whereabouts that consistent internal naming enabled you to use some tricks with getglobal() and Frame:GetName(). This internal naming was all done with templates, so you're just continuing that best practice here.

Rather than calling getglobal() and Frame:GetName() each time you want to find one of these icon objects, you can use a trick to make them a bit more accessible. In the WoW interface, frame objects are simply tables, which means they can store and hold values. These values won't be retained across sessions, but they can be handy for a situation like this, to help reduce repeated code. Add the following to your FocusFrameBuffTemplate after the close of </Layers>:

```
<Scripts>
    <OnLoad>
        self.Icon = getglobal(self:GetName().."Icon")
    </OnLoad>
</Scripts>
```

This code defines an OnLoad handler that is called once for each frame when it is loaded and created from XML. The handler will be passed the self variable, which will be the frame being initialized. You then look up the $parentIcon texture defined in the template by finding out the name of your frame (using self:GetName()) and then adding the text "Icon" to the end, and finally looking that texture up using getglobal().

Tooltip Placement Code

You'll want to borrow some code from Blizzard, from the top of `TargetFrame.xml`. Look at the `TargetofTargetBuffTemplate` virtual frame that is defined near the top of that file, and find the `<OnEnter>` code. You'll use some of that as the basis for your `<OnEnter>` handler. Add the following code to the `<Scripts>` section of your `FocusFrameBuffTemplate`:

```
<OnEnter>
   if ( self:GetCenter() > GetScreenWidth()/2 ) then
      GameTooltip:SetOwner(self, "ANCHOR_LEFT");
   else
      GameTooltip:SetOwner(self, "ANCHOR_RIGHT");
   end
   if ( self.Debuff ) then
      GameTooltip:SetUnitDebuff("focus", self:GetID());
   else
      GameTooltip:SetUnitBuff("focus", self:GetID());
   end
</OnEnter>
```

This code is fairly simple but has a lot going on. The first `if` statement uses the `Frame:GetCenter()` and `GetScreenWidth()` functions to determine if the frame that's being moused over is on the left or right side of the screen. It does so by calling `self:GetCenter()`, which returns the x and y coordinates of the center of the frame's current position. That value is then compared to the screen width divided by two.

Depending on whether the value is greater than the middle of the screen (the frame is on the right side) or less than, you call `GameTooltip:SetOwner()` with either `"ANCHOR_LEFT"` or `"ANCHOR_RIGHT"`. This simply means that if the frame is on the right side of the screen, the tooltip should be anchored on the left, and if it's on the left side, the tooltip should be anchored to the right side. This is just a simple way to ensure that the tooltip is always on the screen, and looks right.

In the second `if` statement, you check the value of `self.Debuff`, and if that is set, the code calls `GameTooltip:SetUnitDebuff()`; otherwise it calls the `GameTooltip:GetUnitBuff()` function. The game separates buffs from debuffs, and you want to be able to display both types in the same template; you use this bit of code so you can use the same frames for both types. You pass the UnitID and a number to these functions, namely the string `"focus"` and the return from `self:GetID()`, which is a number you set in a different block of code.

Finally, make sure the tooltip is hidden when the user stops mousing-over the frame by adding the following after `</OnEnter>`:

```
<OnLeave>
   GameTooltip:Hide();
</OnLeave>
```

Inheriting from Your New Template

Now you have a fancy new template, and you need to use it somewhere. The target-of-target frame displays four buffs, so you want to do the same (you can always add more if you'd like). Open `FocusFrame.xml` and add the code from Listing 15-3, directly after the `</StatusBar>` tag from the mana bar:

Listing 15-3   Buff Frame Definitions

```
<Frame name="$parentBuff1" inherits="FocusFrameBuffTemplate" ↵
id="1">
   <Anchors>
      <Anchor point="TOPLEFT" relativePoint="TOPRIGHT">
         <Offset>
            <AbsDimension x="4" y="-10"/>
         </Offset>
      </Anchor>
   </Anchors>
</Frame>
<Frame name="$parentBuff2" inherits="FocusFrameBuffTemplate" ↵
id="2">
   <Anchors>
      <Anchor point="LEFT" relativeTo="$parentBuff1" ↵
relativePoint="RIGHT">
         <Offset>
            <AbsDimension x="1" y="0"/>
         </Offset>
      </Anchor>
   </Anchors>
</Frame>
<Frame name="$parentBuff3" inherits="FocusFrameBuffTemplate" ↵
id="3">
   <Anchors>
      <Anchor point="TOPLEFT" relativeTo="$parentBuff1" ↵
relativePoint="BOTTOMLEFT">
         <Offset>
            <AbsDimension x="0" y="-1"/>
         </Offset>
      </Anchor>
   </Anchors>
</Frame>
<Frame name="$parentBuff4" inherits="FocusFrameBuffTemplate" ↵
id="4">
   <Anchors>
      <Anchor point="LEFT" relativeTo="$parentBuff3" ↵
relativePoint="RIGHT">
         <Offset>
            <AbsDimension x="1" y="0"/>
         </Offset>
      </Anchor>
   </Anchors>
</Frame>
```

There's nothing special here; you just create four new frames using your template. Each frame is given an id, which is the number that will be returned from Frame:GetID(). These frames are layed out so that the first two are on the top row, and the last two are on the bottom row. All of these frames are hidden by default because the template specifies hidden="true". You'll set the buff textures and show these frames in a bit of code later.

Responding to Events

You have the graphical foundation for your addon, but you need to create the glue that will make the addon actually do something! Open FocusFrame.xml and add the following after the </Frames> tag in your definition for FocusFrame (this should be close to the bottom of your file at the moment):

```
<Scripts>
    <OnLoad>
        FocusFrame_OnLoad(self)
    </OnLoad>
    <OnEvent>
        FocusFrame_OnEvent(self,event,...)
    </OnEvent>
</Scripts>
```

As mentioned in the preceding section, the <OnLoad> function is passed the self variable, which you need to pass to your FocusFrame_OnLoad() function, which hasn't been defined yet. This enables you to use the same function for multiple frames and even though you don't take advantage of that here, it's still a good idea to pass that argument along in case you need it later.

In contrast, the <OnEvent> handler gets the following arguments:

- self: The frame the event originated from

- event: The name of the event as a string ("PLAYER_LOGIN", "UNIT_HEALTH", and so on)

- ... : A special Lua construct that signifies the function may have any number of arguments, and allows you to pass them through to another function without needing to specify how many there are or to name each of them.

You will be using the event handler in your code to handle health updates, mana updates, and buff and debuff changes.

Registering for Events

Right now your XML definitions are pointing to functions that don't exist, so it's a good idea to define those before continuing. Open your empty FocusFrame.lua file and add the following code:

```
function FocusFrame_OnLoad(frame)
    frame:RegisterForDrag("LeftButton");
    FocusFrame_Reset();
```

```
    frame:RegisterEvent("PLAYER_FOCUS_CHANGED");
    frame:RegisterEvent("UNIT_AURA");
    frame:RegisterEvent("UNIT_HEALTH");
    frame:RegisterEvent("UNIT_MANA");
    frame:RegisterEvent("UNIT_RAGE");
    frame:RegisterEvent("UNIT_ENERGY");
    frame:RegisterEvent("UNIT_FOCUS");
    frame:RegisterEvent("UNIT_MAXHEALTH");
    frame:RegisterEvent("UNIT_MAXMANA");
    frame:RegisterEvent("UNIT_MAXRAGE");
    frame:RegisterEvent("UNIT_MAXENERGY");
    frame:RegisterEvent("UNIT_MAXFOCUS");
    frame:RegisterEvent("UNIT_DISPLAYPOWER");
    frame:RegisterEvent("ADDON_LOADED");
end
```

This function is defined to have a single argument called `frame`. In the XML definition you take the `self` variable and pass it to `FocusFrame_OnLoad()`, which means the new variable `frame` will contain the object that was just loaded. The code then uses this object and calls the `RegisterEvent()` method to register for different events. Table 15-2 describes each event. You call `FocusFrame_Reset()` in the first line, which you will define in a moment.

Table 15-2   Events and Descriptions for FocusFrame

Event	Description
PLAYER_FOCUS_CHANGED	Fires when the player's focus unit changes
UNIT_AURA	Fires when a unit's buffs or debuffs change
UNIT_HEALTH	Fires when a unit's health points change
UNIT_MANA	Fires when a unit's mana points change
UNIT_RAGE	Fires when a unit's rage points change
UNIT_ENERGY	Fires when a unit's energy points change
UNIT_FOCUS	Fires when a unit's focus points change
UNIT_MAXHEALTH	Fires when a unit's maximum health points change
UNIT_MAXMANA	Fires when a unit's maximum mana points change
UNIT_MAXRAGE	Fires when a unit's maximum rage points change
UNIT_MAXENERGY	Fires when a unit's maximum energy points change
UNIT_MAXFOCUS	Fires when a unit's maximum focus points change
UNIT_DISPLAYPOWER	Fires when a unit changes mana types (from mana to energy, for example)
ADDON_LOADED	Fires when an addon is fully loaded

Event Handling

You've registered for the events, but you have to write some code that actually does the work. Define this new function at the bottom of FocusFrame.lua:

```
function FocusFrame_OnEvent(frame, event, arg1, arg2, arg3, arg4,↵
arg5, arg6, arg7, arg8, arg9)
    if ( event == "ADDON_LOADED" and arg1 == "FocusFrame" ) then
        frame:UnregisterEvent("ADDON_LOADED");
        -- Create a table for our SavedVariables if it doesn't exist
        if ( not FocusFrameOptions ) then
            FocusFrameOptions = {};
        end
        FocusFrame_Reset();
```

This is a simple bit of code that checks whether the addon is finished loading (it does so by comparing arg1 to the name of the addon "FocusFrame". If it's fully loaded, the code unregisters the event, and initializes the saved variable table. You then call the FocusFrame_Reset() function, which you'll write in a moment, to initialize the portrait, set the text display, and update the mana and health bars.

PLAYER_FOCUS_CHANGED

The PLAYER_FOCUS_CHANGED event fires whenever you change your focus unit, and the code to manage it is relatively simple. Just add the following after the last bit of code you added in FocusFrame.lua:

```
    elseif ( event == "PLAYER_FOCUS_CHANGED" ) then
        FocusFrame_Reset();
```

You'll write the FocusFrame_Reset() function to change all the graphical elements of the frame, so it makes sense to use that here when the player's focus unit changes.

UNIT_AURA

The UNIT_AURA event fires anytime someone's buffs or debuffs change (including your pet, your target, and so on). Buff and debuff scanning can be a relatively nasty process, so you'll write a utility function to handle this, but you need to call that function from here. Add the following:

```
    elseif ( event == "UNIT_AURA" and arg1 == "focus" ) then
        FocusFrame_UpdateAura();
```

Because you're only interested in the focus unit, you can check the arg1 variable to only look at the focus and make sure you're not updating your frame when it's not necessary.

Note Several tools are available that can help you determine how events work, and what arguments they pass to the handling function. You can download DevTools, an addon by Iriel, at http://wowinterface.com, for example. It provides a /dtevents command that can be quite useful for event troubleshooting.

UNIT_MAXHEALTH

When a player gains a buff or changes equipment, the UNIT_MAXHEALTH event may fire if his maximum health has changed. You can use this event to update the minimum and maximum values of the health bar. Because you're only interested in the focus unit, you can check arg1 again to pass on the event if it doesn't interest you. Add the following code to your ongoing function:

```
elseif ( event == "UNIT_MAXHEALTH" and arg1 == "focus" ) then
    FocusFrameHealthBar:SetMinMaxValues(0,↵
UnitHealthMax("focus"));
```

A status bar has only three operational values: the minimum value, the maximum value, and the current value. If a player's maximum health changes, you update the status bar (otherwise it would show more full or empty than it should). This code uses the SetMinMaxValues method on the status bar, to pass the min and max values. The minimum value is 0, and the maximum value can be obtained using the UnitHealthMax("focus") function call.

UNIT_MAXMANA, UNIT_MAXRAGE, UNIT_MAXENERGY, UNIT_MAXFOCUS

Much like UNIT_MAXHEALTH, the UNIT_MAXMANA, UNIT_MAXRAGE, UNIT_MAXENERGY, and UNIT_MAXFOCUS events will fire when a caster, rogue, warrior or pet's maximum power changes. You can lump all these calls together because they use the same function — UnitManaMax("focus") — and all update the same status bar. This is the same code as before, with a few small changes. Add the following to your function:

```
elseif ( event == "UNIT_MAXMANA" or event == "UNIT_MAXRAGE" or ↵
event == "UNIT_MAXENERGY" or event == "UNIT_MAXFOCUS" and ↵
arg1 == "focus" ) then
FocusFrameManaBar:SetMinMaxValues(0, UnitManaMax("focus"));
```

UNIT_DISPLAYPOWER

When a druid shape-shifts, it can change between mana, energy, and rage depending on its form. When that happens, the UNIT_DISPLAYPOWER event fires. Coloring the mana correctly is a quick way to see what form a druid is in, and you should be able to support this. Add this code to your function:

```
elseif ( event == "UNIT_DISPLAYPOWER"  and arg1 == "focus" ) ↵
then
    local color = ManaBarColor[UnitPowerType("focus")];
    FocusFrameManaBar:SetStatusBarColor(color.r, color.g, ↵
color.b);
    FocusFrameManaBar:SetMinMaxValues(0, UnitManaMax("focus"));
```

This first defines a local variable called color, and looks in the table ManaBarColor for an entry equal to UnitPowerType("focus"). This is a global table that the game uses to define the colors for mana, rage, and energy. UnitPowerType() is just a number that corresponds to a specific power type, as described in Table 15-3.

Table 15-3 Unit Power Types from UnitPowerType()

Return	Description
0	Mana
1	Rage
2	Focus (for hunter's pets)
3	Energy
4	Happiness

Source: www.wowwiki.com/API_UnitPowerType

Each entry of the table `ManaBarColor` contains three elements: r, g, and b. The code just passes those to the `SetStatusBarColor()` method on the `FocusFrameManaBar`. When a druid shape-shifts into a bear, the `UNIT_DISPLAYPOWER` event fires, but the `UNIT_MAXHEALTH` event does not, so you need to set the min and max values here to ensure that they're always up-to-date.

UNIT_HEALTH

One of the most important events (arguably the most important for healers), the `UNIT_HEALTH` event tells you when the current health of a unit has changed. It fires for all units that your player is interested in, so you need to filter it out so that it only handles the focus unit's events. When a unit's health changes, it's a good opportunity to check whether the unit is dead (so you can display the Dead text on top of the frame). Add the following code to your function:

```
elseif ( event == "UNIT_HEALTH" and arg1 == "focus" ) then
    -- If the unit has died or become a ghost, clear off the
buffs/debuffs
    -- and display the "Dead" text
    FocusFrame_CheckDead();
    FocusFrameHealthBar:SetValue(UnitHealth("focus"));
```

UNIT_MANA, UNIT_RAGE, UNIT_FOCUS, and UNIT_ENERGY

Short and simple, the `UNIT_MANA`, `UNIT_RAGE`, `UNIT_FOCUS`, and `UNIT_ENERGY` events fire when a unit's current power changes, such as when a caster, rogue, warrior, or pet uses a skill. The last section in `FocusFrame_OnEvent` simply responds to mana changes in the focus unit, and changes the current value of the mana bar. Finish up your function with the following snippet:

```
elseif ( event == "UNIT_MANA" or event == "UNIT_RAGE" or ↵
event == "UNIT_FOCUS" or event == "UNIT_ENERGY" and arg1 ↵
== "focus") then
```

Checking for Death

Because you're calling it in the code you've just written, you need to define the `FocusFrame_CheckDead()` function. Add the following to the bottom of `FocusFrame.lua`:

```
function FocusFrame_CheckDead()
    if ( UnitIsDead("focus") or UnitIsGhost("focus") ) then
        FocusFrame_UpdateAura();
        FocusFrameDeadText:Show();
    elseif ( FocusFrameDeadText:IsShown() ) then
        FocusFrameDeadText:Hide();
    end
end
```

This section is relatively straightforward. It first checks to see if the unit is dead or if it is a ghost. If it's died, the code calls `FocusFrame_UpdateAura()` to clear buffs (otherwise they'd remain showing on the dead character, which could be confusing). `FocusFrameDeadText` is a simple `FontString` you defined, and you show it when the unit is dead. If the unit isn't dead, and the dead text is being shown (say, they resurrected), then you hide the text again.

Initializing the Frame

Each time the player changes his focus, you need to initialize the frame. This involves setting the portrait to the right picture, and updating the name, health, and mana bars. You use the `FocusFrame_Reset()` function to accomplish this, so add the following code to the bottom of `FocusFrame.lua`:

```
function FocusFrame_Reset()
    -- Change the portrait
    SetPortraitTexture(FocusFramePortrait, "focus");
    -- Change the name
    FocusFrameName:SetText(UnitName("focus"));
    FocusFrame_CheckDead();
    -- Set the minimum and maximum values of each status bar
    FocusFrameHealthBar:SetMinMaxValues(0, UnitHealthMax("focus"));
    FocusFrameHealthBar:SetValue(UnitHealth("focus"));
    FocusFrameManaBar:SetMinMaxValues(0, UnitManaMax("focus"));
    FocusFrameManaBar:SetValue(UnitMana("focus"));
    -- Change the mana bar to the correct color
    local color = ManaBarColor[UnitPowerType("focus")];
    FocusFrameManaBar:SetStatusBarColor(color.r, color.g, color.b);
    -- Update any buffs/debuffs the unit might have
    FocusFrame_UpdateAura();
end
```

The code has been commented to make clear what it is doing at each step. A new function is introduced here, called `SetPortraitTexture()`. It takes a texture and a unit name as arguments, and sets that texture with the portrait of the unit. You don't have access to that sort of artwork from Lua, so this call is necessary to ensure that you don't have to draw your own =).

Got Stub?

You must be anxious to look at the frame, but you still have to define the `FocusFrame_UpdateAura` function. (If you load the addon, the game gives an error because you're calling an undefined function.) You can create an empty stub for `FocusFrame_UpdateAura()` that will enable you to load the addon, and see how it works. Add the following to the bottom of `FocusFrame.lua`:

```
function FocusFrame_UpdateAura()
end
```

Putting All the Pieces Together

Load up your game and you'll see FocusFrame listed under your AddOns button, along with the description you gave it in your table of contents. When you select your character and load up in the game, you won't see anything because the frame is hidden by default, and there's one more step necessary to make the frame visible when you gain a focus unit.

Hiding and Showing Secure Frames

Secure frames, you'll recall, cannot be shown or hidden in combat. You can use the following macro to test this out. First show the frame using the following:

```
/script FocusFrame:Show()
```

You should see the empty focus frame in the center of your screen. You can drag and move this frame wherever you'd like it. If you find a low-level mob and aggro them, you will find the following macro fails because of the limitations of secure frames:

```
/script FocusFrame:Hide()
```

Fortunately there is a function specifically designed to show and hide a frame based on unit existence. It's called `RegisterUnitWatch()`. This function combines with the concept of attributes to handle the showing and hiding of your frames behind the scenes, with Blizzard's blessing. Open `FocusFrame.lua` and at the top of `FocusFrame_OnLoad()`, add this code:

```
frame:SetAttribute("unit", "focus");
frame:SetAttribute("*type1", "target");
RegisterUnitWatch(frame);
```

The first line sets an attribute on the frame, called `unit` with the value `"focus"`. This is a special system the secure templates used to store values that can be used to maintain the secure nature of the templates. The `unit` attribute is used by the next two lines.

The second line says, "Anytime the left button is clicked on this frame, target the unit stored in the `unit` attribute." An entire book could be written about the way secure templates work, but the wiki page mentioned earlier in the chapter is a good reference tool.

The third line calls `RegisterUnitWatch()` to set up the visibility you're looking for. This function looks at the `unit` attribute, shows the frame when that unit exists, and hides it when it stops existing. This used to be more difficult to accomplish, and it's nice to have an easy way to do the job.

You should be able to load the game up, and play with the `/focus` and `/clearfocus` commands to show and hide your new frame (everything except the buffs and debuffs should update at this point).

Dragging Your Frame

Now that you can see your frame, you need to make it draggable so you can place it anywhere. Open `FocusFrame.xml`, and find the `<Scripts>` section at the end of your file. Add the following after the `</OnEvent>` for that frame:

```
<OnDragStart>
   if ( not FocusFrameOptions.Locked ) then
      self:StartMoving();
      self.isMoving = true;
   end
</OnDragStart>
<OnDragStop>
   if ( self.isMoving ) then
     self:StopMovingOrSizing();
   end
</OnDragStop>
```

This code checks your saved variable `FocusFrameOptions`, and checks for the Locked setting, so you can't accidentally move the frame while you have it locked. You will define the slash command to toggle that option a little later in the chapter.

Scanning Buffs and Debuffs

There are literally hundreds of different ways to scan for buffs and debuffs, and another hundred ways to display them. This section shows you one method to display buff and debuff icons for your FocusFrame. The code will show up to four buffs and debuffs, counted together. If there are four buffs, no debuffs are shown because in this example buffs have priority. You could easily change these options around and extend your addon.

Open `FocusFrame.lua` and add the following as a new function; the whole function will be broken up, so just continue to add to the bottom as the code is explained:

```
function FocusFrame_UpdateAura()
   local count = 0;
   for i=1,4 do
      local name,rank,texture = UnitBuff("focus", i, 1);
      if ( not name ) then
         break;
      end
```

A local variable called count is defined (so you can easily track how many buff icons you've already filled) and the code loops from 1 to 4. On each step of the loop, the UnitBuff() function is called, and is passed the UnitID, the index i, and the value 1. The second argument is the index of the buff to check on the given unit, and the third argument is a special flag that tells the game to filter buffs. When the flag is set to 1, only buffs that you can cast on someone else will be shown. This function returns the name, rank, and texture file used for that buff's icon. The last block in the code checks whether the variable name has been set; if not, it breaks out of the loop.

Add the following code, which is run when the variable name has been set (meaning the game found a buff on that unit, in that slot):

```
        count = count + 1;
        local button = getglobal("FocusFrameBuff"..count);
        if ( button ) then
            button.Icon:SetTexture(texture);
            button:Show();
            button.Debuff = nil;
            button:SetID(i);
        end
    end
```

Because the code found a buff, it increments the counter by one, and uses that value to getglobal() the buff frame (you defined four of them using the virtual template). Rather than check to see if i >= 1 and i <= 4, the code simply looks to see if getglobal() returned a button; if not, the rest of the if statement is skipped. It's then necessary to set the texture on the icon object and show the frame. Because this isn't a debuff, you need to clear the Debuff flag defined earlier (this is used by the virtual template so it knows which function to call). Finally, the code calls :SetID(i), so the template knows what number to pass to the UnitBuff() function.

The next section is the same, except it uses UnitDebuff() and sets the debuff flag. Add this code to your function:

```
    for i=1,4 do
        local name,rank,texture = UnitDebuff("focus", i, 1);
        if ( not name ) then
            break;
        end
        count = count + 1;
        local button = getglobal("FocusFrameBuff"..count);
        if ( button ) then
            button.Icon:SetTexture(texture);
            button:Show();
            button.Debuff = true;
            button:SetID(i);
        end
    end
```

You need to hide any frames that may have been shown before, but should be hidden (otherwise you'll be displaying buffs that have expired). This simple loop starts at count + 1 and hides any of the frames that should be hidden:

```
for i=count+1,4 do
    local button = getglobal("FocusFrameBuff"..i);
    button:Hide();
  end
end
```

Creating a Slash Command

You're in the home stretch. All that's left to do is configure the few options you have by creating a slash command. Include the code in Listing 15-4 at the bottom of FocusFrame.lua.

Listing 15-4   Slash-Command Handler

```
function FocusFrame_SlashCmd(msg)
    msg = string.lower(msg);
    if ( msg == "lock" ) then
        if ( FocusFrameOptions.Locked ) then
            DEFAULT_CHAT_FRAME:AddMessage("FocusFrame is already ↵
locked");
        else
            FocusFrameOptions.Locked = true;
            DEFAULT_CHAT_FRAME:AddMessage("FocusFrame is locked");
        end
    elseif ( msg == "unlock" ) then
        if ( not FocusFrameOptions.Locked ) then
            DEFAULT_CHAT_FRAME:AddMessage("FocusFrame is already ↵
unlocked");
        else
            FocusFrameOptions.Locked = nil;
            DEFAULT_CHAT_FRAME:AddMessage("FocusFrame is ↵
unlocked");
        end
    elseif ( msg == "reset" ) then
        FocusFrame:SetUserPlaced(nil);
        FocusFrame:ClearAllPoints();
        FocusFrame:SetPoint("CENTER", 0, 0);
    else
        DEFAULT_CHAT_FRAME:AddMessage("Usage: /focusframe {lock | ↵
unlock | reset}");
    end
end
SLASH_FOCUSFRAME1 = "/focusframe";
SLASH_FOCUSFRAME2 = "/fframe";
SLASH_FOCUSFRAME3 = "/ff";
SlashCmdList["FOCUSFRAME"] = FocusFrame_SlashCmd;
```

Nothing here should really be a surprise after all the work you've done. You're defining a slash command that can handle the lock, unlock, and reset commands. The slash command is accessible by the commands `/focusframe`, `/fframe`, and `/ff`. There are literally hundreds of other options you could introduce in this addon, but we're out of space! Feel free to take this addon and customize it to your needs, tweak it, and, if you want to share your changes, upload it to one of the addon distribution sites. You could be on your way to becoming an addon author!

Summary

As you can see from this example, and your prior work on Whereabouts, a simple idea can grow large quite quickly with little details that need to be resolved before you can move on. Understanding the way the graphical widgets are defined and work is certainly half of the battle but that's relatively useless without an understanding of the events system. Once both systems are put together, quite complex addons are possible.

As you went through this project, you undoubtedly had a number of things you might have done differently, or features you might have added. That is where the fun of interface customization comes in; you can take anything you're given and adapt it to suit your own needs.

The next chapter explains all about macros and how to create them.

Creating Advanced Macros

Macros have been around since the beginning of the game, but they've taken on a completely different shape and function with the release of The Burning Crusade expansion.

Formerly, macros made complex decisions in combat by utilizing blocks of Lua code. That's no longer possible. However, a new host of slash commands has been added to replace (and in some cases improve) the lost functionality. These commands allow Blizzard a greater degree of control over what can and can't be done from within a macro.

This chapter describes in detail what's currently possible with the revamped macro system, as well as what was intentionally disabled.

What's the Point of a Macro?

Macros provide a way for the average user to program action buttons to do different things without needing to download a full-scale addon. Macros are often used to reduce the strain of performing a repetitive task. They also are used to make certain kinds of decisions based on the state of your character, and then act accordingly. The game provides a macro-editing window, which can be used to create new macros. The complexity of macros ranges from the simple Polymorph script introduced to you in Chapter 1 to something as complex as the macro discussed next. In general, macros are never more then a few lines long (there's a 255-character limit), although there are some addons that allow you to create longer macros.

Consider the following Warrior-specific macro:

```
/cast [nocombat,stance:1] Charge; ↵
[combat,nostance:3] Berserker ↵
Stance; [nocombat,notstance:1] Battle Stance; ↵
[combat,stance:3] ↵
Intercept
```

This macro performs the following checks in order:

1. If not in combat and in Battle Stance, cast Charge.

2. If in combat and not in Berserker Stance, cast Berserker Stance.

3. If not in combat and not in Battle Stance, cast Battle Stance.

4. If in combat and in Berserker Stance, cast Intercept.

It is designed to let the Warrior use a single button to shift into the right stance, based on whether he's in combat, and then cast either Charge or Intercept, again depending on stance and combat status. The macro can perform only one of the listed actions when run, so it may need to be run twice in some cases: once to change stances, and again to cast the spell.

What Can't Be Done with Macros?

The new macro system has been specifically designed to prevent macros from making certain combat-sensitive decisions. That statement may seem to conflict with the preceding macro, which makes decisions based on a Warrior's stance, as well as whether the character is engaged in combat, but the distinction has been made clear by Blizzard: Macros and addons must be configured prior to combat, and they can only make decisions based on specific factors. Following are some things that explicitly cannot be used to make decisions in a macro:

- The distance from the player to a unit (range)
- The amount of health or mana a player or unit has left
- The remaining cooldown of a spell, item, or action
- The number of combo points the player has on a target
- If a special requirement for a spell is met, such as "Must be behind the target" (Backstab)
- The buffs or debuffs on a unit

In exchange for these restrictions, you now can tell when your character is swimming or flying, and you have a /dismount command and other goodies that were extremely difficult to pull off under the old macro system.

Casting Multiple Spells

The rule of thumb is that you can cast only one spell per macro. However, there's one special case: Any action that doesn't activate the global cooldown can be used in a macro along with other actions.

Note

The global cooldown is a period of time, after casting a spell, when you cannot immediately cast another spell. This limitation was created to set the pace in the game, to ensure that skill wasn't equated with pushing the buttons the fastest, and to help compensate for lower latency connections. Rogues and Druids in cat form have a global cooldown of 1.0 seconds, while the rest of the classes are restricted for 1.5 seconds.

There are a small set of spells and items that don't activate a cooldown, typically spells that have some effect on your future spell casts. For example, casting Nature's Swiftness does not activate the global cooldown. Nature's Swiftness is a Druid/Shaman spell that makes the next Nature spell with a casting time less than 10 seconds cast instantly. If using this spell activated the global cooldown, you wouldn't be able to cast the next spell instantly, thus negating its usefulness. To use multiple spells in a single macro, separate them with the /stopcasting slash command, which tells the client that you're going to cast another spell (or cancel a spellcast if you're currently casting):

```
/cast Nature's Swiftness
/stopcasting
/cast Healing Touch
```

Here are a few examples of spells and items that don't activate the global cooldown:

- **Inner Focus:** A Priest spell. The next spell is free and has an increased chance to critically strike.

- **Nature's Swiftness:** A Druid/Shaman spell that makes the next Nature spell is instant.

- **Talisman of Ephemeral Power:** An Item that increases damage and healing by magic.

- **Cold Snap:** A Mage spell that finishes the cooldown of Frost spells.

- **Preparation:** A Rogue spell that finishes the cooldown of any rogue abilities currently on cooldown.

Macro Syntax

The syntax for each line of a macro looks something like this:

```
/command [conditions] spellname; [conditions2] spellname2; ...
```

For example, you can create a single macro that casts Demon Skin when out of combat, and casts Shadow Bolt otherwise (meaning when in combat):

```
/cast [nocombat] Demon Skin; Shadow Bolt
```

The game evaluates the first condition and, if it evaluates to true, casts the first spell. If a spell doesn't have a condition, it's cast automatically. Keep in mind that once you activate the global cooldown, you can't cast any other spells in the same macro. This means that if the first condition is true (the player is not in combat), the Demon Skin is cast and the macro ends.

Not all macro commands take conditions, and you still have access to all the slash commands you had previously. You can use /p or /ra to send messages to people in your party or raid, and /say or /yell to announce things in a certain proximity. In each of these commands, you can use %t to insert the name of your target. For example:

```
/cast Polymorph
/p I'm polymorphing %t
```

This simple macro sends a message to your party, letting them know whom you are trying to sheep.

Macro Commands

Several slash commands are available when writing a macro, and this section covers commands that are relatively specific to macros. For a full listing of slash commands, type the /help command in the game.

Casting, Using, Attacking

Combat is vital to the game, and that includes casting spells, using items, and initiating attack. Table 16-1 is a list of commands that help you in combat. Each one can take advantage of the conditions described in the "Macro Conditions" section a little later in the chapter.

Table 16-1   Cast/Use/Attack Slash Commands

Slash Command	Description
/cast <spell>	Casts a spell from your spell book, including pet spells
/use <itemname>	Uses an item by name
/use <slot>	Uses an item by slot
/use <bagid> <bagslot>	Uses an item in your bags, by bag/slot number
/equip <itemname>	Equips an item by name
/equipslot <slot> <itemname>	Equips an item into a given slot
/castrandom <spell1> <spell2>	Casts a random spell
/userandom <item1> <item2>	Uses a random item
/stopcasting	Stops spell casting
/startattack [unit]	Starts attacking, optionally a specific unit
/stopattack	Stops attacking

Targeting

The commands described in Table 16-2 all involve targeting. The first four commands are equivalent to using the Tab key to cycle through targets, but they are more specific in that you can reverse the order of the cycle by adding a 1 after the command, that is, `/targetenemy 1` instead of `/targetenemy`. The last few commands accept either a valid UnitID or the name of a player or NPC.

Table 16-2   Targeting Slash Commands

Slash Command	Description
/targetenemy [1]	Targets the nearest enemy, optionally reverse order
/targetfriend [1]	Targets the nearest friend, optionally reverse order
/targetparty [1]	Targets the nearest party member, optionally reverse order
/targetraid [1]	Targets the nearest raid member, optionally reverse order
/targetlasttarget	Targets your last known target
/cleartarget	Clears your target
/clearfocus	Clears your focus unit
/target [UnitID or name]	Targets a unit
/focus [UnitID or name]	Sets a unit as your "focus" unit
/assist [UnitID or name]	Assists a given unit

A UnitID is a special name the game uses to refer to the different characters in your party and group. Table 16-3 describes the most commonly used UnitIDs.

Table 16-3   Valid UnitIDs

UnitID	Description
player	Always refers to your character
pet	Always refers to your pet, if active
party1-party4	Refers to your party members (excluding you)
raid1-raid40	Refers to your entire raid (including you)
target	Refers to your target, if it exists
focus	Refers to your focus, if it exists
mouseover	Refers to the unit currently under your mouse
party1target	Party1's target
party1pet	Party1's pet, if it exists

As the last two entries show, you can append `target` or `pet` to the end of a UnitID to look at a unit's target or pet. You can only view the pet of your raid and party units, but target should work for any valid UnitID. That means that `raid14targettarget` is a valid UnitID, as long as it exists.

Utility and Miscellaneous

These are some utility commands that provide specific functions. From here you can virtually click a button, and even specify a mouse button to send to the frame. You can cancel buffs, change action bars, or stop macro execution entirely. Table 16-4 describes these commands.

Table 16-4   Utility Slash Commands

Slash Command	Description
`/click ButtonName [mouseButton]`	Clicks a given button
`/cancelaura <name>`	Cancels a buff on "player" (your character)
`/changeactionbar <page>`	Changes the action bar to a different page
`/swapactionbar <page1> <page2>`	Toggles between page1 and page2
`/stopmacro`	Stops macro execution
`/dismount`	Dismounts you

Pet Actions

Pets can be controlled purposefully through macros. You can specify the pet's aggressive mode; order it to attack, follow, or stay; and change the autocast status of a given spell. Pet slash commands are described in Table 16-5.

Table 16-5   Pet Slash Commands

Slash Command	Description
`/petattack`	Commands your pet to attack
`/petfollow`	Commands your pet to follow
`/petstay`	Commands your pet to stay
`/petpassive`	Commands your pet into passive mode
`/petdefensive`	Commands your pet into defensive mode

Table 16-5   *Continued*

Slash Command	Description
/petaggressive	Commands your pet into aggressive mode
/petautocaston *<spell>*	Sets a given pet spell to autocast
/petautocastoff *<spell>*	Turns off a given spell's autocast

Other Slash Commands

Along with all the special slash commands, you can use any valid slash command in a macro and have it work. That means you can set up a macro to follow your friend:

```
/follow cladhaire
```

You could compulsively check how long you've been playing on your character:

```
/played
```

If you like to role-play, you can even write messages when casting spells, with something as simple as:

```
/say May the light of the Elune guide you!
/cast Heal
```

You also can use the /script command, which executes a line of Lua code to accomplish a certain task. /script gives you lots of options, but it cannot cast spells, target units, or cause your character to move (among other things).

Macro Options

There is currently only one macro option, which can change the target of a given action or spell. This can be used like the macro conditionals, and can be specified alongside them, but does not factor directly into whether or not the command is run.

You can specify this option to change the target of a spell or action being taken. You can use this to change a /use command so it always is used on yourself (perfect for making self-cast bandages):

```
/use [target=player] Heavy Runecloth Bandage
```

You can set the target to be any valid UnitID, including mouseover, a special UnitID that exists when your mouse is over a unit in the 3D world or a frame that is associated with a unit. Because macros can now be triggered by mouse clicks, this is how you can tell a macro to cast on the unit you're hovering over.

If you supply a UnitID that doesn't exist, such as party1 when you aren't in a party, you won't get an error message. That said, your macro could either display the casting hand, or do nothing at all. If you supply a completely invalid ID, such as praty1 instead of party1, you get the error message shown in Figure 16-1.

FIGURE 16-1: Error message for invalid UnitID.

Macro Conditions

Each of the following sections describes a known macro condition. An example macro is included, along with a discussion of what it means when the option is prefixed with no, which typically negates the condition.

[combat] and [nocombat]

The [combat] condition evaluates to true if the player is in combat. You can use the [nocombat] command as well; it evaluates to true if the player is not in combat. A possible use of these conditions is to create a multipurpose button that casts a spell in combat and a buff out of combat:

```
/cast [nocombat] Power Word: Fortitude; [combat] Lesser Heal
```

This macro casts Power Word: Fortitude if you are not in combat; otherwise it heals your target. You could write the same macro using just the nocombat tag because when you are in combat, the system will fall through to your next condition:

```
/cast [nocombat] Power Word: Fortitude; Lesser Heal
```

[harm] and [help]

The [harm] and [help] conditions can't be negated because they are opposites. [harm] evaluates to true if your target is attackable, and [help] evaluates to true if your target is assistable. Take a look at the following example, which will help you create buttons that can be used against both types:

```
/cast [harm] Smite; [help] Lesser Heal
```

Now take what you already have and put them together to make a more complex macro. You can use the following button to buff, heal yourself, or nuke the enemy:

```
/cast [combat,help] Lesser Heal; [harm] Smite;
[target=player,nocombat] Power Word: Fortitude
```

If you are in combat, and targeting an assistable player, you will heal him. If you are targeting an attackable player, you will cast Smite on him. Otherwise, the button will cast Power Word: Fortitude on you.

The comma (,) between conditions means each condition must match for the spell to be cast. There is no way to say "if combat or help" within the same condition block; you have to use another set for that. For example:

```
/cast [combat] Lesser Heal; [help] Lesser Heal; Smite
```

casts Lesser Heal if you are in combat or if you are targeting an assistable player; otherwise it casts Smite.

[stance], [stance:#], and [nostance]

You've already seen one example of this, with the Warrior macro you wrote previously, but there are other classes that can take advantage of the [stance], [stance:#], and [nostance] conditions, as shown in Table 16-6.

Table 16-6   Stance Descriptions

Class	Warrior	Priest	Druid	Rogue
[nostance]		Normal	Normal	Normal
[stance:0]		Normal	Normal	Normal
[stance:1]	Battle Stance	Shadowform	Bear Form	Stealth
[stance:2]	Defensive Stance		Aquatic Form	
[stance:3]	Berserker Stance		Cat Form	
[stance:4]			Travel Form	
[stance:5]			Moonkin or Tree of Life or Flight Form	
[stance:6]			Flight Form (if player has Moonkin or Tree of Life)	
[stance]	Always true	Shadowform	True in any shapeshift form	Stealth

Source: Neuro_Medivh on the World of Warcraft forums

You can use the [stance] conditional, combined with /cancelaura to make a macro that always returns a Druid to caster form:

```
/cancelaura [stance:1] Dire Bear Form; [stance:2] Aquatic Form;
[stance:3] Cat Form; [stance:4] Travel Form
```

Druids and Their Crazy Forms

Druids can have up to six different shapeshifts (Bear, Aquatic, Cat, Travel, Moonkin, Tree of Life, and Flight Form), so they can potentially use up to [stance:6]. The easiest way to figure out which you should use is to count the shapeshift buttons from left to right, starting at 1. These numbers correspond directly to the stance numbers. If a Druid never did the quest for Aquatic Form, then everything would be moved down a number.

Extending Your Nature's Swiftness Macro

You can the use the [stance] conditionals to make your Nature's Swiftness macro even more powerful. The following snippet uses Nature's Swiftness if it's available, and then casts Healing Touch on you. If Nature's Swiftness is not available, it gives you an error message, but still casts your heal.

```
/cast Nature's Swiftness
/stopcasting
/cast [target=player] Healing Touch
```

Putting this together into one monster macro makes a very nice, all purpose "Oh, Crap!" button, which will put you into caster form on the first click, and heal you on the second click (because shapeshifting normally activates the global cooldown):

```
/cancelaura [stance:1] Dire Bear Form; [stance:2] ↵
Aquatic Form; [stance:3] Cat Form; [stance:4] Travel Form
/cast Nature's Swiftness
/stopcasting
/cast [target=player] Healing Touch
```

If you are already in caster form, you will heal yourself on the first click instead. When you type this in the macro window, ensure that each command in the macro is on a single line, or they won't evaluate properly.

[stealth] and [nostealth]

Use the [stealth] and [nostealth] conditions to make simple macros that change based on whether the player is stealthed. For example, you could have a single macro that does Ambush if you're stealthed, and Backstab if you're not stealthed:

```
/cast [stealth] Ambush; Backstab
```

Because the extra default Blizzard bars don't change when you stealth (only the main bar changes), you can use this to double up on some actions. You can also use this as a Druid when using Prowl in cat form because your bar doesn't change:

```
/cast [stealth] Pounce; Rake
```

[mounted] and [nomounted]

The [mounted] conditional can be used to determine if you're currently on a mount, and it also can be used to cancel your mount buff:

```
/cancelaura [mounted] Swift Grey Ram
```

[swimming] and [noswimming]

You can use the `[swimming]` conditional to create an all-purpose travel macro for Druids; for example:

```
/cast [swimming] Aquatic Form; Travel Form
```

This macro shifts you into Aquatic Form if you're swimming and into Travel Form otherwise. There are a number of different uses for `[swimming]`, including casting Underwater Breathing, and so on.

[flying] and [noflying]

The `[flying]` condition can be used with `/dismount` or `/cancelaura` to ensure that you only take action when you're currently flying. A feral Druid could use the following macro to jump out of flight form, if he's currently flying:

```
/cancelaura [flying] Flight Form
```

[indoors] and [outdoors]

You can use the `[indoors]` condition in a simple check on your Hunter to choose which spell to cast; for example:

```
/cast [indoors] Aspect of the Cheetah; White Ram
```

This will cast Aspect of the Cheetah when you are indoors, and use your mount when you are outside. `/cast` ends up taking items as well as spells, which is very useful.

[modifier], [modifier<:shift|ctrl|alt>], and [nomodifier]

The `[modifier]` conditions enable you to make macros that respond differently based on modifier keys that are pressed when the macro is activated. The only true modifier keys that the game recognizes are the Shift, Ctrl, and Alt keys. You can easily make a button that casts both a group buff and a single-target buff by doing the following:

```
/cast [modifier:shift] Arcane Brilliance; Arcane Intellect
```

You can use multiple modifiers in a single condition by separating them with a comma. For example, the following macro casts Mage Armor when you Alt+Ctrl+click it, Mage Armor when you Shift+click it, and Arcane Intellect if you simply click it:

```
/cast [modifier:alt, modifier:ctrl] Mage Armor; ↵
[modifier:shift] Arcane Brilliance; Arcane Intellect
```

In addition, you can put modifiers together in an or fashion by using the / symbol between them in the same condition. For example, the following macro turns any modified click into a group buff, and any unmodified click into the single target buff:

```
/cast [modifier:alt/shift/ctrl] Arcane Brilliance; [nomodifier]
Arcane Intellect
```

Unlike the conditions themselves, you can use modifiers in both and and or modes. The second macro here casts Mage Armor only if both Alt *and* Ctrl are held down, while the third macro casts it if any of the modifier keys are held down. This makes these macros somewhat complex and tough to understand, but you can customize them as much as you'd like. You can cut down the macro even more by using the [modifier] condition alone:

```
/cast [modifier] Arcane Brilliance; Arcane Intellect
```

[equipped:<slot>|<class>|<subclass>]

You can use the [equipped:<slot>|<class>|<subclass>] condition to take action based on the items you have equipped. The simplest example here is for a raiding rogue who uses both swords and daggers:

```
/cast [equipped:Dagger] Backstab; Sinister Strike
```

Rogues have the most weapon requirements, so it makes sense to use them as examples. [equipped] takes either an item slot (such as Head, Chest, Ranged) or an item class or subclass. Item classes can be found on the tooltip (Dagger, One-Hand).

```
/cast [equipped:Dagger] Ambush; Cheap Shot
```

These macros cannot take an item name, so you have to use the classes and subclasses of an item. There are too many to lists here, but if it appears on the item's tooltip (such as Leather, Head, Chest, Finger, Two-Hand, Held in off hand), then you can probably use it for this command.

[actionbar:<page>]

The [actionbar:<page>] condition returns true if <page> is the current active page. This doesn't have a ton of use, but it does permit complicated toggles; for example:

```
/changeactionbar [combat,actionbar:1] 3; [nocombat, actionbar:1]
4; 1
```

This macro does the following:

1. If you are in combat, and on page 1, change to page 3.

2. If you are not in combat, and on page 1, change to page 4.

3. If you are on any other page, change to page 1.

That gives you a way to use three different toolbars and have a single button to change between them. You could place your general abilities on page 1, your combat specific abilities on page 3, and your out-of-combat spells (buffs, for example) on page 4.

[button] and [nobutton]

[button] returns true if the given numeric button is held down. Table 16-7 shows how the buttons are numbered.

Table 16-7   Button Mappings

Button Name	Button Number
LeftButton	1
RightButton	2
MiddleButton	3
Button4	4
Button5	5

You can use this so the action responds differently when you left- or right-click. Go back to your Priest and cast some buffs:

```
/cast [button:1] Power Word: Fortitude; [button:2] Prayer of
Fortitude
```

This casts the single-target Power Word: Fortitude when you left-click it, and casts the group buff when you right-click it. Again, this just helps you keep your action bars free and saves you from needing as many bars.

You can use the [nobutton] condition to signify that the macro was triggered by a hotkey, instead of being clicked by a button.

[pet:<name>|<type>] and [nopet]

The conditional [pet:<name>|<type>] enables you to cast different spells based on which pet you have summoned (or if you have a pet summoned at all). Hunters could find the following macro useful to have their pet dash or dive:

```
/cast [pet:Owl] Dive; [pet:Cat] Dash; [pet] Growl
```

Warlocks can take a completely different spin on these macros with something like this:

```
/cast [pet:Voidwalker] Sacrifice; [pet:Succubus] Seduction
```

Again, this is just a nice way to have consistent buttons, regardless of which pet you have summoned. You can refer to the pet either by type (Cat, Owl, Voidwalker) or by name (Fluffy, Birdy, Garkol).

You can use the [nopet] condition to trigger a spell cast if you don't have any pet active.

[channeling], [channeling:<spell>], and [nochanneling]

[channeling] enables you to do things based on whether you are channeling a spell. The following will cast Ice Block only if you aren't currently channeling Evocation:

```
/cast [nochanneling:Evocation] Ice Block
```

To not accidentally restart an Arcane Missiles, you could use this command:

```
/cast [nochanneling:Arcane Missiles] Arcane Missiles
```

[exists] and [noexists]

The [exists] condition returns true if the target of the spell exists. You can use it to make some things a bit easier for healers who want to target a boss and heal:

```
/cast [help] Flash Heal; [target=targettarget,exist,help]
Flash Heal
```

This example casts Flash Heal if your target is friendly; otherwise it checks your target's target. Also, if they exist, and are friendly, it will heal them.

[dead] and [nodead]

You could use the following example to make a simple macro for your Hunter:

```
/cast [target=pet,exists,dead] Revive Pet; [target=pet,exists]
Mend Pet; [target=pet,noexists] Call Pet
```

This macro tries to resurrect your pet if it's dead, mend it if it's still alive, and call it if it doesn't exist. The only situation this won't cover is when the pet is dead, but has despawned (if you logged off or reloaded, for example). In that case, you'll get a red error in the center of your screen telling you your pet is dead. You have to manually cast Revive Pet in that case.

[party] and [raid]

The [party] and [raid] conditions evaluate to true if your target is in your party or raid. They can also be used to group buff, versus single target buff:

```
/cast [party,noraid] Arcane Brilliance; Arcane Intellect
```

[group:<party|raid>]

The [group:<party|raid>] expression returns true if you are in a group. You can specify party or raid, and it will only return if you are in that sort of group specifically. Functionally, [group] and [group:party] are the same expression. This is different than [party] because that condition checks your target, not your status.

Using the New Slash Commands

The Burning Crusade introduced several new slash commands that make writing macros much easier, and make them a bit more powerful. This section describes the new commands, and how they can be used.

/use <itemname>, /use <slot>, and /use <bagid> <slotid>

The /use slash command now accepts three different sets of arguments. You can pass it the name of an item, and it will use the item wherever it is in your bags. That makes a bandage macro much easier:

```
/use Heavy Netherweave Bandage
```

You can also pass it a slot number (the most often used are 13 and 14, which are Trinket0 and Trinket1). The following macro uses your first trinket:

```
/use 13
```

Note

Slot numbers can change at any time, so use http://wowwiki.com/API_TYPE_ InventorySlotID to obtain the slot numbers necessary.

You can also go back to the old method of having an item in a specific spot in your bags, and using it from there, for example, the following macro uses the first item in your backpack, regardless of what it is:

```
/use 0 0
```

Bag 0 is your backpack, and slot 0 is the slot in the bottom-left corner.

If /use <itemname> wasn't useful enough, it also equips a given item if it's not currently equipped, and then uses it on the next click. So the following macro would equip your Ramstein's Lightning Bolts, and then use it on the next click:

```
/use Ramstein's Lightning Bolts
```

/equip <itemname> and /equipslot <slot> <itemname>

Use the /equip command to directly equip an item, or to equip an item into a given slot. It lets you easily switch weapons and other gear. You can use it in the basic way, which just equips the item into the first slot available:

```
/equip Royal Seal of Eldre'Thalas
```

You can also shorten the item name as long as it's still unique to your inventory. Instead of having to check the spelling every time, for example, you could just type:

```
/equip Royal Seal
```

As long as that's enough to find a unique match, the game should equip the trinket without any issues. You can also equip an item to a specific slot, by using the slot number before the name; for example, the following puts Brutality Blade into your Main Hand:

```
/equipslot 16 Brutality Blade
```

You can use this command to change between different weapon configurations in your main and offhand slots.

/castrandom <spell1>, <spell2>, <spell3>

While not terribly useful, the /castrandom command does afford you the opportunity to do some fun things. For example, you can write a simple macro to make people wonder if your mage has been drinking too much Dark Dwarven Lager:

```
/castrandom [nochanneling] Arcane Missiles, Frostbolt, Fireball
```

This macro does not check for cooldowns, so if it chooses a spell that's currently on cooldown, it does nothing.

/userandom <itemname1>, <itemname2>, <itemname3>

Since Blizzard introduced the new pricing scheme for mounts, which allows you to purchase many mounts of different types and colors as long as you pay for the more expensive riding skill, many players have become mount collectors. The /userandom command is perfect for those players because it enables them to summon a random mount:

```
/userandom [nomounted] Gray Kodo, Brown Kodo
/dismount [mounted]
```

This command chooses one of your mounts and summons it as long as you aren't already mounted. You can then click it to dismount.

/stopcasting

The new /stopcasting command accomplishes the same thing as the old /script SpellStopCasting(). It enables you to cast multiple spells per macro, as long as the first one doesn't activate the global cooldown. For example:

```
/cast Nature's Swiftness
/stopcasting
/cast Healing Touch
```

You can also use /stopcasting to stop a spell that's being cast — to cancel a heal without needing to hit escape, move forward, or jump, for example. You can simply make a macro and bind that to any key you'd like.

/stopmacro

Blizzard has introduced another new slash command, /stopmacro, which stops a macro's execution if the specified conditions are met. There are a few different ways to do this, including using it on your Priest as a macro for resurrection:

```
/cast Resurrection
/stopmacro [noexists]
/stopmacro [nodead]
/say Resurrecting our close friend %t...
```

This gives you a nice resurrection macro that can be used on dead party members (and it will announce that you're casting it), but it also can be used when someone has already released and you need to use the "hand" to cast on his body. In those cases, it won't announce the resurrection, which is good, because it would say "<no target>". %t is really the only special symbol available right now, and it just displays your current target's name.

/click <ButtonName> <buttonNumber>

Use the /click command to virtually "click" another button. This is most helpful when using custom addons and such, but it has plenty of use in the default UI. Because you can change pages, you can write a macro that clicks a given button regardless of the page you are on. The following macro right-clicks (see Table 16-7 for button mappings) on the 10th action button, regardless of what page you are on:

```
/click ActionButton10 2
```

You could also use it to do something like bind a macro to scroll in and out on the minimap. Create the following macro:

```
/click [modifier:alt] MinimapZoomOut; MinimapZoomIn
```

This creates a macro that when you click it, zooms the minimap in, and when you Alt+click it, zooms the minimap back out. You can already bind these in the key bindings interface, but it illustrates what you can do with /click.

/cancelaura <buffname>

As you've seen in some of the prior examples, the /cancelaura command enables you to cancel a buff by name. This is particularly useful for Druids who can use the command to cancel their shapeshift forms. Now that /dismount is available, you don't need to use this for mounts, but it's still rather handy.

/changeactionbar <page>

You can use /changeactionbar to change to a given page on your action bars. This command accepts conditions (as you saw earlier in this chapter), so it can give you lots of functionality, and an easy way to switch your action bars.

/swapactionbar <page1> <page2>

The /swapactionbar command swaps between two action bars, taking conditions as well. This enables you to swap between the two pages specifically, instead of just changing to a given page.

Comments in Macros

Because macros are capable of handling increasingly complex things, it can be helpful to document what you are trying to do with each line of the macro. You can do so using either the - (hyphen) character or the # character at the beginning of a line:

```
- Call "Mend Pet" if you have a pet
/cast [target=pet,exists] Mend Pet
# Cast "Call Pet" if you don't have a pet
/cast [target=pet,noexists] Call Pet
```

There are two commands that, used in a # comment, will change the display of the button, so it's best to use the - character for comments, and "#" for those commands.

Icons and Tooltips and Cooldowns, Oh My!

You've created more than 25 different macros now that are probably sitting — with random names and icons — all over your character's bars. You may have noticed that if you choose the question mark icon, the game replaces that icon with the first spell or item found in the macro. It also displays the cooldown and range requirements of that spell. Sometimes this is appropriate, and saves you the effort of searching through the long list of icons, but at other times it can be confusing.

Luckily, Blizzard has provided two commands to help these macros make a bit more sense. You now have the capability to change the icon, cooldown, and tooltip of a given macro using comments. You can use the #showtooltip <name> comment to choose which spell's tooltip to show (along with its icon and cooldown). If you specify just #show <spellname>, the game displays the name of your macro in the tooltip, but shows the icon and cooldown of the specified spell. The cooldown and icon are tied together, but you can always choose another icon when creating the macro itself.

Using #showtooltip overrides any #show command you have, so you use only one of them.

The following code changes the quick heal macro to show the range of Healing Touch, so you can use it to gauge the distance:

```
#showtooltip Healing Touch
/cast Nature's Swiftness
/stopcasting
/cast [target=mouseover] Healing Touch
```

You can see the difference in Figure 16-2, which shows the cooldown of Nature's Swiftness, and in Figure 16-3, which shows the Healing Touch.

FIGURE **16-2: Nature's Swiftness cooldown and icon.**

FIGURE **16-3: Healing Touch icon, same macro.**

Creating Cast Sequences

Many times you'll want to cast a number of spells in order, without needing to use modifiers or multiple buttons. You can do this using the new /castsequence command, which has the following syntax:

```
/castsequence [<options>] reset=<conditions> <spell1>,
<spell2>, <spell3>
```

Ignoring the reset portion for now, take a look at a sample Warlock macro:

```
/castsequence Corruption, Immolate, Curse of Agony
```

This simple macro rotates among three spells, moving forward only when you successfully cast one of them. When you define a sequence like this, the icon and tooltip change as you step through the sequence so you know what step you're on. Here's what to do:

1. Type /macro to open the macro window.

2. Select the ? icon, click New, and then name your macro in the pop-up window (see Figure 16-4).

FIGURE **16-4: Name your macro.**

3. Click OK. Then type your code into the Enter Macro Commands field at the bottom of the Create Macro dialog, as shown in Figure 16-5.

FIGURE 16-5: Define your new macro
with the set of spells you would like.

4. Drag the macro to a button on your hotbar so you can click it.

5. Click Exit to close the macro window.

As you use the new macro, the icon (see Figures 16-6, 16-7, and 16-8) changes to reflect the next spell set to be cast in the sequence, so you always know where you are.

FIGURE 16-6: Corruption icon.

FIGURE 16-7: Curse of Agony icon.

FIGURE 16-8: Immolate icon.

Adding Reset Conditions

These sequences work quite well, but you could occasionally end up in the wrong part of the sequence, and might want a way to reset it. For example, let's say you have the following macro:

```
/castsequence Corruption, Curse of Agony, Fear, Immolate
```

If someone comes along and helps you kill the mob you're fighting, you could end up on the Fear step when you go to kill the next mob. Because your strategy is to get as many spells as possible cast before they get to you, this puts you at a disadvantage. Thankfully, there's an easy way to reset the sequence to the first step. Table 16-8 describes the valid reset conditions. The syntax of /castsequence is:

```
/castsequence [<options>] reset=<conditions> <spell1>, ↵
<spell2>, <spell3>
```

Table 16-8   Valid Reset Conditions

Condition	Description
<num>	Can be any number; sequence resets after X seconds
target	Resets the sequence when you change or lose target
combat	Resets the sequence when you enter or exit combat
alt	Resets the sequence if its clicked with the Alt key held down
ctrl	Resets the sequence if its clicked with the Ctrl key held down
shift	Resets the sequence if its clicked with the Shift key held down

You don't want to use a timed reset, but the target reset is exactly what you need! Reset conditions do not get placed in brackets — they're simply placed after the /castsequence command, like this:

```
/castsequence reset=target Corruption, Curse of Agony, ↵
Fear, Immolate
```

The sequence will now reset anytime you change or lose targets. You can also use multiple conditions by separating them with the / symbol:

```
/castsequence reset=target/combat Corruption, Curse of Agony, ↵
Fear, Immolate
```

That resets the sequence if any of the conditions are met.

If you have your reset set to a modifier key (Alt, Ctrl, Shift) and you reset the macro using the modifier, it resets the sequence and casts the first spell.

Adding Timed Resets

You also can reset a sequence after a given period of time. This could be useful to a mage trying to escape:

```
/castsequence reset=24 Frost Nova, Blink
```

This command will, quite simply, use Frost Nova when it is up, and then the button will change to show Blink. If you use Blink while it is up, the macro will then display Frost Nova, and the cooldown remaining on the button. If you don't use Blink within 24 seconds, the macro will reset to Frost Nova (because it will be available again).

You might think that these timed resets give you a ton of power, but they are limited, just as much of the rest of the code, to enforce the design philosophy. Every time the command is run, the timer resets. It's actually acting as more of an idle timeout instead of a timed reset.

This slash command is *not* meant to give the user a way to cast a spell every time the cooldown is up, and some other spell every other time, and it can't be used as such.

What's Next?

Where do you go from here? Hopefully, this book has given you an understanding of the core concepts of addon development, such that you can get started on your next project whenever inspiration strikes! However, there's a lot more to learn by examining other addons, researching online, and talking to other gamers.

Looking at Source Code

There's a tremendous amount you can learn by reading other people's source code, especially in WoW modding, where good documentation isn't always easy to come by. For example, if your addon needs a drop-down menu and you don't know how to define one, your best option is to download a simple addon that you know has a drop-down menu, search the code for the appropriate sections, and dissect it. If you're not used to reading source code, this could be difficult. Sometimes it just takes a while to make sense of someone else's code.

You can't copy and paste the code exactly, but for many tasks you can reuse and recycle code that's already out there, modifying it to suit your purposes. If you use anyone else's code (even if you modify it pretty heavily), you should contact the original author and ask permission. Let him know what you're working on and that his code came in handy. He might even be interested enough to help you. At the very least, include his name in your source code or readme file.

Examining Blizzard's Files

One of the best resources at your disposal is the source code for Blizzard's default interface, which is written exactly the same way that addons are: XML and Lua. Normally, all these files are packed up in Blizzard's MPQ archives, but there are a couple of ways you can examine them.

First, Blizzard provides a small program (for Windows and Mac) called the Interface AddOn Kit, which you learned about in Chapter 15.

Second, there are a number of programs that enable you to explore the MPQ archives. One called MyWarCraftStudio (created by linghuye) provides a nice interface for browsing through the contents of each file and optionally extracting pieces of them (see Figure 16-9). MyWarCraftStudio also allows you to view any of the textures without extracting them. Once you've opened the program, you need to point it to the MPQ file you want to open. WoW's MPQs are stored in the Data directory. Note that files in any of the patch MPQs override their equivalents in other archives. Also, you can't run MyWarCraftStudio at the same time as the WoW client.

On the Web
Even though MyWarCraftStudio is available from a number of places online, you should grab the latest version from linghuye's blog at `http://cnitblog.com/linghuye`. The page isn't English, but you should be able to find the download link without too much trouble.

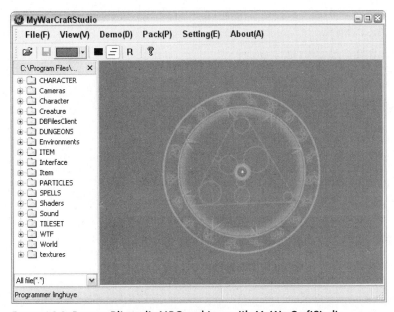

FIGURE 16-9: Browse Blizzard's MPQ archives with MyWarCraftStudio.

Internet Resources

Despite the fact that very little *official* WoW API documentation exists, there's a wealth of information out there, and many people who are willing to help you as long as you approach them amiably and intelligently. More than any other site, you're going to be visiting WoWWiki regularly, the home of all unofficial WoW API documentation.

Websites

WoWWiki has been around since 2004, and has evolved miraculously over that time; becoming the definitive source for Addon development related documentation, guides, examples, FAQs, and tutorials. In addition, the site contains a staggering amount of information about the game itself. There's enough information there to last you days, and because it's a wiki you can contribute as well. The API documentation here is your bible.

The site's homepage is `http://wowwiki.com`, and all addon-related material can be found at `http://wowwiki.com/Interface_Customization`.

Forums

When you can't find the information you need, ask other people! WoW addon developers and users are friendly and helpful, as long as you ask intelligent questions and do your homework before posting. The fastest way to get brushed off or ignored is to ask other people to do your work or research for you. Make sure you've scoured the Internet before asking for help. Here are some active addon-related forums.

- The official Blizzard UI and Macros Forum:

  `http://forums.worldofwarcraft.com/board.html?forumId=11114`

- The WoW Community Mod Site's UI Customization Forum:

  `http://forums.worldofwar.net/forumdisplay.php?f=107`

- Curse Gaming's Addon Discussion:

  `http://forums.curse-gaming.com/forumdisplay.php?f=47`

- WoWInterface's Forums:

  `www.wowinterface.com/forums/`

- WoW Guru's User Interface Customization Forum:

  `www.wowguru.com/forums/forumdisplay.php?f=148`

IRC

You can also talk to other addon developers in real time using IRC (Internet Relay Chat). Once again, forum guidelines apply: Be polite and do your research first. A few IRC channels out there are related to WoW modding, but the most useful is the `#wowi-lounge` channel on Freenode (`irc.freenode.net`).

Index

How to take it to the Extreme.

If you enjoyed this book, there are many others like it for you. From *Podcasting* to *Hacking Firefox*, ExtremeTech books can fulfill your urge to hack, tweak and modify, providing the tech tips and tricks readers need to get the most out of their hi-tech lives.